D0814772

CONTENTS

blandly—as if he regularly arrived in the marble halls of Grosvenor House, complete with riding kit—and then disappearing quite quietly at the height of the party. Actually, Ariels dropped the starting flag at about the third cocktail: outside was a pouring wet evening but, by nightfall, the rain had abated and "WOH 363," *Motor Cycling's* model, had by then exchanged its place in the carpeted Grosvenor House lobby for the Great North Road.

On several other roads doubtless my "hated rivals" also would be haring off into summer-night darkness distinctly thankful for the protection given by the generously proportioned screen—though the taller men would have noted that the rim of the Perspex left the tops of their heads out in the breeze! Wet roads revealed an immediate impression of good steering and handling and the facilities for adjusting the headlamp made it possible to get just the right degree of tilt to the beam. I felt that just a little more light would have been useful but let us reserve judgment here.

The model had started well: the tick-over was pleasant though a little resonant, with a metallic ring that could be associated with pristine exhaust pipes and silencers. This was reasonable because new equipment had been fitted to "WOH 363"—one of the 10,000-mile test models—for our purposes.

This earlier performance history, equal to about a year of private ownership, had resulted in virtually no engine wear. Neither piston revealed slap and the power-unit pulled better at town speeds than any other British-made "250" that I have ridden.

But the test of so unique a machine is not a thing to be rushed to keep up with a Press schedule and the needs of a printing machine. These few paragraphs, therefore, are to say that *Motor Cycling's* very strenuous and extended test is well under way: it started with a visit to the Motor Industries Research Association (MIRA) proving track at Lindley, with good results, and by the time this page appears in print, the machine and rider, plus a pillion passenger, are due to have left this country for a spell of hard going over the fast and often not-so-good roads of the Continent.

RIDING THE "LEADER"

First Stage of "Motor Cycling's" International Test of the Sensational New Ariel "250"

THERE has been fierce rivalry between fact-seeking Pressmen anxious to tell how the new Ariel "Leader" runs and handles on the road. The far-sighted ones started wheedling as long ago as last March, and, over the subsequent period, have been joined by others, each with a hard-hitting argument, fair words and blandishments, all calculated to swing Ariels into permitting a premature and *exclusive* release.

But they are tough, mighty tough, at Selly Oak and although *Motor Cycling's* plans were well laid and approved several months ago, the handing-over ceremony resembled the start of a race rather than anything else! That was why at the Press reception last week (see page 388 in this issue) more than one guest could have been seen smiling

A dream comes true and the new Ariel takes to the road. The handling, says the author, conjures up memories of lightweight racers in the Isle of Man

Wotton Sees the Leader

The Pipe-dream Two-fifty

Ariel Twin on the Road

Proves a Certain Winner

By GEORGE WILSON

THE twin-boom jet was being flung about the sky with incredible *élan*. If that crew, I mused, is having as much fun as I am, then they're enjoying themselves. I was watching the aerobatic display from the forecourt of a filling station in Bibury, as grey-stoned and old-world a village as you'll find in all the wide Cotswolds. The dual-seat was raised and a gallon of petroil was going into the Leader's tank. The sun shone and I was floating on air. My course was set for Wotton-under-Edge, Gloucestershire, to see a general-practitioner buddy—a dispenser of cough cure to the local villagers. And the Leader was behaving in magnificent style. So well, in fact, that I had visions of the Isle of Man Mountain lap and a lightweight racer. Yes, the handling was every bit as good as that and impressed more and more on each of the 250 miles covered that afternoon.

The Leader had been collected the evening before, when thunder rolled round the heavens, lightning flashed wickedly and heavy hammers of rain had knocked daylight for six by the time tables were being laid for tea. I was going in at the deep end and no mistake—I wouldn't be curious about the Ariel's weather-proofing for very much longer! But when I cocked my leg over the seat the rain had eased, though it was drizzling dismally. I was wearing gents' natty office suiting, protected only by a lightweight plastic mac. No more wet-weather gear was needed. On roads that were literally awash the Leader was ridden the 16 miles home, and the only dirty marks on my shoes when we arrived had been there before the run began. And my trews were spotless.

That first evening run and the gallop next day were vastly different, not only because of the weather, but because I'm something of an old woman where delivery tune is concerned. And certain details were far from being to my liking! The pilot mixture was much too weak, twistgrip movement was far too heavy and there was about an eighth of an inch of backlash in the cable. Details to you, perhaps, but to me molehills like that assume Everest proportions.

So off came the right-hand engine panel; in by about a turn and a half went the pilot air screw; up by $\frac{1}{8}$in came the throttle cable

5

adjuster; and down the cable went a very great deal of oil. These jobs done, I was very much happier. That panel, by the way, came off and went back with delightful ease. The five securing bolts are held captive by cross pins behind the panels and they married up with their holes to a tee. There was no need to push and "spring"; to be careful to insert one particular bolt first. For that I awarded Ariels ten marks out of ten.

That 250-mile run I mentioned earlier: the original idea had been not quite to squeeze it into an afternoon. But one thing at the desk led to another, like you I have to eat in the middle of the day and by the time I got away it was half-past-one. And the weather was excellent. My route lay out of London by a westward dormitory exit to Hampton Court, and then by way of Staines, Windsor, Maidenhead, Henley-on-Thames, Oxford, Cirencester, Stroud, past the Cotswold Scramble course and on to Wotton-under-Edge, to the honeysuckle-clad cottage in which my old friend lives. We were out to break no records, nor even, indeed, to carry out a full-scale road test, but the progress chart is impressive for all that. I was home again at 8.45 p.m., which makes an overall average for the 250 miles of 34 m.p.h. If you knock off time for tea and a chinwag, stops for fuel and to take eight photographs the result becomes more than significant. Yes, the Leader goes well. In the first hour in thickish traffic it covered 32 miles. In the second hour on open roads it covered 46 miles. But enough of statistics. Back to the run.

Previously, wearing a peakless helmet, I had found that air eddying round my eyes had suggested that the screen height or rake, or both, were not quite right for a rider of my particular build. But I had forgotten a lesson learned long ago. Remember it? Hardly any screen provides complete freedom from draughts unless your helmet is peaked—peaked so as to collect the air stream from the top of the blade and guide it over your head. So it was in this case. The peak was fitted soon after the trip began and there was not the slightest need for goggles for the remainder of the day. I looked over the top of the screen, too, not through it.

Soon after starting out, the plastic mac was discarded. Cautious to a degree, I had the locker filled (or filled I thought) with additional tools of my own, a pair of overtrousers, goggles and a camera. Eventually the mac went in, too; the capacity of that box is incredible! For the whole afternoon and until Stroud was

Above: The men chiefly responsible for the Leader—Val Page, designer, left, and Ken Whistance, Ariel director and general manager

Above: A pause by the Oxfordshire-Gloucestershire border. Some three minutes after this stop was made a hand could be held on the cylinder-head fins. Below: Private-road interlude!

Above: On the evening on which the Leader was collected rain was falling and the roads were awash after a downpour. The weather-shielding proved first class

#311
$5.00

ARIEL
LEADER-GOLDEN ARROW ARROW

Limited Edition Extra

Compiled by
R.M.Clarke

ISBN 1 85520 6242

BROOKLANDS BOOKS LTD.
P.O. BOX 146, COBHAM,
SURREY, KT11 1LG. UK
sales@brooklands-books.com

www.brooklands-books.com

A-A58BX2   Printed in China

ACKNOWLEDGEMENTS

For more than 40 years, Brooklands Books have been publishing compilations of road tests and other articles from the English speaking world's leading motoring magazines. We have already published more than 700 titles, and in these we have made available to enthusiasts some 25,000 stories which would otherwise have become hard to find. About seven years ago we were asked if we could produce a similar reference series for motorcycles and as a result over 40 titles are now available. For the most part, our books focus on a single model, and as such they have become an invaluable source of information. As Bill Boddy of *Motor Sport* was kind enough to write when reviewing one of our Gold Portfolios - the Brooklands catalogue "must now constitute the most complete historical source of reference available, at least of the more recent makes and models."

Even so, we are constantly being asked to publish new titles on bikes which have a narrower appeal than those we have already covered in our Portfolio series. The economics of book production make it impossible to cover these subjects in our main series, but Limited Edition and Limited Edition Extra volumes, like this one, give us a way to tackle the less popular but no less worthy marques.

Both the Limited Edition and Limited Edition Extra series maintain the same high standards of presentation and reproduction set by our established range. However, each volume is printed in smaller quantities - which is perhaps the best reason we can think of why you should buy this book now. We would also like to remind readers that we are always open to suggestions for new titles; perhaps your club or interest group would like us to consider a book on your particular bike?

Finally, we are more than pleased to acknowledge that Brooklands Books rely on the help and co-operation of those who publish the magazines where the articles in our books originally appeared. For this present volume, we gratefully acknowledge the continued support of the publishers of *British Bike Magazine, Classic Bike, Classic Bike Guide, Classic Racer, Motor Cycle, Motor Cycling, Motorcycle Enthusiast, Motorcycle Mechanics, Motor Cyclist Illustrated* and *The Classic Motorcycle* for allowing us to include their valuable and informative copyright stories.

R.M. Clarke.

The old and the new are typified by this picture of the Leader in front of the Cirencester Parish Church, built in the 15th and 16th centuries. The style is Perpendicular, though there are many Norman details

The machine invites you to take liberties and it could be cranked over as far as even you, Mr. Bob McIntyre, would be likely to want, without anything scraping.

That factor, allied to the powerful braking and the exceptional stability when the brakes are used hard, contributed largely to the Ariel's willingness to tuck 40 and more miles into almost any hour that did not involve city traffic. Both brakes were delightfully light, smooth and progressive in operation. There was no fork judder when the front brake was used viciously, no rear-wheel flutter when real pressure was applied to the left pedal. It is no exaggeration to say that the new Ariel is over-braked—and very, very pleasant a feeling, too.

So we were able to corner fast and stop fast. What of the acceleration? What about speed, and the ease or otherwise of slipping up and down through the gear box? Using the engine normally and changing up at relatively modest r.p.m., the acceleration was unexceptional—no more than you would expect from any goodish present-day roadster two-fifty. But if the engine was really gunned, taken up to 50 m.p.h. (or some 5,550 r.p.m.) in the 7.8 to 1 third gear, then things really happened. As for the gear change, it was really first class—light and so effortless that for much of my riding I just didn't bother to use the clutch, so smoothly did the dogs slide in and out of engagement. No degree of skill whatever was needed for clutchless changes. I was cogging up and down on corners, on roundabouts, any old where, at will, without once hearing a scrunch. Pedal movement is slightly long by contemporary standards. Neutral could be selected without fumbling.

Positioning of the controls could hardly be better. The handlebar levers are extremely short, measuring only 5½in from fulcrum to tip and they require a reach of only 3½in (as measured from the back of the grip to the front face of the lever). The grips are swept back slightly and allow the wrists to assume a natural angle. Relationship between the handlebar and twin-seat brought on no discomfort at the end of my six and more hours at the controls. Perhaps I would have preferred the foot-rests farther forward by an inch.

As for what I call the lesser controls, positioning the dip switch under the bar is a master stroke, for it can be operated at a turn of the left hand, flicking it forward with the thumb, pushing it to the rear with the tip of the forefinger. It is as though one were operating a twistgrip. And the beam-setting arrangement—a neat lever through the instrument panel—is a boon. Switches are carried on the panel and the light switch is on the left—just where it ought to be.

I made other runs besides the afternoon jaunt and it was with genuine regret that I handed the machine back to the rightful owners earlier this week. Fuel consumption overall, including running about London and my 250 miles with the needle generally between 55 and 60 m.p.h., worked out at about 75 m.p.g. I gather that if the machine is cruised a shade more gently the figure becomes about 85 m.p.g.

With any enclosed machine such as the Leader two distinct snags might be expected: lack of manoeuvrability owing to some restriction—however slight—in the steering lock, and some degree of difficulty in carrying out, say, primary and rear chain adjustment. Yet the Ariel could be wheeled round in the passage-way alongside my house as easily as many naked models—and perhaps more easily than most—and all normal routine adjustments, yes, including those for the chains, could be carried out incredibly simply. Never before in my experience has so much intelligent design gone into providing accessibility.

What do I think about the Leader generally? I think it a winner all the way, from the foremost tip of its white-walled front tyre to the rearmost point of its shapely silencers. It is a machine that exudes planning and forethought, a motor cycle in which pipe-dream features have been reduced to down-to-earth proportions and *incorporated!* After experience with any new design I put to myself the 64,000-dollar query—would I have one for my own? The answer in this case is a very, very emphatic, "Yes, please."

reached on the return run at about 6 p.m. the mac stayed there. Behind the screen and weathershield I (as John Surtees would have said), "simply sat there and piloted the thing." The freedom from wind pressure was a novel experience. Freedom from wind roar was, too, yet reflected mechanical noise was obtrusive only when the engine was well and truly on the bugle, pushing the Leader along at 60 or more.

Starting was effortless, so much so that at traffic lights I found myself rolling the grip right back and killing the engine. (I had set the throttle stop to allow the slide to close completely—just as, in my view, all two-stroke throttles should be set so as to avoid four-stroking on down-grades.) One gentle prod brought the engine to life without fail. With the switch in the emergency-start position the result was equally good. An interesting point is that on emergency start, which one would use just to get going if the battery were flat, all the generator's output is fed to one coil and one plug. I have frankly never experienced such easy emergency starting.

The miles quickly totted up. The model was being heeled through Gloucestershire swervery almost before I knew we had started out. And, as mentioned earlier, the handling was proving sheer delight. The suspension is firm without being hard; powerful return damping ensures complete freedom from pitching. In the past 10 years I have ridden many machines faster than the Ariel. But two-fifty Moto-Guzzi racing models excepted, I have not straddled anything that held its line so well on corners, could be swung this way and that with the same degree of effortlessness.

IN laying out the Leader, Ariels aimed at a roadster providing a new level of refinement in motor cycling. The sprightly performance and superlative handling of the thoroughbred solo were considered essential features, but were to be married to cultured manners and the sort of conveniences demanded ever more insistently, such as built-in weather shielding, accommodation for luggage, enclosure of mechanism, sleek lines and cleanliness in use.

The makers have achieved their aim and more. A pressed-steel, beam-type frame of great torsional rigidity, in conjunction with a very ingenious trailing-link front fork and a conventional pivoted rear fork, contributes to a magnificent blend of steering and comfort. The potentialities of the parallel-twin two-stroke engine have been thoroughly exploited to combine pep with sweetness. Not only are the conveniences mentioned inherent in the basic layout; they are supplemented by a host of other highly practical features—such as extensive thief proofing and a lever for

ROAD TESTS OF NEW MODELS

249 c.c. Ariel Leader

Sprightly Two-stroke Twin with Excellent

Roadholding and Steering : Built-in Weather

Protection : Many Practical Features

trimming the headlamp beam—and an extraordinarily useful range of items available at extra charge.

Most of the Leader's attractive features have, at some time or other, been incorporated in earlier designs or offered as accessories, but never before has a motor cycle provided a more complete and coherent answer to the plea for progression along " civilized " lines.

For some 1,500 miles the model under test was used, with and without a passenger, for business and pleasure trips varying in length from a few miles to a few hundred. For much of the mileage the weather was wet and the roads were often awash. With the exception of a peaked safety helmet, no special clothing was normally worn—just a lounge suit, light raincoat and kid gloves. In other words the rider dressed as he would to travel in an open sports car; and he arrived at his destination just as clean and dry. Only when riding through a succession of freak storms was it found desirable to wear a really waterproof coat and, perhaps, light leggings. (Riders who do not wear spectacles found it an advantage to use goggles in rain.)

On the longer journeys the Leader's comprehensive luggage capacity was greatly appreciated. The test model was equipped with the full range of extras, including panniers and carrier. Normal weekend kit, with spare shoes and change of clothing, was comfortably stowed in the detachable, shaped plastic bags in the lockable panniers. On the cast-aluminium carrier behind the dual-seat two suitcases could be secured by the adjustable, 1in-wide rubber straps provided. No less useful was the box, with lockable hinged lid, incorporated in the upper mid-section of the body. Its capacity for holding items which might be required during an outing—maps, flask, sandwiches, waterproof overalls and so forth—was remarkable. When the Leader was parked the box was handy for holding the rider's helmet, and there was room left for oddments such as scarf and gloves.

The steering lock and the securing clip for the hinged dual-

Left: A cast-alumin-ium carrier, complete with rubber straps, is available at extra charge. An idea of the amount of gear that could be accommodated is evident from this picture

Fuel-tank filler cap, battery and tool compartment are reached simply by hinging up the dual-seat which has a moulded plywood base

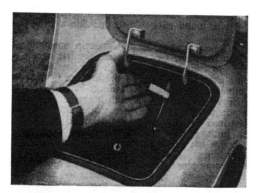

The steering lock (seen here) and the lock for the dual-seat are operated from the box in the body top

seat are both operated from inside the box; hence, by locking the box lid, not only can the model be rendered proof against theft but the fuel tank, battery, tools and tyre pump (all housed under the seat) can be safeguarded, too.

When the Leader was delivered for test the engine was only partially run in. Nevertheless an effortless cruising speed of about 50 m.p.h. on a quarter throttle was soon being used. The performance figures shown in the information panel were compiled when the total mileage was only 1,500; and though by then the model was quite capable of withstanding full throttle indefinitely, it was felt that slightly better figures could probably be obtained after two or three times that mileage. (Incidentally,

contrary to the usual practice with a naked machine, all perform-ance data were obtained with the rider normally seated.)

Except when revved to the limit the engine was delightfully smooth and revelled in hard work. Under average conditions a cruising speed of a genuine 60 m.p.h. could be maintained as long as desired—which is praiseworthy for a two-fifty two-stroke—and required a throttle setting of around two-thirds to three-quarters. (On full throttle, the Leader lapped the Motor Industry Research Association's high-speed circuit at an average speed of over 64 m.p.h.) Yet the engine two-stroked excep-tionally well under light load and was perfectly happy and unobtrusive when one was burbling along at well below 30 m.p.h. in top gear.

The torque peak of the engine occurs fairly high up the r.p.m. scale and this tends to give the Ariel Leader a dual personality. If upward gear changes are made early to keep engine speed low, it is a model of docility; but if the engine is allowed to spin fast by suitable use of the gear box, then accelera-tion and climb are quite sprightly. Indeed, it was commonplace to cover 140 to 145 miles in three hours, inclusive of normal traffic delays and fuel stops. The usual drill when refuelling was to take on 1½ gallons of petrol and a half a pint of oil—those being the largest convenient quantities approximately con-sistent with the recommended petroil ratio of 25 to 1.

INFORMATION PANEL

SPECIFICATION

ENGINE: Ariel 249 c.c. (54 x 54mm) two-stroke twin with separate iron cylinder barrels and light-alloy heads. Roller big-end bearings. Crank-shaft supported in three ball bearings. Compression ratio, 8.25 to 1. Petroil lubrication; mixture ratio, 25 to 1.

CARBURETTOR: Amal Monobloc with strangler for cold starting. Felt air filter.

IGNITION and LIGHTING: Coil ignition with fixed timing. Lucas RM13/15 50-watt alternator driven by right-hand end of crankshaft. Lucas 6-volt, 13-ampere-hour battery charged through rectifier. Lucas 6in-diameter headlamp with pre-focus light unit.

TRANSMISSION: Four-speed gear box in unit with the engine; positive-stop foot control. Gear ratios; bottom, 19 to 1; second, 11 to 1; third, 7.8 to 1; top, 5.9 to 1. Multi-plate clutch with Neolangite facings operating in oil. Primary chain, ⅜ x 0.225in in cast-aluminium oil-bath case. Rear chain, ½ x 0.305in in pressed-steel case. Engine r.p.m. at 30 m.p.h. in top gear, 2,650.

FUEL CAPACITY: 2½ gallons.

TYRES: Dunlop white-wall 3.25 x 16in; rear, Universal; front, Lightweight Reinforced ribbed.

BRAKES: 6in diameter x 1⅛in wide front and rear; fulcrum adjusters.

SUSPENSION: Ariel trailing-link front and pivoted rear forks, both employing Armstrong hydraulically damped shock absorbers.

WHEELBASE: 51in unladen. Ground clearance, 5in unladen.

SEAT: Ariel dual-seat; unladen height, 31in.

WEIGHT: 330 lb equipped with all available extras (pannier cases and bags, luggage carrier, prop and front stands, trafficators, parking light, Smiths' eight-day clock, neutral indicator and inspection lamp) but without fuel.

PRICE: £168. With purchase tax (in Great Britain only), £209 11s 7d. Price does not include extra equipment mentioned.

ROAD TAX: £1 17s 6d a year.

MAKERS: Ariel Motors, Ltd., Selly Oak, Birmingham, 29.

DESCRIPTION: The Motor Cycle, 17 July 1958.

PERFORMANCE DATA

(Obtained at the Motor Industry Research Association's proving ground, Lindley)

MEAN MAXIMUM SPEED: Bottom: 24 m.p.h.
Second: 40 m.p.h.
Third: 57 m.p.h.
Top: 67 m.p.h.

HIGHEST ONE-WAY SPEED: 69 m.p.h. (conditions: negligible wind; rider normally seated).

MEAN ACCELERATION:

	10-30 m.p.h.	20-40 m.p.h.	30-50 m.p.h.
Second	6 sec	5.5 sec	—
Third	10 sec	9 sec	9.5 sec
Top		16.6 sec	16 sec

Mean speed at end of quarter-mile from rest: 57 m.p.h.
Mean time to cover standing quarter-mile: 22 sec.

PETROIL CONSUMPTION: At 30 m.p.h., 90 m.p.g.; at 40 m.p.h., 82 m.p.g.; at 50 m.p.h., 73 m.p.g.

BRAKING: From 30 m.p.h. to rest, 33ft (surface, dry tarmac).

TURNING CIRCLE: 14ft 6in.

MINIMUM NON-SNATCH SPEED: 13 m.p.h. in top gear.

WEIGHT PER C.C.: 1.32 lb.

A front view of the Leader gives an excellent impression of the weather protection provided. The windscreen is attached to the top of the weathershield and supported by substantial vertical rods. Flashing - light indicators flank the headlamp

Not adjustable for load, the springing proved to be a remarkably good compromise for riding with or without a passenger. In the former instance it was only a shade on the firm side and in the latter well-nigh perfect. In both cases roadholding was exemplary. Complementary to the fine roadholding was steering of a lightness and precision which were a joy to the connoisseur and a source of great confidence to the beginner. Another aspect of performance to reach the same high standard was braking, which was smooth, powerful and controllable. A sensible innovation is a second stop-light switch so that use of either brake operates the light.

Well shaped and deeply padded, the dual-seat was praised by both riders and passengers. The riding position was relaxed and comfortable though short riders might prefer a slightly lower seat and a footrest setting two or three inches farther forward. There is an ample range of adjustment for the rear-brake and gear pedals and, though the positions of the clutch and front-brake levers on the handlebar cannot be altered, they are reasonably well sited just above the plane of the rider's forearms. To clear the windscreen, the levers are comparatively short; consequently it was found advisable to maintain a close setting in the control cables.

Worthy of special praise is the fingertip positioning of the dipswitch and trafficator switch beneath the left handlebar grip. (Trafficators are extra.) The trimmer for the headlamp beam operates in a slot in the middle of the instrument panel and has a range suitable for all machine loadings between the extremes of a light rider and two persons with luggage. Intensity of the beam was adequate for normal speeds after dark and full lamp and ignition load on the battery was balanced by the alternator at 30 m.p.h. in top gear.

Clever design has ensured ease of maintenance in spite of extensive shielding. The brake adjusters are readily accessible, as are the sparking plugs (from the front of the engine). Removal of the side panels—which involves undoing five coin-slot screws on each side and first detaching the gear pedal and kick-starter on the right—gives access to the carburettor, contact breaker and gear box, and to clutch and primary-chain adjustments. The tail of the body may be hinged upward for rear-wheel removal and, if panniers are fitted, that is a necessary preliminary to rear-chain adjustment, too, unless a box spanner is available to fit the spindle nut.

A retractable lifting handle can be brought into use when pulling the machine on to its centre stand; the prop stand is extra, as is the two-piece, detachable front stand normally stowed in the tool tray. Other extras not already mentioned were a speedometer trip recorder, eight-day clock, low-consumption parking lamp and inspection lamp with 4ft of flex.

The Leader's elegant lines are enhanced by white-wall tyres and a two-tone finish combining light Admiralty grey with oriental blue or cherokee red. Such is the appeal of the model's outstanding convenience, cleanliness, roadworthiness and appearance that the Leader cannot fail to be the forerunner of a new trend and a yardstick by which future designs will be judged.

The exhaust note had a crisp edge, which mellowed slightly as the miles totted up and carbon formed in the silencers, but was by no means objectionable. Mechanical noise was negligible and an air silencer (formed by the rear engine-attachment bracket) subdued induction roar.

Little effort was required to spin the engine by means of the kick-starter and cold starting was child's play. Provided the strangler was closed and a few moments were allowed for the carburettor to fill after the tap was turned on, a first-kick response was the rule, but in any case no more than three or four prods were ever required. (The strangler control and petroil tap protrude through the left-hand side panel.) Only about a quarter-mile had to be covered before the strangler could be opened fully; restarting, with the engine warm, required only a light thrust on the pedal.

Idling was better than average for a two-stroke and, with the engine ticking over slowly, bottom gear could be engaged noiselessly—with the sole proviso that, before the first gear engagement of the day, the clutch plates were freed by operating the kick-starter with the clutch withdrawn. Clutch engagement was smooth. A leisurely technique was required for a clean change from bottom gear to second; the other two upward changes could be made more quickly and well repaid careful matching of the control movements. Clean downward changes demanded a synchronized blip of the throttle; the best results were achieved by setting the throttle stop for idling and removing every trace of backlash from the throttle cable, so that the response to blipping was a mite quicker than if the throttle was set to close completely. Neutral was easily selected from bottom or second gear. The indicator light (an extra) in the instrument panel serves also as an ignition warning light when the gears are in neutral—a minor but appreciated feature. Slight transmission noise was audible in the indirect gears.

Left : The flashing-light indicators are actuated by a long, easily operated lever. Right : Plan view of the facia which houses the ammeter, speedometer, clock (or medallion), light and ignition switches and, between them, the manual beam-setting lever for the headlamp

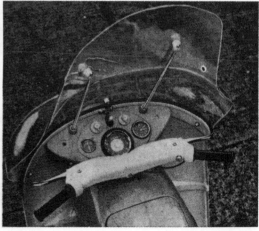

The 249 c.c. Twin Two-stroke

Ariel "Leader"

Motorcycle Performance and Handling Combined with Rider Protection, Full Enclosure and Modern Styling

A raincoat and gloves was all the outer clothing that was really needed on the "Leader." Overboots were never worn. Full frontal protection from the weather and rider comfort are characteristics of the Ariel.

NO new post-war machine has been greeted with more publicity than the Ariel "Leader." A premier manufacturer had interpreted in modern terms the enthusiast's ideal of the fully-enclosed motorcycle—and had put the result on the production line. The Press ran out of synonyms for "revolutionary." The practical motorcyclist wondered what it would be like on the road.

To that question, two months of testing under conditions of everyday use provide a convincing answer. Ariels have pulled it off. Motorcycle performance and handling have been coupled successfully with the styling,

TESTER'S ROAD REPORT

Maximum Speeds in :—

Top Gear (Ratio 5·9 to 1) 66 m.p.h. = 5,900 r.p.m. — Time from Standing Start 44 secs.

Third Gear (Ratio 7·8 to 1) 59 m.p.h. = 6,900 r.p.m. 25 secs.

Second Gear (Ratio 11 to 1) 50 m.p.h. = 8,100 r.p.m. 13 secs.

Speeds over measured Quarter Mile :—

Flying Start 65½ m.p.h. Standing Start 43 m.p.h.

Braking Figures On DRY TARMACADAM Surface, from 30 m.p.h.:—

Both Brakes 35 ft. Front Brake 57 ft. Rear Brake 68 ft.

Fuel Consumption :—

30 m.p.h. 106 m.p.g.   40 m.p.h. 86 m.p.g.   50 m.p.h. 80 m.p.g

[Graph: M.P.H. vs SECONDS. Curve labelled "SPEED AT END OF STANDING ¼ MILE", "MAX IN 3RD", "MAX IN 2ND", with "CHANGE" markings and gear labels TOP, 3RD, 2ND, 1ST]

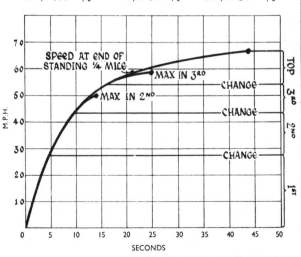

(Above) Maintenance under way after removal of the nearside body panel. The twin contact-breakers have been exposed by unscrewing and swinging back their cover-plate. The inspection plate has been removed for access to the primary chain, the slipper-type adjuster of which is being operated by the screwdriver (arrowed).

(Right) The rear bodywork hinges upwards for wheel removal.

weather protection, luggage accommodation, cleanliness and other amenities usually associated with the luxury scooter.

Features which might have been suspect for their novelty came through the test with flying colours. The " Leader " has no frame in the accepted sense, but welded steel pressings, forming a box-section " spine " with lugs for attachment of the engine and the swinging fork. Thanks to this rigid structure, and the carefully matched characteristics of the unusual trailing-link front fork and conventional rear suspension, the machine has excellent roadholding, steering and comfort.

The weather protection and enclosure is as effective as it is strikingly styled. The test mileage—3,000—was considerably greater than that given to most machines, and it is to the " Leader's " credit that the longer the machine was ridden, the more enjoyable became the experience. Riding fatigue was never experienced, even at the end of a journey of hundreds of miles through rain and wind, with a sporting event sandwiched between the outward and homeward runs. On the move, the windscreen and integral legshields gave almost complete protection so that a raincoat was the only riding kit really required. Overboots were never worn.

On the panel are ammeter, speedometer, clock, ignition and lighting switches, headlamp trimmer and "flasher" and neutral indicator lights. "Flasher" control lever is below the left grip.

The screen was not quite wide enough to stop rain driving on to the rider's sleeves and gloves. Taller riders also found it rather low and, after obtaining what relief they could by varying the angle—the only adjustment possible—were obliged to tuck themselves out of the airflow by sliding farther to the rear of the very comfortable dual seat.

The Ariel-designed engine had all the smoothness and buoyancy expected of a good twin two-stroke. Starting could be achieved on the first " power stroke " after two or three priming prods, once one had mastered the rather critical setting of the butterfly-type choke. Performance left nothing to be desired for a quarter-litre lightweight, whether burbling at 30 m.p.h. on a quiet Sunday afternoon jaunt or hurrying at a constant 60 m.p.h.-plus on a hundred-mile journey.

For a really fast getaway, second gear was held until 30 m.p.h. showed on the speedometer and third gear up to 50 m.p.h. Vibration set in only when the engine was revving almost at the absolute limit in the lower gears. Upward changes could be made silently, if slowly, but downward changes demanded a high degree of co-ordination between the throttle, clutch and road speed if a " clonk " was to be avoided. Clutch

The excellent styling of the " Leader " is well seen in this broadside view.

take-up was always smooth once the rider had become familiar with the movement of the short clutch lever.

Silencing was effective at all engine speeds. Overall fuel consumption for town-and-country going, including main-road cruising at 45-50 m.p.h., averaged about 80 m.p.g. The range offered by a tank holding 1½ gal., plus ½ gal. reserve, was rather meagre.

The resilient comfort of the suspension has been combined with excellent handling. At 65 m.p.h. along a winding road the machine could be violently banked from left to right, over every variation in surface from long ripples to deep potholes, without the rider having any fear of pitching or losing his line.

Lighting was excellent. The headlamp beam, although adequately spread, was very penetrating and had a clean cut-off when dipped. The speedometer was substantially correct below 45 m.p.h., but read 6% fast at 50 m.p.h. and above. The mileage recorder showed a constant error of + 6%.

General accessibility proved to be surprisingly good. Removal of the two side panels would lay bare the engine, gearbox, clutch and primary chaincase, while rear-wheel removal was facilitated in ingenious fashion by loosening two pivots and hinging up the whole of the rear body pressing, below and behind the dual seat.

Many accessories, some of them new to motorcycle practice, are available on the " Leader." The flashing direction indicators (an optional " extra ") proved a boon in traffic, or in wet weather when it was inconvenient or inadvisable to let go of the handlebars. The panniers and rear carrier (also " extras ") would have been large enough to accommodate the luggage of two riders on a Continental tour and the tanktop parcels locker (standard) would hold a safety helmet and gauntlets. Three other items of standard equipment much appreciated were the retractable lifting handle for pulling the machine on to the centrestand, the headlamp beam trimmer and the steering-head anti-thief lock.

BRIEF SPECIFICATION

Engine: Ariel 249 c.c. twin-cylinder two-stroke; bore 54 mm. by stroke 54 mm.; iron cylinders; light-alloy heads; c.r., 8.2 : 1; claimed b.h.p., 16 at 6,400 r.p.m. with choke and felt air-filter. Amal Monobloc carburetter, type 375/33,

Transmission: Four-speed gearbox in unit with engine; positive stop foot-change; overall ratios, 5.9, 7.8, 11 and 19 : 1; built-in vane-type shock absorber; primary drive by ⅝-in. pitch chain; final drive by ½-in. pitch chain.

Frame: Steel pressings fabricated by welding, forming box structure with three engine-fixing lugs and pivot for rear suspension; frame supports outer shell pressing, panels and hinging rear bodywork.

Wheels: WM 2-16 rims carrying 16-in. by 3.25-in. Dunlop whitewall tyres. Full-width hubs incorporate 6-in. diameter brakes front and rear.

Lubrication: Petroil (25 : 1 " straight " mineral oil or 20 : 1 " ready-mix " proportion).

Electrical Equipment: Lucas RM 13/15 generator; full wave rectifier for AC/DC set; Lucas plastic-case ML9E 13 a.h. battery; separate 6-v H.T. coils; 6¼-in. Lucas pre-focus headlamp; combined tail-stop lamp; stop warning operated by rear and front brakes.

Suspension: Ariel designed trailing-link front suspension and swinging fork at rear, both hydraulically controlled by Armstrong spring units.

Tank: Welded steel fuel tank inside frame " box "; capacity 2 gal. (½ gal. reserve.)

Dimensions: Wheelbase, 51 in.; ground clearance, 5 in.; unladen seat height, 30 in.; dry weight (with all available extras), 330 lb.; overall length, 73½ in.

Finish: Cherokee red and Admiralty grey.

General Equipment: Full kit of tools; pump; Smiths 85 m.p.h. speedometer; ammeter; centre stand and lifting handle; headlamp beam trimmer; parcels locker; pillion footrests; steering-head lock.

Price: £168 plus £41 11s. 7d. P.T. = £209 11s. 7d. Extras on machine tested: Parking lamp and switch, 19s. 8d.; inspection lamp, 15s. 7d.; carrier with two straps, £1 19s. 11d.; prop stand £1 8s. 1d.; front stand, 12s. 6d.; pannier cases, £9 7s. 2d. pair; pannier bags, £2 9s. 11d.; neutral gear indicator, £1 4s. 4d.; flasher set, £7 9s. 8d.; eight-day clock, £5 12s. 3d.; trip on speedometer (can only be supplied with new machine) 10s. 1d.; dual seat waterproof cover, 9s. 4d.

Annual Tax: £1 17s. 6d.

Makers: Ariel Motors, Ltd., Grange Road, Selly Oak, Birmingham, 29.

AND NOW— THE

The Square Four fades away, and emphasizing the new trend in motor cycle design comes the latest product of the Ariel stable, the Arrow 250 c.c. twin, a companion to the company's successful Leader of 1959. It will sell at £167 13s. 5d. Ariel claim that cost-savings have been made by advanced and rationalized production methods, making this the cheapest 250 c.c. on the market.

Obviously, too, the use of features from the Leader, has been a large factor in the low price. Most important of these, apart from the engine unit now developed to give maximum power consistent with durability, fuel economy and maintenance, is the boomerang-shaped, box-section beam chassis, from which the engine is underslung.

A tail pressing which forms a neat rear mudguard. Above this is a skirted dual seat, hinged to give access to the fuel filler cap and battery. A dummy petrol tank pressing blends in with the general lines and extends forward to hold the headlamp. Those who know the Leader will have no need to be told that the chassis principle employed now by Ariel gives strength, rigidity and a low centre of gravity. This in turn results in good handling.

The front forks are also incorporated from last year's "Machine of the Year" and a patented trailing link design with two-way, car-type hydraulic damping. They ensure a constant wheelbase, another important factor in giving good handling. The powerful, smooth brakes have full-width hubs and the steel brake shoes are faced with a large area

of non-fade linings. Ribbed front (3.25-in.) tyre and studded rear are mounted on 16-in rims (white walls extra).

Features of the Arrow are a large capacity air cleaner and a full enclosure, by a two-piece pressing, of rear chain, both standard fittings and included in the basic price. The

Continued on next page

And Now—The Ariel Arrow Continued from previous page

cleaner has a replaceable filter and, mounted on the right of the machine, is readily accessible.

The filler cap to the petrol tank, which is contained in the chassis, is reached by lifting the hinged skirted dual seat. Between the rider's knees is a pressing which contains a removable tool-box and space for gloves, waterproofs. The Arrow will do 70 m.p.h. and fuel consumption at 30 m.p.h. is 110 miles to a gallon of petrol/oil mixture. Standard colour scheme is two tones of grey, in best quality stove enamel.

Technical Details

That's the general picture of a machine that is likely to start motor cycle enthusiasts talking in the coming weeks and months. But take a further, more technical look at the Ariel Arrow.

Engine: Robust 250 c.c. twin-cylinder, two-stroke, operating on loop scavenging principle. Separate ported cast-iron cylinders and alloy heads. Deep directional finning arranged for maximum cooling, each pair being secured to crankcase by four studs and high tensile steel sleeve nuts. Built-up crankshaft mounted on three heavy-duty ball bearings. Taper and key-coupling in middle of shaft secured by bolt, easily accessible throw hollow main shaft for servicing. Crankcase pressure held by four self-adjusting rubber oil seals. The Lucas 50-watt a.c. generator is spigot-mounted on the offside of the crankcase with twin contact-breaker assembly near side. The $\frac{3}{8}$-in. pitch endless chain is fitted with a rubber-covered spring steel adjuster for silent running. Amal Monobloc carburetter has cold-starting device. Lubrication, by petroil system.

Gearbox and Transmission 4-speed with foot control. Ariel clutch incorporates rubber cush drive and is of three-plate wet type. The $\frac{1}{2}$-in. pitch rear chain is automatically lubricated from the primary chaincase.

Frame and fitting Engine underslung and fixed by three long bolts. The lower high tensile bolt also carries swinging arm of rear suspension, which pivots on rubber bushes. Unscrewing all three bolts frees engine-gearbox unit with rear wheel and chaincase. Rear frame extension forms air intake silencer which has the carburetter connection at front and air filter with replaceable element on offside.

Front Forks: Trailing link, long coil suspension springs supporting two-way hydraulic dampers and contained within two large diameter stanchion tubes. All swivelling points have anti-friction nylon bushes.

Hubs: Full-width, fitted with heavy-duty ball bearings. Wheels quickly detachable. Brakes 6-in diameter.

Mudguards: Front guard deep valance with concealed fixing to the fork stanchion tubes. Rear tail section forms rear guard.

Dual Seat: Sponge rubber interior shaped. Trimmed with high quality waterproof material.

Standard equipment: Easy-lift central stand, 100 m.p.h. speedometer, ammeter, ignition and lighting switch, lightweight 13 amp hour 6-volt Lucas heavy-duty battery; a.c. generator and rectifier; 6-in. diameter pre-focus headlamp with double filament and pilot bulbs, electric horn, folding pillion footrests, licence holder, knee grips, set of tools and tyre inflator.

Price: £167 13s. 5d.

There it is. Another new machine rolling off the production lines. Optional accessories are of course available: windscreen, front stand, carrier, and so on. All to sharpen the appetite of the prospective Arrow rider and to justify Ariel's claim to have given the customer "low-priced luxury".

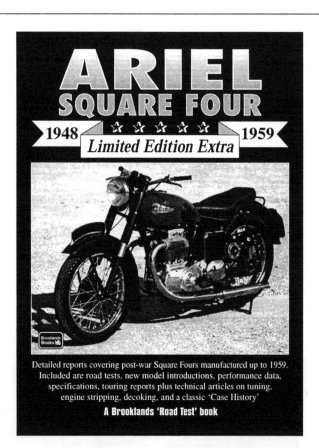

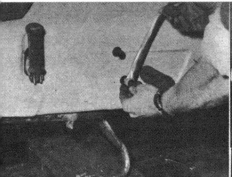

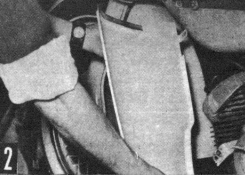

To remove the gearchange lever slacken the nut and pull the lever out a little. It can then be turned up and withdrawn

2 After removing both side panels the leg shields are free to come off after the two nuts securing them have been undone

3 Undoing the cylinder head nuts with the special Allen key provided in the tool kit. Removing the plugs simplifies this

SERVICING the LEADER

Bob Crofts shows

the easy way to maintain

your Ariel Leader

OF all bikes on the road, the Leader is probably the easiest to maintain. It was designed with this aim in view, and anybody who can ride the machine is capable of servicing it.

In this MM Photo Guide we show how to do some of the little jobs that have to be done from time to time. First, a decoke. This usually becomes necessary every 5,000 miles, though for top performance the silencer should be cleaned out every 2,500 miles.

The contact breaker points should be checked and cleaned at the same time as the silencer. It doesn't take a moment to do this job, and the difference in performance makes it well worth while.

Front brakes and hubs need attention at regular intervals, and we have shown how to remove the front wheel. This is somewhat different from other machines owing to the unusual front suspension.

Maintenance on the Leader is so simple that there is no excuse for neglecting it. Remember that only by regular servicing will you be sure of trouble-free riding at all times. ●

CONTINUED OVER ▶

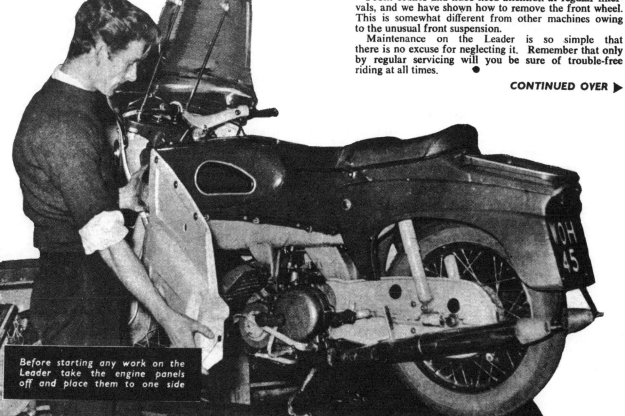

Before starting any work on the Leader take the engine panels off and place them to one side

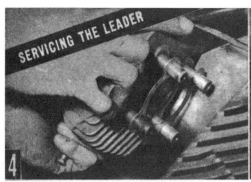

4 Removing one of the cylinder heads. Note the bottoms of the four sleeved nuts and the head gasket coming away with them

5 Removing carbon from the cylinder head with an old hacksaw blade. The Leader needs a decoke about every 5,000 miles

6 Bring each piston in turn to the to its stroke and carefully scrape off carbon deposits from the piston c

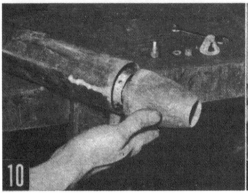

10 The silencer must be cleaned more often than the engine, say every 2,500 miles. Start by removing the chrome end piece

11 If silencer baffles are stiff push piece of wood A into pipe B and hold in vice. Silencer body C can now be pulled off

12 Scrape all carbon off the baffles. holes in the end usually become blo to an extent, and must be poked

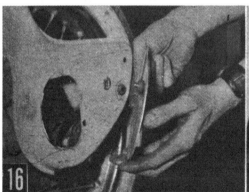

16 Tyre changing or attention to the front brake involves removal of front wheel. Start by taking off the two fork panels

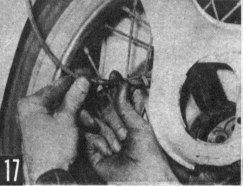

17 Next disconnect the front brake cable by slackening off the adjuster and slipping it out of the slotted outer cable stop

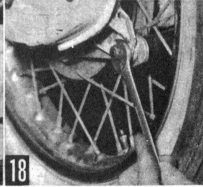

18 Release the fulcrum arm by undoing bolt at the front. You will have to two spanners for this job. Note wa

22 Withdraw the spindle from the nearside. If necessary gently tap it out with a soft drift. Do not damage the threads

23 With the spindle out the front wheel can now be completely removed. Block up the front of the bike to prevent it tipping

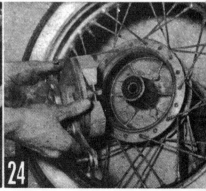

24 The brake plate complete with the s pulls straight off the wheel. Change grease in hub at 5,000 mile inte

must unsling the exhaust pipe and
...ncer before the barrel will come off.
...connect at barrel and beneath engine

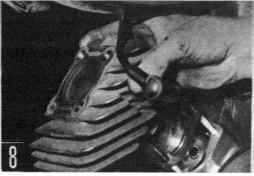

8 The barrel can now be pulled straight
off for cleaning the ports. Scrap the
gasket and fit a new one when replacing

9 It is most important to check that the
piston rings are free in their grooves
and not stuck. Get pegs in right place

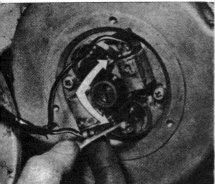

...ecking the points. The gap should be
...tween .014 and .016 inch. Both sets
...ould be checked (arrowed) not just one

14 Adjusting the clutch. With cover plate
removed turn the adjusting screw in or out
to get 1/16 inch slack at clutch lever

15 Adjusting primary chain. Screw the nylon
adjuster in or out to give ⅜ inch up
and down movement at the inspection cap

...fore the spindle nut is undone depress
...rks and insert peg in each side of the
...rk stanchions to keep them in place

20 With the forks locked in the depressed
position undo the spindle nut on offside
of the machine with box spanner from kit

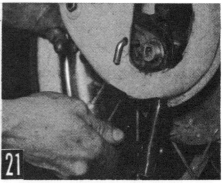

21 Before the spindle can be knocked out it
is necessary to loosen the spindle pinch
bolt on the nearside, using box spanner

...e brake linings on the Leader must not
...chamfered, but must have a clean-cut
...ife edge on the leading edges as shown

26 Remove all traces of lining dust from
the brake drums with a clean rag. Dust
on the linings causes brakes to grab

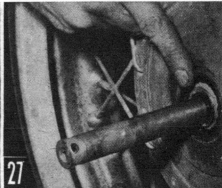

27 When replacing spindle line up the wheel
carefully so that step on spindle does not
catch and damage the lip on the hub

450-DAY MAIN[T

An Ariel "Leader's"

17,000 Miles

on Assignment to

"Motor Cycling"

Reported by

MIKE BASHFORD

FEW motorcyclists can escape the flattering inquisitiveness of the fellow-rider who asks, "How does the bike go?"

Nor the inevitable follow-up, delivered with a knowing look, "Ah, but how reliable is it?" And all of us have wanted to know these things about a prospective purchase.

To the first question a *Motor Cycling* road test can, of course, provide the complete answer. To the second, in the nature of things, it can't. If only every test could be followed by. . . . Well, for once, it has been.

The 250 c.c. twin-cylinder two-stroke Ariel "Leader" was the subject of a road test in our issue of December 18, 1958. The test machine, WOV 802, is actually my staff mount, and for the past 17,000-odd miles and 18 calendar months I have been keeping a maintenance, mileage and fuel log-book—the record of an extended reliability test and the answer to question number two.

We took delivery of the "Leader" on August 24, 1958, and the table of maintenance covers all work carried out on it in the past 450 days up to February 24 last (which makes four days more than 18 lunar months). "WOV" was one of the very first production "Leaders" to come off the Selly Oak assembly line and, like most early production machines, it differed in minor details from later models. So certain components have been modified by the manufacturers to bring it up to the latest specification.

The table reflects the fact that maintenance was not carried out at regular periods or, necessarily, at the mileage figures recommended by the factory—a non-ideal state of affairs enforced by the everyday routine of the writer and, probably, of the average owner. The machine was not run in when supplied. The mileage figures, taken at the time of maintenance and at the end of every month, have been corrected for a mileometer error of plus six per cent.

The final mileage figure of 17,131 does not, of course, approximate to my personal mileage, which was considerably higher.

Much of the maintenance work noted in the log is self-explanatory. Since this is not an article upon "Leader" maintenance, but merely a reliability check, only those components which have been modified or replaced and those items of maintenance which demand explanation have been noted in the text. It was not thought necessary to refer to the regular topping-up of oil in the primary chaincase and gearbox and of water in the battery.

It must be borne in mind that a *Motor Cycling* staff machine leads an arduous life. Constant speeds of between 55 and 65 m.p.h. are normally demanded of the "Leader" on the way to and from sporting events or other urgent assignments. It also suffers from having to negotiate muddy tracks while covering trials. Under these conditions the "Leader" has always given me all that I would ask in reliability, performance and road-holding.

Here is a short commentary on the table:—

ENGINE

Routine decarbonizing of cylinder heads, pistons, exhaust and transfer ports was carried out three times in the 18-months' period and the piston rings were renewed at 10,000 miles because of wear and consequent poor cylinder-bore contact. There are no signs of cylinder or big-end wear.

GEARBOX

Apart from periodic topping-up of the oil level and an oil change about every 5,000 miles, the gearbox has needed no attention.

TRANSMISSION

Both primary chain and secondary chain have been replaced —at virtually the same time. I expected to have to renew the secondary chain at about 10,000 miles because of its uneven and fast wear, but the breakage of a primary chain roller came as a complete surprise, the general condition of the chain being otherwise excellent. A modified internal clutch operating lever, replacing the earlier pattern, has also been fitted.

WHEELS

When the "Leader" was introduced in 1958, its brakes featured alloy shoes and the well-known Ariel fulcrum adjusters. Modifications resulted in the fitting of steel shoes and the adoption of cable and rod adjustment. The "pre-production front brake" fitted at 4,000 miles was a one-off anchor of this type; both it and the original rear brake were afterwards replaced by components of the later production pattern.

EXHAUST SYSTEM

The "Leader" is using its third set of silencer baffles. The original baffles were replaced by a later pattern which improved the performance and deepened the exhaust note. Both the replacements became irreparably damaged when I removed them for decarbonizing.

FUEL SYSTEM

The new pattern fuel-tank cap contains a simple ball-valve to prevent petroil leakage; it was fitted when the carburetter air filter element was renewed at the factory-recommended mileage.

IGNITION

On all "Leader" engines from No. T.251A, the top hole for the contact-breaker cover fixing screw became a "through hole" and the engine flywheel was drilled so that, with the aid of a timing peg and the inspection lamp, the ignition timing could be accurately fixed. We asked that this improvement should be applied as a "mod" to *Motor Cycling's* "Leader."

Replacing the contact-breaker assembly cured a high-speed misfire which had defied all ordinary attempts at analysis. Eventually the insulating plate of the top contact-breaker spring was found to have been incorrectly positioned, causing an electrical short and a softening of the spring. Result: something akin to valve float, but in this case applied to the right-hand cylinder contact-breaker points.

SUSPENSION

The pivots of the trailing-link front forks have been greased periodically, but no other attention has been given to either front or rear suspension.

CONTROLS

No trouble—only "mods." The new pattern clutch-operating cable provided for adjustment at the gearbox end of the cable instead of at the handlebar, and the modified throttle cable and spring gave a lighter action.

ELECTRICAL FITTINGS

Incorrect wiring, threatening an electrical short, accounted for the replacing of the inspection light—another pre-production component. The trafficator unit and horn were replaced because of faulty operation.

FRAME FITTINGS AND ACCESSORIES

Hamfistedness in the garage accounted for damage to the windscreen and seat strap; the former must be debited to myself and the latter to a dealer who mistook the strap for a lifting handle. The panniers originally fitted to the "Leader" were hand-made and equipped with very uncertain locks—pre-production types. The replacement pair are stoutly made, easily lockable and a boon.

Replacement nylon eye-bolts for attaching the windscreen stays to the screen and a new parcels compartment lock have also been fitted—the eye-bolts because of slight damage and the lock to replace an early production version. A curious item was the sign-writing of the front and rear number plates; I am not in favour of transfer-numbers when they peel off after 376 miles.

*   *   *

Well, that's the picture. You can see that of the hundreds of "Leader" components very few have required attention. I will go so far as to say that of all the machines I have ridden, the "Leader"—despite its comprehensive equipment and novel structure—has given by far the least cause for spanner work and has been one of the easiest to maintain. In return for no more than the minimum of necessary maintenance, it has done 17,131 exemplary miles on assignment to *Motor Cycling.*

P.S. Forgot to mention that the eight-day clock has stopped—water in the works, I think. Trouble is, I'm having some difficulty in removing it from the dashboard. Can't think what the jeweller's going to say when I wheel the "Leader" into his shop!

> ## For Tables of Maintenance, Mileage, and Fuel Consumption, see overleaf

(*Left*) *Once in 17,000 miles: removing the contact-breaker cam before taking off the primary chaincase. The cam is self-extracted from its taper as the centre fixing screw is loosened.*

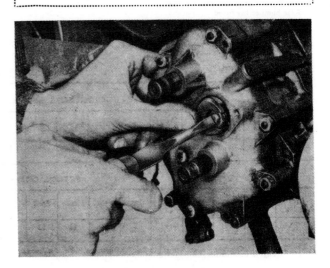

(*Right*) *Seven times in 17,000 miles: adjusting the clearance between clutch push-rod and internal operating lever.*

ARIEL "LEADER" — MAINTENANCE TABLE

(See "450-day Maintenance Test" on preceding pages)

	SPEEDOMETER READINGS (Corrected)									
	1958			1959						1960
	Aug. 24–Sept.	Oct.–Nov.	Dec.–Jan.	Feb.–March	April–May	June–July	Aug.–Sept.	Oct.–Nov.	Dec.–Jan.	Feb. (to 24th)
Engine										
Decarbonization of heads, ports and pistons	—	—	4,430	—	—	10,321	—	—	—	16,841
Piston rings replaced	—	—	—	—	—	10,321	—	—	—	—
Gearbox										
Oil changed	—	—	—	5,951	—	—	10,943	—	—	16,954
Transmission										
Primary chain adjusted	1,250	2,021	—	5,951	8,094	—	11,396	13,928	—	16,954
Primary chain replaced	—	—	—	—	—	9,989	—	—	—	—
Secondary chain adjusted	1,250	2,021	4,430	5,951	8,094	9,989	10,943	13,928	15,327	16,954
Secondary chain replaced	—	—	—	—	—	—	10,321	—	—	—
New pattern clutch operating lever fitted	—	—	4,430	—	—	—	—	—	—	—
Clutch push-rod adjusted	1,250	—	4,185	—	8,094	9,989	10,321	13,928	—	16,954
Primary chaincase oil changed	—	—	5,010	—	—	9,989	—	—	—	16,954
Wheels										
Pre-production front brake fitted	—	—	4,430	—	—	—	—	—	—	—
Production front and rear brakes fitted	—	—	—	—	—	—	10,782	—	—	—
Front brake adjusted	698	2,021 2,326 2,638	4,640	—	8,094	10,240	—	13,928	15,839	—
Rear brake adjusted	698	—	4,640	—	8,094	10,240	—	13,928	—	16,841
Front and rear brake cam spindles and front brake plate bush greased	—	2,425	4,640	—	8,094	10,240	—	13,928	—	16,954
Front wheel hub, brake and bearings dismantled, cleaned and greased	—	—	—	—	8,094	—	—	—	—	16,954
Rear wheel puncture repaired	—	—	—	—	8,094	—	—	—	—	—
Exhaust System										
Decarbonization of silencers and pipes	—	—	4,430	—	—	—	10,321	—	—	16,841
New pattern silencer baffles fitted	—	—	—	—	—	—	10,321	—	—	—
Silencer baffles replaced	—	—	—	—	—	—	—	—	—	16,841
Fuel System										
Air filter element replaced	—	—	—	—	—	—	10,782	—	—	—
Carburetter dismantled and cleaned	—	2,788	—	5,790	—	9,842	—	—	—	—
New pattern fuel tank cap fitted	—	—	—	—	—	—	10,782	—	—	—
Ignition										
Primary chaincase and flywheels modified to include timing device	—	—	4,430	—	—	—	—	—	—	—
Contact-breaker assembly replaced	—	2,021	—	—	—	—	—	—	—	—
C.B. points adjusted and cleaned	1,321	—	—	—	—	9,989	—	—	—	16,954
C.B. cam felt pad lubricated	—	—	4,185	—	—	9,989	—	13,123	—	—
Sparking plugs replaced	—	3,988	—	—	—	—	—	—	—	16,841
Sparking plugs cleaned and gapped	1,580	2,788	4,430	5,790	—	9,842	—	13,123	—	16,841
Suspension										
Front hydraulic unit pivots greased	—	1,956	—	5,920	—	10,200	—	—	—	16,954
Controls										
New pattern clutch operating cable fitted	—	—	4,430	—	—	—	—	—	—	—
New pattern throttle cable and spring fitted	—	—	4,430	—	—	—	—	—	—	—
Brake pedal spindle and centre stand bush greased	—	1,956	—	5,920	—	9,989	—	13,928	—	16,841
Handlebar and dashboard controls, levers and cables oiled and adjusted	—	2,321	—	5,560	—	9,756	—	—	15,839	—
Throttle cable replaced	—	—	—	—	—	—	11,396	—	15,939	—
Electrical Fittings										
Inspection light replaced	—	2,021	—	—	—	—	—	—	—	—
Trafficator unit replaced	—	2,021	—	—	—	—	—	—	—	—
R.H. trafficator bulb replaced	—	—	—	—	—	9,407	—	—	—	—
Horn replaced	—	—	—	4,430	—	—	—	—	—	—
Headlamp bulb replaced	—	—	—	—	—	—	10,514	—	—	—
Frame Fittings and Accessories										
Windscreen height extension fitted	—	—	—	—	—	—	11,396	—	—	—
Rear bumper bar fitted	—	—	—	—	—	—	11,778	—	—	—
Windscreen replaced	—	—	—	—	—	—	—	13,928	—	—
Parcels compartment lock replaced	—	—	4,430	—	—	—	—	—	—	—
Panniers replaced	—	—	—	—	—	—	10,782	—	—	—
Sign-writing of number plates	376	—	—	—	—	—	—	—	—	—
Windscreen eye-bolts replaced	—	—	—	—	—	—	10,782	—	—	—
Seat strap replaced	—	—	—	—	—	—	10,943	—	—	—
Rear-view mirror fitted	—	—	—	—	7,518	—	—	—	—	—

MILEAGE PER CALENDAR MONTH

Aug. (from 24th)	Sept.	Oct.	Nov.	Dec.	Jan.	Feb.	March	April	May	June	July	Aug.	Sept.	Oct.	Nov.	Dec.	Jan.	Feb. (up to 24th)
348	1,246	1,304	1,126	991	237	625	964	954	1,120	937	469	947	510	1,592	856	1,713	951	341

PETROL CONSUMED (Gallons)

Aug. (from 24th)	Sept.	Oct.	Nov.	Dec.	Jan.	Feb.	March	April	May	June	July	Aug.	Sept.	Oct.	Nov.	Dec.	Jan.	Feb. (up to 24th)
4	17	18	15	13½	3	8½	13	13	15	12½	6	13	7	21½	12	23	13	4

Engine Lubrication: Self-mixing oil in 20 : 1 proportion.   Total mileage: 17,131.   Petrol consumed: 232 gal.   Average consumption: Approx. 73 m.p.g.

The 249 c.c. ARIEL 'ARROW'

Superb handling and brisk performance from a low-priced twin

Specification

ENGINE

Type	Parallel-twin two-stroke
Bore	54 mm.
Stroke	54 mm.
Cubic capacity	249 c.c.
Compression ratio	10 : 1
Carburetter	Amal type 375/33 "Monobloc," ⅞-in. choke
Ignition	Battery and dual coils
Generator ..	Lucas RM 13/15 50-w alternator
Makers' claimed output ..	17 b.h.p., at 6,500 r.p.m.
Lubrication	Petroil at 24 : 1 ratio
Starting	..Kickstarter

TRANSMISSION

Ratios	5.8, 7.6, 10.9 and 17.6 : 1
Speed at 1,000 r.p.m. in top gear ..	11½ m.p.h.
Speed equivalent to revs. at maximum power rating :	
Second gear	42 m.p.h.
Third gear	57 m.p.h.
Top gear	74 m.p.h.
Primary drive..	Single row chain in oilbath
Final drive ..	Single-row enclosed chain
Clutch	Multi-plate in oilbath
Shock-absorber	Torsion-type in clutch centre

CYCLE PARTS

Frame ..	Box structure of steel pressings, fabricated by welding
Front suspension ..	Trailing-link forks with coil springs hydraulically damped
Rear suspension ..	Swinging fork with two hydraulically damped spring units
Tyres	Dunlop 3.25 × 16-in. ribbed front and studded rear
Brakes	6 in. dia. full-width hubs front and rear. Total brake lining area, 24½ sq. in.
Fuel Tank ..	3 gal. welded steel ; single tap
Lamps	30/24w. head ; 3-w. pilot ; 3/18-w tail/stop
Battery	Lucas 12 a.h. MLZ9E
Speedometer	Smiths 100 m.p.h.

Seating	Side hinged dual seat
Stands	Centre
Tool kit	Spanners : 4 open-ended, 3 box, 1 special ring, 1 C-type ; 2 Allen keys ; Phillips screwdriver ; tyre lever ; feeler gauge/screwdriver ; 2 locating pegs (front suspension)
Toolbox	Detachable container in top panel pressing
Standard finish	Seal grey and light Admiralty grey

OTHER EQUIPMENT

	Tyre pump

PRICES

Machine	£171 17s. 10d. (inc. £29 7s. 10d. P.T.)
Extras :	
Carrier with straps	£1 5s. 9d.
Prop stand	£1 7s. 0d.
Total as tested	£174 10s. 7d.
Tax	£1 17s. 6d. p.a.
Makers	Ariel Motors Ltd. Selly Oak, Birmingham, 29.

'Motor Cycling' Test Data

Conditions. *Weather: Cold, damp. (Barometer 29.60 Hg. falling to 29.40. Thermometer 44° F.) Wind: S.S.W., 5-10 m.p.h. Surface: (braking and acceleration): damp asphalt. Rider : 11½ stone, 5 ft. 8½ in. ; wearing coat, overboots and safety helmet, normally seated. Fuel : Premium grade (96 research method octane rating).*

Venue : *Motor Industry Research Association Station, Lindley.*

Speed at end of standing 1,000 yd. :

East	65.1 m.p.h.
West..	57.4 m.p.h.

Best certified M.I.R.A. maximum (rider prone) .. | 72.8 m.p.h.

Braking from 30 m.p.h. (all brakes) .. .. .. | 9½ yd.

Fuel consumption :

At constant 30 m.p.h. ..	104 m.p.g.
50 m.p.h.	80 m.p.g.
500-mile overall figure ..	84 m.p.g.

Speedometer

30 m.p.h. indicated	= 29.4 m.p.h. true
40 m.p.h. indicated	= 39.6 m.p.h. true
50 m.p.h. indicated	= 49.4 m.p.h. true
60 m.p.h. indicated	= 58.6 m.p.h. true
70 m.p.h. indicated	= 68.7 m.p.h. true

Mileage Recorder : Accurate

Electrical Equipment

Top gear speed at which generator output balances :

Ignition only	12-15 m.p.h.
Minimum obligatory lights	18 m.p.h.
Full lights	20 m.p.h.

Weights and Capacities

Certified kerbside weight (with oil and 1 gal. fuel) .. .. .. | 291 lb.

Weight distribution, rider normally seated :

Front wheel	35 %
Rear wheel	65 %

Tank capacity (metered) :

Total	3 gal.
Reserve	Nil

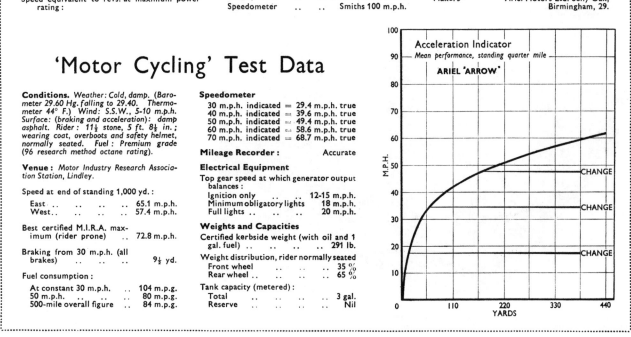

WHEN it first appeared, nearly a year ago, the Ariel "Arrow" made news largely because of its sheer novelty. The usual order of things had been reversed and a new model produced by "stripping" an enclosed machine. And the newcomer's price was sensationally low because the costly tooling for its basic presswork had already been carried out for the parent "Leader."

But neither novelty nor price has had anything to do with the reputation which the "Arrow" has established since that time. It stands on its own merits as a lively quarter-litre with exceptional handling and an engine which has proved capable of development for racing.

In the 1961 model, subject of this test, that engine has been modified in the light of racing experience by raising the compression ratio from 8.3 : 1 to 10 : 1 and fitting squish-type heads and oval-section connecting rods. Chief change in the cycle parts is an improved front brake.

The new model retains the immaculate handling of its predecessor, and of the "Leader."

'Mods' Tell

Absolute maximum speed is up, but the chief benefits of the engine "mods" are improved acceleration and better pulling power all the way up the speed range. Making fullest use of the increased power available resulted, at one stage, in a corresponding rise in the fuel-consumption rate, but the overall figure of 84 m.p.g. was better than that claimed by the makers.

The engine was a satisfactory starter, requiring temporary use of the butterfly-type choke to give a rich mixture. But within about 30 seconds that setting could be dispensed with and the unit would settle to a pattering rhythm, breaking into a steady, smooth two-stroke note as soon as a load was applied.

Ignition and lighting switches are located in the headlamp shell and a separate emergency-start circuit is incorporated. This standby had, in fact, to be used at an early stage in the test after a kerbside viewer had played with the switch and left it turned on.

That incident demonstrated the very satisfactory charging rate of the RM13 alternator, feeding through a full-wave rectifier to the battery. It balanced the ignition's demands on the battery at between 12 and 15 m.p.h. in top gear, which is about the

minimum non-snatch speed obtainable with the engine turning over barely above 1,000 r.p.m. The full lamp load was balanced at just below 20 m.p.h., so that even cautious country-lane running entailed no drain on the battery.

The Smiths speedometer, calibrated in multiples of 20 m.p.h., is mounted in the headlamp shell, together with an ammeter. Both are clearly visible. The speeds recorded "felt" about right and it was no surprise, therefore, to find by the standard check at M.I.R.A. a high degree of fidelity over most of the scale. Readings were optimistic by about 2 m.p.h. at ceiling pace.

Flexibility

An attribute of the "Arrow" was its flexibility. The acceleration indicator graph shows the gearchange speeds likely to be used by the average owner, but it was practicable to slip rapidly through second and third ratios to engage top before 20 m.p.h. had been attained. From that speed the model would pull away steadily without sign of distress. On premium grade fuel with a 1:24 proportion of two-stroke oil, it was impossible to make the unit pink.

The alternative technique of extracting the last ounce of power by hanging on to each gear up to the limit of useful r.p.m., was equally well accepted. In logging the standing-start quarter-mile figures, for instance, "third" was retained to within a few yards of the finish-line, when rapidly swapping to "top" served to swing the speedometer needle around to a fraction over 63 m.p.h. Against the wind, on the opposite run, staying in third gear produced best results.

The acceleration curve flattened above 60 m.p.h. and more than the nominal 1,000-yd. distance was needed to work up to speeds of more than 70 m.p.h. It was in such circumstances that the "Arrow" showed signs of

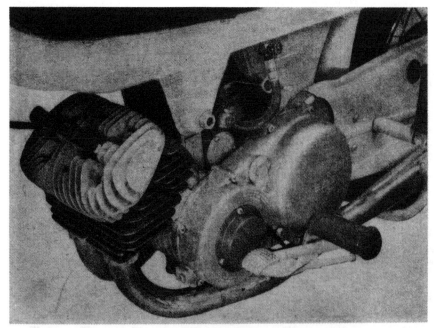

The sparking plugs are placed centrally in the new squish-type heads. The push-pull control of the butterfly-pattern choke is immediately below the petrol tap.

(Left) The pull-out filler cap is under the dual seat ; a corner of the battery is just visible above the hand. (Above) Ignition and lighting switches, ammeter and speedometer are mounted in the headlamp shell

thirst. Under these conditions—considerably more exacting than those of, say, a fast but constant-speed motorway journey—the fuel record showed 69 m.p.g.

Wet weather during almost the whole of the test period produced road conditions in which the well-nigh perfect steering and weight distribution of the " Arrow " were experienced at their best. The generally low construction of the machine, in conjunction with 16-in. diameter wheels, added to the rider's sense of security. All but the most short-legged can easily " touch down " with both feet. The kickstarter crank can be operated virtually from a sitting position and the machine is light to manhandle.

Braking

Apart from the engine modifications, the most outstanding 1961 improvement is seen in the performance of the front brake. With a new link-type anchorage, little braking effect is lost through torque reaction. Finger pressure at the handlebar lever is sufficient to check progress ; a firmer application reveals forward braking almost to racing standards. The " Arrow " could easily be stopped by both brakes within the accepted 10 yards from 30 m.p.h. and from high speeds the machine could be pulled up with-

out falter. There was no evidence of fade or drum distortion and the equipment was as reliable in wet weather as in fine.

The exhaust note was an inoffensive burble. The induction silencer, incorporated in the centre lug box structure, was effective in its main task and also trapped any fuel blow-back, so helping to keep the engine clean. There was a smear of oily exhaust on the two main silencers. The ends were fouled ; but the dark-finished tail pieces were easily cleaned.

On the near-side, the centre and prop-stand extensions wrap around the exhaust system but can be operated without the rider's toe-cap contacting the pipe. The fully enclosed rear chain retained its original tension and good condition throughout.

Weather protection was good. Deep mud-guards kept surface water at bay though, naturally, the absence of legshields made waders a " must."

With the tank hidden away, as it is, beneath the dual seat, there is a risk of filling up and forgetting which, in the absence of any kind of reserve supply, becomes a serious matter. It seems odd that so useful and widely accepted an item as a two-level tap should be included among the list of *extras*—at a mere 4s., too. An elec-

tric fuel gauge, similar to that now fitted to several British-made scooters, would be another way of eliminating the problem and adding a further touch of refinement to this already well-equipped machine.

Maintenance

Accessibility is excellent and a full kit of tools makes the normal maintenance an easy chore. The kit is carried in the " false tank "—within the upper body shell—which also encloses the two H.T. ignition coils. All spanners are to U.N.F. standard, and Allen and Phillips tools are also supplied. together with such special gadgets as the locking pegs required for front spindle removal. A 41-page instruction book (supplied wrapped in a polythene envelope) leaves the novice in no doubt as to what work he has to do and when.

Primary chaincase and gearbox fill-up points are indicated by references on the die-cast crankcase housing. Removal of three Phillips screws uncovers the contact-breaker, leaving the wiring intact. The near-side Ariel nameplate pulls away, allowing access to the rectifier. The battery is beneath the dual seat.

In short, nothing has been spared in making this quality lightweight as easy to maintain as it is exhilarating to ride.

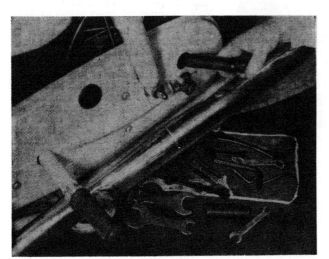

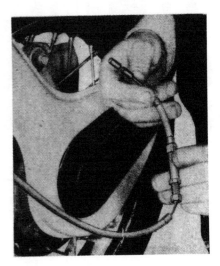

(Left) Access to the three bolts securing the rear sprocket to the wheel is obtained through a hole, normally sealed by a rubber plug, in the rear chaincase.

(Right) In addition to the normal adjuster, the front brake has a " free " nipple which, when considerable play has developed, can be used as a distance-piece between the fixed nipple and the operating lever.

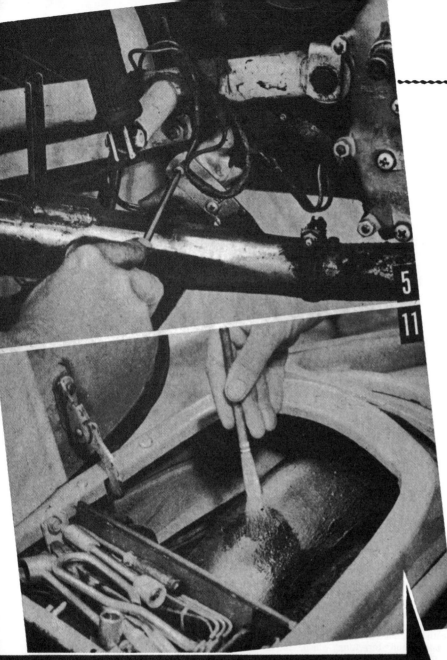

20 HINTS FOR THE ARIEL LEADER

These ideas and modifications will make your riding and maintenance easier, says E. BURRETT

THESE IDEAS SAV

1 The top ends of the front hydraulic dampers chafe the cable outers when the front wheel is on full lock. It can be stopped by fitting over them the neck cut from a small polythene bottle.

2 The front brake cable adjuster gets water into it and rusts the cable. Build up the cable outer with a few rounds of insulation tape just above the adjuster, smother the adjuster in grease and slide a length of rubber gas tubing over the adjuster and the tape.

3 Replace the wire which holds on the air cleaner with a No. 2 Jubilee Clip.

4 Fit a No. 3 Jubilee Clip round the rubber air intake where it fits on to the carburetter.

5 The rear stop light switch lets in water and shorts the battery. Re-wire so that both wires go into the switch from below. Then cover the switch and operating spring completely with a length of cycle inner tube in which a couple of slots have been cut to allow the fixing lugs to come through.

6 Before undoing the nut under the speedometer head to enable the cable to be greased, put a few turns of insulation tape an inch below the nut round the outer cable to stop the nut sliding down. It will save having to take off the side plate to retrieve it.

7 Replace the plastic petrol pipe with one which contains a filter. You then have a visible check on the sediment and it can be easily washed out by connecting the filter end of the pipe to the petrol tap and running a little petrol to waste through it. The carburetter will only then require dismantling for examination for wear.

8 If panniers are fitted the "tail" becomes too heavy to stay up without support. Make a "jack" with 24 inches of bamboo cane. Cut in the middle and join for use with a piece of dowel glued into one of the pieces (for easy carrying).

9 Cut a piece of cane 4 inches long for use in knocking out the front spindle. It can also be used to start the sprocket wheel nuts if it is put into "your end" of the box spanner.

10 The tank lock freezes in winter. If it is unfrozen with hot water before you leave home the wind whistling through the headlamp cowl will freeze it again before you reach your destination. Isolate it by taping back the tang and use a hawser lock to secure your machine during "a freeze up."

11 If you really want to preserve your machine. underseal *everywhere* where you don't polish.

12 If you have a screen extension, make a couple of polythene washers the size of half a crown to go between the extension and the large screen. They will prevent the two screens from scratching and scraping each other.

13 Put a roll of cloth between the end of the petrol tank and the plug leads where they enter the coils. It will stop the leads vibrating out of the coils, and soaks up any petrol that creeps along the tank seam.

14 Decarbonize the silencers at intervals of not more than 2,500 miles. If you leave it longer you will find it difficult to draw out the baffle plates without damage. If you remove the stay from the rear number plate and work from the back it is not a long job.

15 When decarbonizing the silencers, immerse and soak the baffle plates in a quart tin of Gunk from which the conical top has been removed with a tin opener, swish the baffle plates in a bucket of water and brush the carbon off with a piece of wire file card (obtainable from a tool shop). It makes a filthy job easy.

16 When reassembling a silencer after a decoke, the centre fixing rod slips back when the baffle plates are slid on. Wrap a piece of thin wire round the thread of the rod, feed the wire through the centre tube of the baffle plates and, holding the wire lightly, slide the plates back.

17 When the side panel fixing screw washers " go " make new ones from plastic garden hose (it can be bought by the foot).

18 The parcel locker lid tends to vibrate at speed. It can be cured by wiring a spring between the hinge arms (it doesn't show). You *may* be able to stop the vibration by re-positioning the fixing screws on the lid.

19 If you want your tools in the tool tray instantly accessible, stick a thick piece of foam plastic to the underneath of the seat, over the tray. It will hold them down and prevent rattle.

20 Engine noise can be absorbed considerably by putting a piece of old carpet on the bottom of the parcel locker. Cut it generously, using the fibre linings laid out flat as a pattern. Cut in one piece. Do not stick it down or you will not be able to get to the coils.

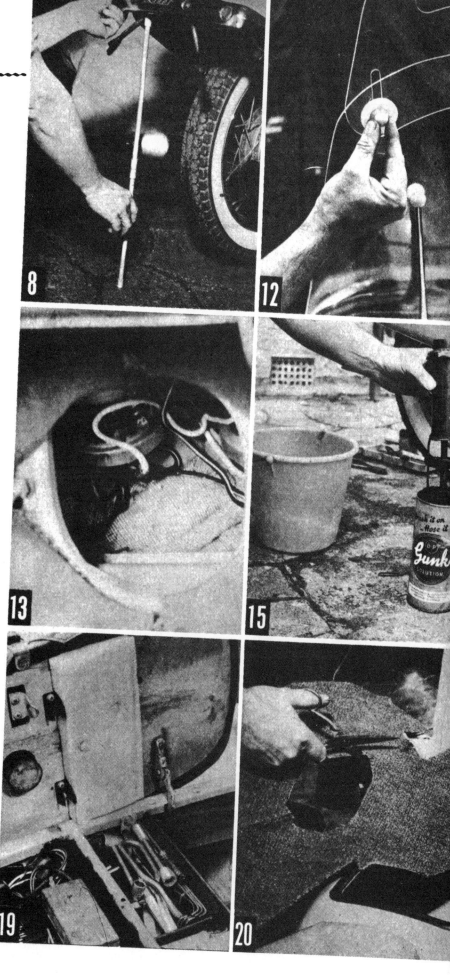

249 c.c. Ariel Leader

ALL-WEATHER LIGHTWEIGHT WITH LIVELY PERFORMANCE, EXCELLENT ROADHOLDING, GOOD BRAKES AND LUXURY EQUIPMENT

Above: A side panel is removed to show the engine drive side. Left: Front-brake anchor location

TWO years ago the Ariel concern took an imaginative step into the future by introducing the revolutionary Leader. The long-established models in the range—singles, twins and the legendary Square Four—were all shelved. And how that master-stroke has paid off! The Leader has become—and that right deservedly—one of the most popular motor cycles on British roads. It has set an example which other makers, in due time, must inevitably follow.

Constructional details are unorthodox by any standard. Beneath the immensely rigid, beam-type frame is slung a parallel-twin two-stroke engine-gear unit and that, in turn, is concealed by easily detachable side panels. Front suspension is by a trailing-link fork and the rear wheel is carried in a pivoted fork. Within this basic layout are ingenious features by the score to delight experienced riders as well as newcomers. And for those who want to gild the lily, a vastly comprehensive list of extras is available.

The 1961 Leader incorporates several detail improvements. Cylinder heads have squish-type combustion chambers,

Luxury plus: panniers, cast light-alloy carrier, flashers and reflector-equipped bumper bar

10 to 1 compression ratio, and an axial plug position. These new heads give an increase of 1.5 b.h.p.—power output is now 17.5 b.h.p. at 6,400 r.p.m.

Fuel-tank capacity has been increased to three gallons (originally the capacity was 2½ gallons); the front-brake anchorage has been repositioned to achieve smoother braking while retaining the pivoted linkage that isolates wheel suspension from brake reaction. Hubs are now cast-iron, of the type introduced for the Arrow—the Leader's stablemate—and have shallow external ribs to improve rigidity. The benefit of the more powerful brakes and nippier engine was immediately obvious on the road.

At all times, second-kick or third-kick starting was certain provided, for the first start of the day, the strangler was closed and half a minute or so was allowed for the carburettor float chamber to fill after the tap had been opened. When the engine had fired the strangler could be opened. When the power unit was warm it would idle slowly and reliably, two-stroking exceptionally well.

As with most two-stroke twin units, real power became apparent in the middle and upper parts of the r.p.m. scale, and only moderate punch was available at low engine revs. The engine was so docile that the machine would potter on level ground in top gear at 20 m.p.h., firing sweetly and without a trace of transmis-

sion snatch. At town speeds the exhaust was no more than a well-trained mutter. Mechanically, the engine was to all intents and purposes noiseless.

Making full use of the intermediate ratios introduced another side of the Leader's character. The revs soared up the scale, with a surge of power from 10 m.p.h. in bottom, 18 m.p.h. in second, 25 m.p.h. in third and 33 m.p.h. in top. Except at maximum speeds in the gears there was no trace of vibration.

With the engine spinning rapidly, the exhaust was felt to be a little healthy for lay-public ears in built-up areas. The silencers, of course, were new and carbon deposit would mellow the tone. With a genuine 60 m.p.h. cruising speed within the scope of this superb machine, the Leader is obviously well able to cope with long-distance touring. And, with panniers and a rear carrier as fitted to the test model, the luggage-carrying problem is overcome.

Provided the controls were manipulated intelligently, the gear change was of the knife-into-butter order. With the engine ticking over slowly, bottom could be noiselessly engaged and neutral could be equally easily selected from bottom or second gear. An indicator light in the dash (available at extra charge) simplifies selection of neutral and also acts as an ignition warning.

Light and positive, the steering in all its aspects proved above reproach. Any chosen line on any bend could be taken with the certain knowledge that, irrespective of bumps or potholes, it would be held precisely. Both front and rear suspension characteristics are perfectly matched; there was no suggestion of pitching or weaving at any time, and bumpy surfaces were ironed out as if they weren't there.

Viewed broadside, the Leader gives the impression of having a high centre of gravity. Yet there was no impression of top hamper, a factor which enabled the machine to be "chucked around" at will. Traffic threading was child's play. Although the effect of strong winds could be felt, there was never any suggestion of the machine deviating more than fractionally off course.

Carefully tailored, the riding position is comfortable for average or tallish riders. The clutch and front brake levers are non-adjustable but afford a sensible wrist angle. Reach to the levers is well within the span of the smallest hand. The gear-change and rear-brake pedals are both simply (and widely) adjustable for height. A worth-while safety feature is that the front brake, as well as the rear, is coupled to the warning light.

Ample protection is furnished by the windscreen and weathershield. Except in really heavy rain, there was never any need to wear overboots. Even the rider's hands were adequately protected. The screen extension for tall riders (available at extra charge) proved most effective, especially in wet weather.

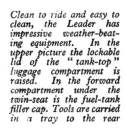

Clean to ride and easy to clean, the Leader has impressive weather-beating equipment. In the upper picture the lockable lid of the " tank-top " luggage compartment is raised. In the forward compartment under the twin-seat is the fuel-tank filler cap. Tools are carried in a tray to the rear

First-class visibility is given by the headlamp. Intensity and spread of the beam is sufficient to allow daylight cruising speeds to be used after dark. The dipswitch is mounted below the handlebar, where its trigger is easily operated by the left thumb. The headlamp beam may be set in a jiffy by fore and aft movement of a small lever protruding through the facia. A loud, clear warning is given by the horn.

A particularly useful feature is the locker in the top of the body; it is large enough to accommodate a safety helmet and several medium-size parcels besides. Of those many extra items, the twin rear-view mirrors, mounted on each side of the weathershield, were most effective and totally vibration-free.

Trafficators, operated from a switch located under the left handlebar, were reliable and added their share to the relaxation of riding in dense traffic. Then, too, the parking light did away with nagging doubts about leaving the machine in unlit areas. An inspection lamp, which plugs into a socket on the facia, also proved its worth, especially when routine maintenance tasks had to be carried out in poor light.

Undoing five slotted screws (and, on the right, removing the kick-starter and gear pedal) allow the side panels to be removed for access to the engine and gear box. And pivoting the tail of the body makes rear-wheel removal a simple job.

White side-wall tyres enhance the already smart lines of the Leader, a peppy lightweight that has just about everything the experienced rider, or learner, could require. The model's appeal is world wide; its potentialities are enormous.

SPECIFICATION

ENGINE: Ariel 249 c.c. (54 x 54mm) two-stroke twin with separate iron cylinder barrels and light-alloy heads, having squish-type combustion chambers. Roller big-end bearings. Crankshaft supported in three ball bearings. Compression ratio 10 to 1. Petroil lubrication; mixture ratio 25 to 1.

CARBURETTOR: Amal Monobloc with strangler for cold starting. Felt air filter.

IGNITION AND LIGHTING: Coil ignition with fixed timing. Lucas RM13/15 50-watt alternator driven by right-hand end of the crankshaft. Lucas 6-volt, 13-ampere-hour battery charged through rectifier. Lucas 6in-diameter headlamp with pre-focus light unit.

TRANSMISSION: Four-speed gear box in unit with the engine; positive-stop foot control. Gear ratios: bottom, 19 to 1; second, 11 to 1; third, 8.5 to 1; top, 5.9 to 1. Multi-plate clutch with Neolangite facings operating in oil. Primary chain, ⅜ x 0.225in in cast-aluminium oil-bath case. Rear chain, ½ x 0.305in in pressed-steel case. Engine r.p.m. at 30 m.p.h. in top gear, 2,650.

FUEL CAPACITY: 3 gallons.

TYRES: Dunlop white-wall 3.25 x 16in; rear, Universal; front, Lightweight Reinforced ribbed.

BRAKES: 6in diameter x 1⅛ wide front and rear.

SUSPENSION: Ariel trailing-link front and pivoted rear forks, both employing Armstrong hydraulically damped shock absorbers.

WHEELBASE: 51in unladen. Ground clearance, 5in unladen.

SEAT: Ariel dual-seat; unladen height, 31in.

WEIGHT: 351 lb equipped with all available extras (pannier cases and bags, luggage carrier, prop and front stands, trafficators, parking lamp,

Smiths eight-day clock, neutral indicator, inspection lamp) and tools but without fuel.

PRICE: £165 15s 0d. With purchase tax (in Great Britain only), £199 18s 9d. With extra equipment fitted, £236 10s 8d.

ROAD TAX: £1 17s 6d a year.

MAKERS: Ariel Motors, Ltd., Selly Oak, Birmingham, 29.

DESCRIPTION: *The Motor Cycle,* 6 October 1960.

PERFORMANCE DATA
(Obtained at the Motor Industry Research Association's proving ground, Lindley.)

MEAN MAXIMUM SPEED: Bottom: 25 m.p.h.
Second: 42 m.p.h.
Third: 57 m.p.h.
Top: 63 m.p.h.

HIGHEST ONE-WAY SPEED: 67 m.p.h.
(conditions: windless; rider normally seated)

MEAN ACCELERATION:	10–30 m.p.h.	20–40 m.p.h.	30–50 m.p.h.
Second	6.6 sec	6.2 sec	
Third	9.4 sec	9.8 sec	9.0 sec
Top	—	16.2 sec	18.0 sec

Mean speed at end of quarter-mile from rest: 59 m.p.h.
Mean time to cover standing quarter-mile: 22 sec.

PETROIL CONSUMPTION: At 30 m.p.h., 80 m.p.g.; at 40 m.p.h., 78 m.p.g.; at 50 m.p.h., 62 m.p.g.

BRAKING: From 30 m.p.h. to rest 34ft (surface, dry tarmac).

TURNING CIRCLE: 14ft 6in.

MINIMUM NON-SNATCH SPEED: 12 m.p.h. in top gear.

WEIGHT PER C.C.: 1.41 lb.

ARIEL ARROW

ROAD TEST

THE National Rally is a pretty tough test for any machine. Six hundred miles (nearer nine hundred by the time I got home again) all crammed into one wet weekend. This year I chose to do it on an Ariel Arrow—the naked version of the famous Leader.

You pick your own route on this Rally. I decided on one that included main roads, country lanes, London traffic, the Derbyshire Peak District and finished with a tour of the Industrial North. There were dry roads and wet roads, smooth roads and Lancashire cobbles. And of course I drove through the night.

Such a test told me pretty well everything I wanted to know about the Arrow—its bad points as well as its good ones. Let's start with the things I liked about it—and there were plenty.

First, the handling. This was superb. It is light, and after 36 hours in the saddle I can honestly say that I suffered from no physical fatigue whatsoever. No ache across the shoulders, no sore seat, no stiff arms. Show the Arrow a corner and she goes round as if on rails.

In the wet I found that I was pressing on with greater confidence than I have ever experienced with any other machine. The brakes are first class. At no time did I experience any form of grabbing or fade. This is probably the safest motorcycle I have ever ridden.

The two-stroke twin motor gives good acceleration in all gears, provided you keep the revs up. But I wasn't very keen on the gearchange. I found that the travel of the lever was too long. The gears went in all right, but the whole selector mechanism seemed a bit rough, and I was finding false neutrals all over the box.

The fuel consumption was disappointing—just over 53 m.p.g. during the whole test. On the Rally itself I never exceeded 60 m.p.h., and usually cruised at 50 to 55 m.p.h.

Most routine maintenance jobs can be done easily enough, but the carburetter and ignition coils are rather inaccessible, the coils being hidden in the middle of the box frame.

So there you have it—a machine with many excellent points and a few bad ones. But you can't have it all ways—after all the Arrow only costs £168. If you want a machine suitable for town work or for the open road, a machine with exhilarating performance and perfect handling, then you should think seriously about an Arrow.—D.F.

HOW LONG DOES IT TAKE ?

Remove and replace rear wheel	18 minutes
Remove both cylinder heads...	14 minutes
Adjust both brakes................	½ minute
Check points........................	2½ minutes
Adjust rear chain.................	1½ minutes
Check battery level...............	½ minute

'M.M.' MACHINE TEST REPORT No. ....15.....

Machine ...ARIEL........ Model ...ARROW.... c.c. ..249..

TEST Mileage ...1278... Price new ...£168...... Examiner...DF...

Supplied by ...ARIEL MOTORS LTD..........

Maximum Points 10 (compared with machines in same c.c. and price range)

Brakes (front)	10	Lights	9
Brakes (rear)	9	Engine accessibility	7
Brakes (both)	9	General performance	9
Steering at high speed	10	Overall finish	8
Steering at low speed	9	Electrical layout	6
Gearbox action	7	TOTAL	93

OVER WHOLE TEST
Fuel consumption ...53¼.. m.p.g.

Acceleration 0-50 .....9.... secs.

Top speed ....72... m.p.h.

Remarks...*..Rider flat... ...on tank..

BRAKING GRAPH

M.P.H. (100 95 90 85 80 75 70 65 60 55 50 45 40 35 30 25 20 15 10 5)

STOPPING DISTANCE IN FEET
(0 5 10 15 20 25 30 35 40 45 50 55 60 65 70 75 80 85 90 95 100)

ARIEL stripdown

BOTTOM-HALF MAINTENANCE FOR THE ARROW & LEADER

HOW TO . . .
- ▶ Strip the Clutch
- ▶ Remove Primary Chain
- ▶ Withdraw Flywheel Assembly
- ▶ Renew Main Bearings

THE Leader has been on the road long enough now for some to have done more than 50,000 miles. And inevitably a few will soon need a bottom end overhaul. Here we show you how to do it.

You will want a few service tools for this job. None of them is expensive, and they make a most worth-while investment. Get them from your local Ariel dealer.

You don't *have* to take the engine out of the frame to remove the mains and big-ends, but it is a very simple operation if you choose to do so.

We dealt with the top overhaul of the Leader and Arrow engines in the April, 1960 issue of MM, so for the purposes of this article we can carry on from where we left off.

tart by removing generator from he offside. Undo three Phillips crews and take off the cover and hen undo three nuts holding the tator plate. Note washers beneath

Over on the nearside remove the contact breaker cover. With a big screwdriver remove the large screw in the centre and remove the cam from off the end of the crankshaft

The contact breaker cam coming off (left). Now to remove the chaincase. First the eight chaincase screws, (Phillips headed again) and then the drain plug bolt with spanner

ARIEL

WORKING ON THE BOTTOM HALF . . .

Remove Phillips headed self-tapping screw from the front of the chaincase and then unscrew the primary chain adjuster plug with a screwdriver. Put plug on one side, but not the screw

With the plug out of the way gently screw the self-tapping screw into the nylon chain adjuster and use this to pull it out of the chaincase. The chaincase cover can now be removed

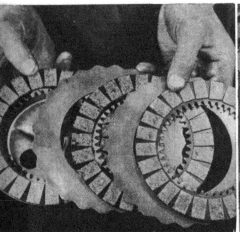

Pull off the endplate (which has cork inserts) and the rest of the clutch plates. Note the order: endplate, plain, cork, plain, cork. In other words two plains, two corks and cover

Replace the three thimbles, springs, etc., and fit service tool (the clutch " banjo ") to lock clutch. Now undo the thin locknut and then the centre nut beneath it. Note position of washer

Remove the clutch centre. This picture shows the back of the clutch centre assembly, showing how the sleeve nut hold the two parts together. Place all clutch parts carefully to one side

Now to remove the other bearing plate on opposite side of engine. Undo the three nuts and Woodruff key. Replace rotor retaining bolt and use the same flywheel extractor to pull plate off

A special tool in three parts is now required to separate the two parts of the crankshaft. Locking plate (1) goes on to studs, bar (2) locks flywheel, and key (3) undoes the extractor bolt

With the extractor bolt undone pull out the offside flywheel assembly. will have to be juggled a bit. Take care and be patient, and do not force Now repeat with the nearside assembl

he rotor is the next item to come ff. To do this you must first undo he rotor securing bolt, which means ocking the flywheel with a service ool as shown. When locked undo bolt

Unscrew the rotor securing bolt and pull rotor off shaft. Note position of the two washers under head of bolt and the key on shaft as well as the rubber "O" ring on end of the shaft

Now for the clutch. First remove the three sleeve nuts, washers, springs and thimbles. Note on reassembly that the washer must go between the bolt-head and the spring, and nowhere else

he primary chain comes off complete ith clutch backplate and flywheel, hich has the sprocket attached to it. ock flywheel again, undo shaft nut nd pull flywheel off with extractor

Now withdraw flywheel complete with chain and clutch backplate. If they are stubborn ease with a screwdriver. Take care not to lose any of the ¼in. rollers from the clutch centre (right)

Removing the bearing plate on primary side. First undo the three nuts, two screws and one bolt from the plate, and the key from the shaft. Screw in flywheel extractor and withdraw plate

o remove the main bearings from the adplates is simplicity itself. Take out e circlip on the offside plate (there n't one on the nearside) and dip hot water for a few moments

To remove the centre main bearing you need the last of the special tools. This consists of a long bolt with a tommy-bar on the end. On the offside a boss fits into the centre bearing

Picture showing the centre bearing extractor from the nearside. Note the way it has been assembled. Tighten long bolt to withdraw bearing. This is also used for fitting new bearing

GOLDEN ARROW

Sports Version of Popular Ariel 249 c.c. Twin

Golden indeed: finish of the new model is almost startlingly gay

ARIELS, that factory with the happy knack of producing sure-fire winners at will, have done it again. There are now *three* 249 c.c. two-stroke twins in the Selly Oak line-up, and the latest creation—officially the Sports Arrow but almost certainly destined for fame as the Golden Arrow—is as eye-popping a model as ever brought a crowd flocking round a showroom window.

Nor is it in appearance alone that the newcomer earns a place as a model in its own right, for to replace the standard $\frac{7}{8}$in-choke Amal Monobloc carburettor of the Arrow there is a $1\frac{1}{16}$in-choke instrument, with the inlet passages in the crankcase casting specially opened out.

Power output is boosted to a claimed 20.2 b.h.p. at 6,650 r.p.m., with a maximum road speed in the region of 75 to 80 m.p.h.

Just how gorgeously a gold-finish tank shell and rear-number-plate fairing tones with the light Admiralty grey of the Ariel frame beam and mudguards, no mere black-and-white photograph can show. And that is by no means all, for the primary chaincase and the silencer end caps are brightly polished—and there are acres of chromium plating on the right-hand-side engine cover, front-fork link covers, tool-box lid, contact-breaker cover and lifting handles. Polished light-alloy trim plates set off the knee-grip rubbers. Whitewall tyres complete the picture.

Specification of the sportster extends to a low-level handlebar, equipped with plastic grips in bright red p.v.c. and with ball-end Doherty front-brake and clutch levers; the effect is heightened by a special M.P.C. sports screen. The kick-starter pedal is of folding type and there is a two-level fuel tap. Both prop and centre stands are fitted. Extra equipment available embraces a front stand, rear carrier (and rubber luggage straps), a dual-seat cover and seat strap.

The Sports Arrow is already in production. Indeed, Midland Editor Bob Currie sampled the first production model last week.

Left: Low-level handlebar, ball-end levers, sports wind-screen: all are featured on the new model

Right: The primary chaincase, dull-finished on the standard Arrow, is buffed to give a mirror-like surface

Model	Capacity, Bore, Stroke and Type of Engine	Comp Ratio	Ign	Gear Ratios				Capacity Fuel Oil	Susp F R	Size of Tyres Front	Rear	Wt lb	Basic Price £ s d	Total Price £ s d
Sports Arrow	249 c.c. 54×54 mm t.s. twin	10:1	C	5.9	8.5	11.0	19.0	3g —	TL PF	3.25×16	3.25×16	278	155 10 0	187 11 5

MANUFACTURERS: Ariel Motors, Ltd., Grange Road, Selly Oak, Birmingham, 29. EXTRAS: Front stand, 12s 8d; dual-seat cover, 9s 4d; carrier and straps, £1 11s 1d; dual-seat strap, 6s 3d. ABBREVIATIONS: C, coil; TL, trailing link; PF, pivoted fork. Total price includes British purchase tax.

Straight Off the Line

THE ARIEL SUPER SPORTS ARROW
AND D.M.W. DEEMSTER ARE PUT
THROUGH THEIR PACES

By BOB CURRIE

PRETTY so-so sort of time, the middle of January. Any other year, I'd be glad to swap it for just a couple of hours of mid-July—but look what this week has brought! Two brand-new two-fifties; and better still, much better still, the opportunity of trying both of them on the road. When I say brand-new I mean just that, for the Ariel Super Sports Arrow and the D.M.W. Deemster were both straight-off-the-assembly-line jobs with nil mileage on their respective speedometers. In fact, at Sedgley I had to cool my heels in patience until they'd finished building the model, the very first production example of the kick-starter Deemster. But the wait was worth while, as you shall hear.

Quite a coincidence that both the machines which make their bows this week should be 249 c.c. two-stroke twins. But there the resemblance ends, for they are aimed at different sections of the market and, on the road, proved as different as spice from sugar. Spice; that was the slick and sporty Arrow. Sugar; that was the gentlemanly Deemster, as sweet and luxurious a touring mount as ever pottered down a country lane.

Each of us has his own opinion on the dropped-handlebar question. You either like 'em, or you don't. I don't; so on that score I viewed the Golden Arrow with something of a jaundiced eye when the Selly Oak folk first wheeled it out of the factory. But you can get used to anything and before I had covered many miles of my native Worcestershire roads I was thoroughly at home, in more ways than one.

Brand-new that engine may have been, but there was no suggestion of tightness anywhere. Here was a mount eager to get going, a model to have fun with, and the merest tweak of the grip would send the revs zizzing up the scale. "Keep her buzzing to get the best from her," so ran Ariel boss Ken Whistance's parting words, "and use the gear box to keep her on the boil." Fair enough.

Gingerly at first, more confidently later, I gave the Ariel its head, letting the revs mount where they would while restraining the throttle opening to prudent limits. The needle swung round the clock; 50 came and went, then 60, and soon the needle wavered round the 70 mark. There was plenty more medicine in the bottle even then, but I was ever the cautious one. It was enough to indicate that, given a fully-run-in engine, the Ariel would certainly justify the Super Sports label. Yes, indeed!

Stark against the setting sun, the black bulk of the Malvern Hills made an irresistible goal, with a chance to try out the hill-climbing ability of the little golden beauty. And you know what? There's nothing top-end-only about the Arrow sportster.

Midlanders, anyway, will know that long drag up from Malvern to the Wyche Cutting, a saddle through the crest of the hills. Third gear and half-throttle all the way is a most respectable climb for a two-fifty, any day of the week. Looking westwards from the hillside road, the red-

Above: A shot which shows off the sporting lines of the Sports Arrow to perfection. Left: Wheel removal on the Deemster is facilitated by a simple strut which engages with built-in sockets at front or rear of the floorboard sub-frame

The new D.M.W. offers first-class weather protection. And by the way, the stop light has a mercury-actuated switch

tinted hills of Herefordshire made a scene which only an artist's brush could have captured. But already the valleys were in darkness and it was time to turn for home.

The average sports model sings its song a mite too loudly for comfort; but not the Ariel. This one has a soothing lullaby of an exhaust note, deeper, quieter even than that of the Arrow. Why that should be so I wouldn't know, for the silencers are similar. I merely offer the comment.

So all right, here's my summing up. First-prod starting, no vibration anywhere in the rev range, outstanding road-holding (with that Ariel trailing-link fork you don't steer—you just think at the model), and a finish that is truly glamorous. If ever a

machine was destined for the hit parade it's the Golden Arrow.

Something entirely different from Sedgley, a design which takes the best of scooter and motor-cycle practice and marries them into a machine which has just about everything—the Deemster. And I'll say one thing right away; it's one of the most comfortable mounts I've ever had the good fortune to try. Deep-cushioned seat, footboards which offer the chance to shift one's feet—just to relieve the monotony from time to time—sensibly wide legshields and a screen to keep off the rain and cold.

Seating position? Yes, it is a bit scooter-like; but get on the road and the balance and handling of the Deemster are 100 per cent motor cycle. The big tank between the knees, and the Villiers engine out in the fresh air; both help to dispel the scooter illusion. Fog in the hollows, icy patches here and there on the early-morning roads didn't exactly fill me with confidence as I headed the D.M.W. out into Warwickshire but I needn't have worried. Not once did the wheels show any tendency to wander.

The Deemster, like the Ariel, is remarkably quiet. The large silencers, positioned below the footboards, have Villiers internals in D.M.W. shells and they mute the exhaust to a note pleasant to the ear. Something else, too; the D.M.W. intake silencer really does a good job and when the throttle is opened there is no accompanying roar from the neighbourhood of the carburettor. While on the subject of noise, you might expect legshields to act as sounding boards, magnifying the various taps and rustlings of the engine and throwing them back to the rider. Nothing of the sort. That Villiers twin sounded as quiet as if it had been hidden under the rear panels.

For certain starting, particularly on a

cold morning, the air lever must be closed. Flood the carburettor, an exploratory swing on the kick-starter pedal—then one good kick and that's it. Easy. But all the same, the pedal is mounted rather high and I found it best to stand at the side of the model and operate from there.

That roomy bin under the seat was amply large enough for me to stow my waders (who needs waders on a Deemster, anyway?); and with the seat raised it was but the work of a second or two to slip off either side panel, with no fiddling little catches to undo. Nor was there any suggestion of chattering or drumming.

Certainly, I tried the Deemster at night. And for those twin headlamps I have nothing but praise. True, they don't throw the light any farther than would a single lamp, but the parallel beams give a really wide pool of illumination so that the whole width of the road, from verge to verge, can be seen. What's more, the beam-adjuster knob, by means of which the whole lamp panel can be tilted, works like a charm. And those D.M.W.-Girling brakes—they are simply terrific!

Came Saturday morning, and a jaunt to the shops proved the model thoroughly town-trained. The pillion passenger, too, found plenty of room for her feet and commented most favourably on the length and comfort of the seat. Oh, and those lovely windtone horns! Loud and melodious (even though this was the 6-volt model), they could grace a Bentley.

I'll let the final comment come from a scooterist who stopped me in Solihull, and who positively drooled as I pointed out to him the many ingenious features which Mike Riley has packed into the design (I even demonstrated the jack for him). "When'll they be in the shops?" he asked eagerly. "How soon can I have one?" Patience, chum, patience; they're coming off the line right now.

Left: Winter morning. Bob pilots the Deemster over ice-covered roads, twin headlamps piercing the chilly mist. Right: And here he heels the Sports Arrow through a Worcestershire bend

The old and the new heads. That on the left is the standard one, that on the right the high compression squish head

Poor performance or difficult starting can often be traced to faulty condensers (arrowed). If in any doubt fit new ones

TUNING TIPS FOR A
FASTER ARROW

JIM CALVERT of Writers Ltd. tells how to get up to another 10 m.p.h. from Arrow or Leader

THE Ariel Leader hit the motorcycle world like a bombshell in the summer of 1958. Since then it has gone from strength to strength, together with its naked sister, the Arrow.

Despite the nippy performance of the engine, many owners want to go even faster. Others want greater economy. Whatever your choice, you can do the same modifications. They give greater engine efficiency, which can be used to give more speed or more miles per gallon. That part of it depends on your riding methods.

Most of the following modifications have been evolved in the development department at the factory, and some of them are incorporated in the latest models. This article is for the chap with a Leader or Arrow made before October, 1960, that is *before* engine number T17591B on the Leader, or T17441T on the Arrow.

These were the "slow" machines, the ones with a compression ratio of $8\frac{1}{4}$:1 that would only jog along at around the 70 m.p.h. mark. If you have one of these and you want to bring it up to 1961 specification without doing any skilled tuning, then read on.

Cylinder Heads

The most dramatic difference performance-wise between the old and the new engines is obtained by use of the new

Some models may be fitted with the old type carburetter jet block (left). The new one (right) has chamfered spray tube

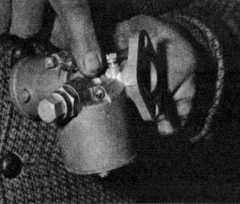
Pilot jet setting is critical as regards economy. In certain cases it is possible to change standard jet for smaller one

It is essential to get ignition timing accurately set on both cylinders, not just one. Use rod supplied in tool

A well-tuned motor cannot be expected to give of its best with a dirty air cleaner. Wash clean, or better still, fit new one

Power can be lost through badly adjusted cycle parts. Are the brakes binding? Is the primary chain tight? Check regularly

Silencers need cleaning at least every 2,500 miles. If you leave it any longer it may be difficult to remove baffle

"squish" cylinder heads, with their compression ratio of 10:1. These will fit straight on to pre-October, 1960, machines, both Leader and Arrow, and no other modification is necessary. Just throw the old heads away and fit the new ones.

Cost? Much less than you think—a mere £3 a pair. Many owners are fitting them, and your local Ariel dealer should have plenty in stock. The improved head gives better combustion and more power, resulting in higher speed for the same throttle opening. or a smaller throttle opening for the same speed (i.e., greater economy).

Carburetter

Some of the early models—particularly the Leaders—had a brass tube sticking out of the bottom of the carburetter block, into which the main jet was screwed. The top of this tube stands about a quarter of an inch into the air stream. On later models this tube was chamfered on one edge, giving better atomisation. The old block carries a 170 main jet, the modified block a 140 main jet. Never change one without the other. The price is 14s., including the main jet. The angled spray tube gives greater economy and improved acceleration.

The pilot jet setting is extremely critical as far as economy is concerned on these machines. Sometimes they are set on the rich side when delivered from the factory, which is always a good thing when run-ning-in a two-stroke.

When the engine has done at least a thousand miles, adjust the pilot air screw to give the most economical setting. Screw it out as far as it will go without giving an erratic tickover. Sometimes it is possible to screw it right out without it making any appreciable difference to the speed of the engine. If this is the case you can well fit a smaller pilot jet. The standard fitting is a 30 pilot jet—try a 25 and see if it makes any difference.

Ignition

Another critical factor in getting the best out of your Leader or Arrow is the ignition, particularly the timing. For all practical purposes the peg in the hole method is quite satisfactory, but for that extra urge you must make sure that it is absolutely spot on. The most important thing is to get the timing on both cylinders exactly right—there is no point in having one right and the other slightly out.

You *can* use a timing disc, but provided there is no backlash you can use the rod in the hole. First clean the contact-breaker points, and set each at the correct gap—.015 inch. Now connect up the light gadget as described in the handbook. Poke the rod into the top contact-breaker cover hole and turn the engine *forwards* until the rod passes through the hole drilled in the flywheel. At this very moment the light should just glow, or flicker, as the points start to open. If

it doesn't, slacken the mounting plate screws and move it until you get the correct setting. Tighten the screws—and check that you haven't altered the timing in doing so.

Now you know that one cylinder is perfectly timed. But how about the other? Turn the engine 180 degrees, connect the light to the other set of points and poke the rod through the hole. If the light flickers as the rod goes home, then well and good.

If not, you can take up the adjustment by altering the gap on the contact-breaker points by making them either smaller or larger. A thou. or two either way isn't going to affect performance as much as having the timing slightly out on one cylinder.

The condensers on these machines sometimes cause trouble. Missing on one pot at any speed could well be due to a faulty condenser. If the points are blackened and worn, this would confirm it. The only remedy is to fit a new condenser—they cost 8s. 3d. each.

Plugs

It is important to fit the recommended plug. This is Lodge 2HLN, or equivalent. On no account fit a softer one. If you are more interested in top speed than anything else and go belting all over the country flat out, then you may use a harder plug—say, a 3HLN. But don't grumble if it oils up in traffic.

continued on page 83

The 247 c.c. ARIEL 'ARROW SUPER SPORTS'

A fast twin two-stroke

of unorthodox design

with excellent handling

Specification

ENGINE
Type .. .. Twin-cylinder two-stroke
Bore .. .. 54 mm.
Stroke .. .. 54 mm.
Cubic capacity .. .. .. 247 c.c.
Piston-controlled cylinder-wall ports.
Compression ratio .. .. .. 10 : 1
Carburetter .. Amal Monobloc 1 1/16-in. bore
Ignition   Battery-powered coil, with separately adjustable contact-breaker timings
Generator   Lucas RM18 6-v. 55-w. alternator with rectifier for battery charging and lighting
Makers' claimed output .. 20 b.h.p. at 6,500 r.p.m.
Lubrication .. .. Petroil at 20 : 1 ratio
Starting .. .. Kickstarter, folding crank

TRANSMISSION
Four-speed unit gearbox with footchange.
Ratios .. .. .. 5.9, 7.8, 11.0, 19.0 : 1
Speed at 1,000 r.p.m. in top gear .. 11½ m.p.h.

Speed equivalent to revs at maximum power rating:
Second gear .. .. .. 41 m.p.h.
Third gear .. .. .. 58 m.p.h.
Top gear .. .. .. 76 m.p.h.
Primary drive   Single-row chain in oilbath
Secondary drive .. .. Fully enclosed single-row chain

CYCLE PARTS
Frame .. Beam type: pressed-steel box-section main member
Front suspension   Trailing-link forks with coil springs and two-way hydraulic damping
Rear suspension .. Swinging fork with two Armstrong hydraulically damped spring units
Tyres .. Dunlop 3.25 × 16-in. whitewalls; ribbed front, studded rear
Brakes .. Full-width type, 6-in. dia. front and rear. Total lining area 24½ sq. in.
Fuel tank .. Located within main frame pressings; three position tap
Lamps .. 30/24-w. head, 3-w. pilot, 18/3-w. stop/tail, 1.8-w. speedometer

Horn .. .. .. Lucas high-frequency
Battery .. .. .. Lucas 13 a.h.
Speedometer   Smiths 100 m.p.h., non-trip type
Seating .. .. Dual seat
Stands .. .. .. Centre and prop
Toolkit: Spanners: 3 open-ended, 3 box, 1 ring, 1 "C." Phillips screwdriver. Tyre lever. Allen key. Tommy bar. Front suspension tools.
Toolroll housing .. In centre of main frame pressing
Finish .. .. .. Gold and ivory

OTHER EQUIPMENT
Sports handlebars; Perspex flyscreen; rear chain enclosure; twin lifting handles; ball-ended levers.

PRICES
Machine   £190 15s. 7d. (inc. £35 5s. 7d. P.T.)
Extras .. .. None
Total as tested .. .. £190 15s. 7d.
Tax .. .. £2 5s. p.a.
Makers .. Ariel Motors, Ltd., Selly Oak, Birmingham 29

'Motor Cycling' Test Data

Conditions. *Weather: Dry, mild (Barometer 30.00 in. Hg. Thermometer 50°F.). Wind: Easterly, not more than 2 m.p.h. Surface (braking and acceleration): Dry asphalt. Rider: 11½ stone, wearing two-piece suit, boots and safety helmet, normally seated except where stated. Fuel: "Super" grade (101½ research method octane rating), with diluent two-stroke oil at 20 : 1 ratio—also, see text.*

Venue: *Motor Industry Research Association Station, Lindley.*

Speed at end of standing 1,000 yd.:
East .. .. .. 66.4 m.p.h.
West.. .. .. 69.0 m.p.h.
Mean .. .. 67.7 m.p.h.
Speed at end of standing 1,400 yd. (rider prone):
East .. .. .. 75.0 m.p.h.
West .. .. 75.4 m.p.h.
Mean .. .. 75.2 m.p.h.
Braking from 30 m.p.h. (all brakes) 11½ yd.
Fuel consumption:
At constant 30 m.p.h. .. 116 m.p.g.
50 m.p.h. .. 80 m.p.g.
500-mile overall figure .. 68 m.p.g.

Speedometer
30 m.p.h. indicated = 28.4 m.p.h. true
40 m.p.h. indicated = 38.8 m.p.h. true
50 m.p.h. indicated = 49.1 m.p.h. true
60 m.p.h. indicated = 60.2 m.p.h. true
70 m.p.h. indicated = 70.0 m.p.h. true

Mileage Recorder .. .. Accurate

Electrical Equipment
Top gear speed at which generator output balances:
Ignition only .. .. 22 m.p.h.
Minimum obligatory lights.. 24 m.p.h.
Headlamp main beam .. 29 m.p.h.

Weights and Capacities
Certified kerbside weight (with oil and 1 gal. fuel) .. .. 308 lb.
Weight distribution (rider normally seated):
Front wheel.. .. .. 44%
Rear wheel 56%
Tank capacity (metered):
Total .. .. .. 2.8 gal.
Reserve .. .. .. 1¼ pints

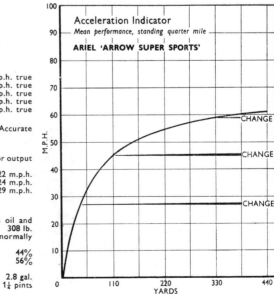

Acceleration Indicator
Mean performance, standing quarter mile
ARIEL 'ARROW SUPER SPORTS'

(vertical axis: M.P.H.; horizontal axis: YARDS; markers: CHANGE, CHANGE, CHANGE)

THE Ariel "Arrow Super Sports" is indeed an exhilarating addition to Britain's growing range of 250 c.c. "work-and-pleasure" mounts. Sprung as a "mid-season" surprise early this year, it is a logical development of the established "Leader" basic design—a twin-cylinder inclined two-stroke engine, with unit four-speed gearbox, mounted below a deep beam structure of welded steel pressings.

Producing a creditable 20 b.h.p. at 6,500 r.p.m., the "Arrow Super Sports" checked out at M.I.R.A. with a performance which, a decade ago, would have been impossible from a silenced "250," and which today is virtually as good as that of many "350s "—topping 75 m.p.h. mean speed for the two-way runs through the electronic timing gear.

Downhill on the open road, it would gallop up to 80 m.p.h. Here is thrilling performance, partly due to completely spot-on gearing.

Fine Acceleration

The Ariel also shone at acceleration. Once the high-compression unit was "on song" it ran up the rev scale as only a tuned two-stroke does. It was more than zestful, it was *sudden*. Almost before the rider was aware that the revs had begun to soar, they had reached the change-up point for the next cog.

The change was slick, and reapplication of the drive revealed the motor to be well into the "go" band for the next upward thrust to a power-peaking crescendo. There was no "dead period" during which acceleration would lag while the revs built up.

The acceleration curve on the opposite page is an excellent one for a 250 c.c. machine. To reach 60 m.p.h. in less than a quarter of a mile from rest is quite a feat for a quarter-litre.

As already mentioned, the twin had to be put "on song." Low down in the rev band, worth while power was lacking, which was not surprising with a tuned engine of this type. But farther up the scale the "Arrow" had the useful, and most unusual, attribute that results were produced *according to throttle opening* rather than according to revs. For example, when dawdling along at 33/34 m.p.h. in top, a really good handful of twistgrip would yield a quick response.

The twin silencers (which can be dismantled for cleaning) were notably efficient at the engine speeds normally used in built-up areas.

At large throttle openings, "Arrow" noise was compounded of some muted background whine, induction hiss, and exhaust yowl—all totalling nothing over a reasonable level for open-road work.

But there was an exhaust discharge of another kind that could come about. The makers recommend the use of two-stroke oil *with* diluent at 20:1 ratio, or oil *without* diluent at 24:1. Using non-diluent lubricants at ratios richer than ½ pint to 1½ gal. produced copious smoke that definitely constituted an annoyance to other road-users, and a couple of experiences in our 1,400 miles taught us to adhere exactly to the handbook's instructions.

In deference to the high compression ratio of 10:1, super grade petrol was always employed; probably premium grade would also have been suitable—but, now that the price difference is down to a couple of coppers, we opted for safety.

Staying on Tune

With high-octane fuel, there was no trace of detonation, the unit remained on tune, and on full-throttle bursts did not get tired. The standard Lodge plugs fitted were perfectly able to withstand all the heat developed during the speed tests, the rigours of which the "Arrow Super Sports" passed with flying colours.

The test drill at M.I.R.A. involves repeated accelerations from rest through the "magic eyes" and return trips to the timing mechanism (which has to be reset); each sequence requires the tester to dismount from the machine, for he works without an assistant. A couple of score of these jaunts tell all that one needs to know about prop or centre-stand serviceability, idling, and hot starting. Under the last two headings, full marks were awarded; the stands, however, were less satisfactory.

The prop stand would do its job reliably only so long as the resting surface was tolerably level and hard. The tread-on ball of the centre-stand tended to pierce thinnish soles of soft shoes. More serious, the grounding of this stand set a limit to the angle of

"Underslung" engine installation gives free airflow to the cylinder heads and barrels.

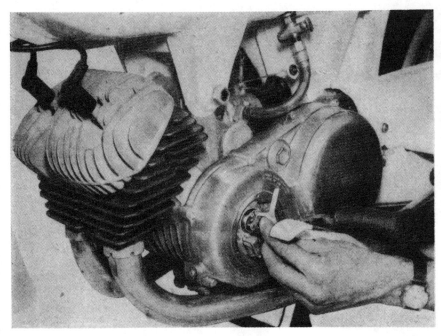

(Left) Checking the contact-breaker points. (Above) A special tool prevents extension of the front suspension to facilitate wheel removal.

bank—an annoying handicap upon such an agile machine. A lazy holding-up spring permitted the stand to bob up and down on rough roads.

The " Arrow's " steering and roadholding were excellent ; and there seemed no doubt that the mount would stick to the line on corners at much acuter angles than its ground clearance permitted, so well did the two suspension systems harmonize. The trailing-link front fork and well-damped rear end gave real comfort when driving hard over roughish roads.

The front suspension and the rubber-bushed reaction linkage to the full-width anchor are so laid out that hard application of either the front brake alone, or both 6-in. units together, brought no change in trim. For the truly hard rider, who leaves his braking late, a rather more powerful front brake would be desirable. But for everyday use, on wet and dry roads, the brakes were well up to their work. Sensibly, the rear-brake pedal can be set for height by an adjuster.

The gear pedal is of the long-travel type and conveniently placed in relation to the footrest. Cog-swopping was easy and fool-proof. Upward changes were slick and fast ; they could be done clutchless if desired, and indeed often were, particularly third-to-top. Downward movements were also easy, but not quiet. The most assiduous synchronization of revs to road speed could not eliminate some grating. For the man with sensitive ears, double-declutching is the answer. Thanks to the Ariel's delightful clutch, and easily found false and true neutrals, this procedure was little hardship. In fact, the tester found very considerable pleasure in doing it quickly in jerk-free silence.

Electrically, the " Arrow " earned praise. Plenty of sparks were forthcoming for quick cold starts, since the battery was always kept up ; the new Lucas higher-output generator is fitted. At night the lights did all that they should. The headlamp beam was found to be of the " spot "—rather than spread—type, and none the worse for that. The new Lucas high-frequency horn was above the usual motorcycle standard ; the button was conveniently placed close to the right grip, the dip switch being on the left.

To match the dropped handlebars, the footrests should be placed farther to the rear ; as it is, the riding position is a slightly uneasy compromise. The Doherty plastic grips could be kept spotlessly clean, but tape had to be wound round the bar itself before they would stay put.

Surmounting the bars is a wide Perspex flyscreen that gives plenty of protection to the prone rider. For those who dispense with this shielding a slight speed bonus is available. For the record, the test " Arrow " set up speeds of 75.7 and 76.4 m.p.h. at the end of the standing 1,400 yd. after the screen had been detached.

The Smiths speedometer was exceptionally accurate. Its slight deviation actually became less as the speed rose ; at 70 m.p.h. it was reading dead true.

Hard driving of the kind which this type of machine invites produced the very reasonable overall fuel consumption figure of 68 m.p.g.

Fast, robust and handling like a thoroughbred, the " Arrow Super Sports " goes into the record as one of the most pleasant sports mounts to pass through our hands in recent years.

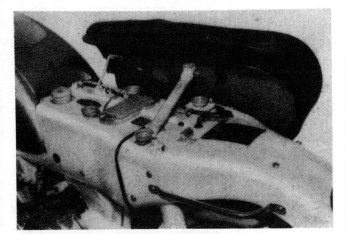

(Left) Under the clip-down dual seat are the tank filler and battery. (Below) Handlebar and instrument layout; the headlamp-mounted ignition switch has a detachable key.

1 Remove clutch springs and nuts and withdraw clutch thrust plate. Then replace the springs and nuts so that rest of clutch can be removed

5 Now to the other side of gearbox. Drain oil, undo nuts and pull off outer case complete. Do not let kickstart spring unwind suddenly

9 The first job in removing gears is to withdraw the layshaft, which is a free sliding fit. Pick the gears off the shaft as it is withdrawn

13 Although both selector shafts are the same length, the forks are set at different heights. Note which is which to ensure proper assembly

ARIEL BOX STRIPDOWN

How to overhaul the Arrow and Leader gearbox

THE Leader and Arrow are not only different from anything else on the outside, but also on the inside. This applies to the gearbox just as much as to the other engine components.

To do a full job on the gearbox, it is necessary to strip the clutch and primary drive. This is because both mainshaft and layshaft are attached to the inner gearbox cover, and the whole gubbins is held together by the clutch nut. There is no need to take the engine out of the frame, however—we did so merely because it was easier to get the pictures. Though goodness knows the engine comes out easily enough, and most people prefer to work on the bench rather than crouch on the floor.

You need three special tools for this job, if you have not got them already. First the Clutch Banjo (Part No. T3540S) to lock the clutch whilst undoing the clutch nuts (see picture 2). You will also want the Flywheel Strap (Part No. T3552S) to hold the flywheel still whilst using the Flywheel Extractor (Part No. T3545S)—see pictures 3 and 4.

Once inside the box note that the gear pinions are all clearly numbered. The correct order on the layshaft, reading from the kickstart case end, is 30, 20, 24 and 17. No. 17 has a raised shoulder on one side which must face the kickstart end.

The three pinions on the mainshaft should be in the following order (reading from the kickstart end again) —16 (raised shoulder towards kickstart case), 26 and 22.—JOHN STURMAN.

2 Prise out the rest of the clutch plates, and slip the special tool over the splines. Holding clutch with this undo both centre nuts

3 Lock flywheel with strap and undo flywheel nut and washer. Before fitting the extractor remember to place protector cap over the shaft

4 Tighten extractor to free flywheel and then pull off flywheel primary chain and clutch all as one unit. Don't lose clutch rollers (arrowed)

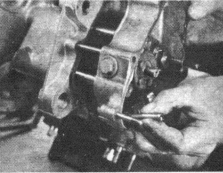

6 The only component likely to need replacing inside case is kickstart spring. Don't overtighten. Wind up fully, then unwind one revolution

7 Examine the clutch adjusting screw. This and the ball bearing are one unit, and may need replacing from time to time. It is not expensive

8 To remove the gear cluster undo single cheese-headed screw inside the inner cover and pull cover and gear cluster off the gearbox shell

10 Here is the layshaft and layshaft gears. They all have numbers on them. See the introduction for correct method of assembling them

11 Before removing mainshaft gears you must undo the nut and washer (1), ratchet (2), pinion (3), bush and spring (4), distance piece (5)

12 The mainshaft and the mainshaft gears can now be removed as shown. All are numbered, 16 being on the left of the picture, then 26 and 22

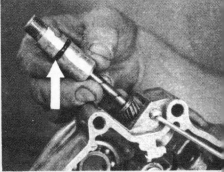

14 Slide selector forks out after the split pins and dowels have been removed. Knock back tab-washer and undo gearchange cam nut (arrowed)

15 The cam (1) is a light press-fit and can be removed with a gentle tap from a soft hammer. Always renew the cam plunger spring (2)

16 To remove speedo drive undo grub screw as shown and withdraw whole unit. You should always renew the rubber O-ring oil seal (arrowed)

41

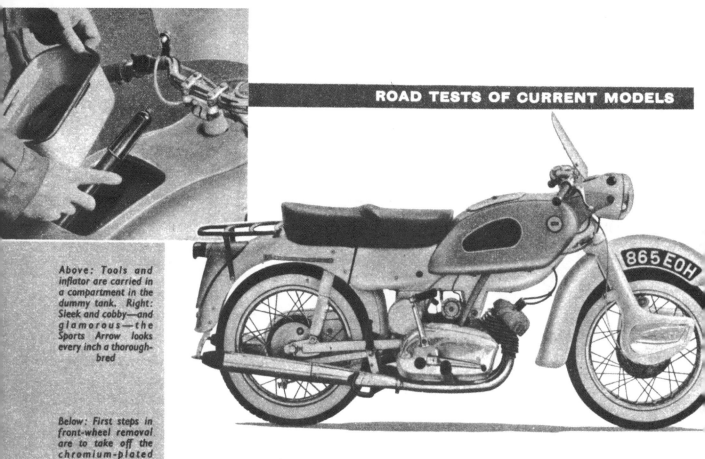

Above: Tools and inflator are carried in a compartment in the dummy tank. Right: Sleek and cobby—and glamorous—the Sports Arrow looks every inch a thoroughbred

Below: First steps in front-wheel removal are to take off the chromium-plated covers at the base of the fork legs and to insert the special tools through the holes provided and into the links. Bottom: Fuel filler and battery are revealed by raising the hinged dual-seat

247 c.c. Ariel Sports Arrow

HIGH-PERFORMANCE TWIN WITH SUPERB HANDLING

IT is not so very long ago that Ariels, renowned for their range of four-strokes, took a bold and somewhat unexpected step. Casting their established models—including the illustrious Square Four—on the scrapheap they staked their all on the success of an unconventional two-stroke twin; it was, of course, the lavishly-equipped Leader two-fifty. The gamble paid off, and soon there was a second version of the same basic design in the lively but low-cost Arrow. And that, too, hit the jackpot.

Could Ariels do it yet again? Indeed they could, for just over a year ago a third variation of the theme was revealed. Gaily finished with gold-enamelled tank shell and rear-number-plate pressing, it was the Sports Arrow. Chromium plating brightened the front-fork cover plates, tool-box lid and right-hand engine cover. White-wall tyres were specified at front and rear. The cast, light-alloy primary chaincase was highly polished. An abbreviated flyscreen graced the rakish, low-level handlebar. Control levers were of ball-end pattern.

Nor was the beauty merely skin deep. This was a true sports mount, fitted with a larger-diameter carburettor than the roadster model, and with corresponding modifications to the cylinder-wall porting which boosted the power output to a healthy 20 b.h.p. at 6,500 r.p.m. As tested in its 1962 guise, the machine appears even more glamorous, for now the gilded tank shell is allied to an ivory finish for the frame, forks and mudguards, so producing almost a "Regency" effect.

And what of the overall impression of the Sports Arrow? Favourable, most favourable. Speed the test machine produced, and then some, but the charm lay in the manner in which the model produced its performance. Its range-mates, the Leader and Arrow, had already achieved a reputation for rock-steady steering and this attribute is, of course, equally applicable to the sports version. Normally, a tuned two-stroke can be a thirsty little beast but the Ariel turned out to be surprisingly light on fuel and, in give-and-take going throughout the test, produced an average figure of about 70 m.p.g.

However, there were also one or two points to be noted on the debit side of the ledger. Starting from cold, for instance, usually called for a dozen or so prods of the

42

Specification

ENGINE: Ariel 247 c.c. (54 x 54mm) two-stroke twin. Separate iron cylinders and light-alloy heads. Roller big-end bearings. Crankshaft supported in three ball bearings. Compression ratio, 10 to 1. Petroil lubrication; mixture ratio, 20 to 1 (except Shell 2T or B.P. Zoom, 25 to 1).

CARBURETTOR: Amal Monobloc with $1\frac{1}{16}$in choke. Rod-operated strangler. Mesh-type air filter.

TRANSMISSION: Four-speed, foot-change gear box in unit with engine. Ratios: bottom, 19 to 1; second, 11 to 1; third, 7.8 to 1; top, 5.9 to 1. Three-plate clutch operating in oil. Primary chain $\frac{3}{8}$ x 0.225in in oil-bath case; rear chain $\frac{1}{2}$ x 0.305in, in pressed-steel case. Engine r.p.m. at 30 m.p.h. in top gear, 2,600.

IGNITION and LIGHTING: Lucas 50-watt RM18 alternator. Coil ignition. Lucas 13-ampere-hour battery. 6in-diameter headlamp with 30/24-watt main bulb.

FUEL CAPACITY: 3 gallons, including reserve.

TYRES: Dunlop 3.25 x 16in whitewall; studded rear, ribbed front.

BRAKES: 6in diameter x $1\frac{1}{8}$in wide, front and rear.

SUSPENSION: Ariel trailing-link front fork, hydraulically damped. Pivoted rear fork controlled by two Armstrong spring and hydraulic units.

WHEELBASE: 51in unladen. Ground clearance, 5in, unladen. Seat height, $28\frac{1}{2}$in unladen.

WEIGHT: 305 lb, including approximately one gallon of petroil.

PRICE: £190 15s 7d, including British purchase tax.

ROAD TAX: £2 5s a year.

MAKERS: Ariel Motors Ltd., Grange Road, Selly Oak, Birmingham, 29.

DESCRIPTION: *The Motor Cycle*, 19 January 1961.

Performance Data

(Obtained at the Motor Industry Research Association's proving ground, Lindley, Leicestershire.)

MEAN MAXIMUM SPEED: Bottom: 30 m.p.h.
Second: 49 m.p.h.
Third: 64 m.p.h.
Top: 78 m.p.h.

HIGHEST ONE-WAY SPEED: 81 m.p.h. (conditions: light three-quarter breeze, 10-stone rider wearing helmet, riding boots and two-piece trials suit).

MEAN ACCELERATION:

	10–30 m.p.h.	20–40 m.p.h.	30–50 m.p.h.
Bottom	2.1 sec	—	—
Second	3.9 sec	4.5 sec	—
Third	—	8.0 sec	7.7 sec
Top	—	15.4 sec	13.2 sec

Mean speed at end of quarter-mile from rest: 70 m.p.h. Mean time to cover standing quarter-mile: 17.6 sec.

PETROIL CONSUMPTION: At 30 m.p.h., 108 m.p.g.; at 40 m.p.h. 82 m.p.g.; at 50 m.p.h., 74 m.p.g.; at 60 m.p.h., 56 m.p.g.

BRAKING: From 30 m.p.h. to rest, 30ft (surface, dry asphalt).

TURNING CIRCLE: 12ft 10in.

MINIMUM NON-SNATCH SPEED: 18 m.p.h. in top gear.

WEIGHT PER C.C.: 1.23 lb.

Handling of the Arrow is already a byword—almost a criterion. The machine is one of the most inherently stable on the roads today

pedal with the strangler fully closed. Once the engine was warm a first-kick start could be guaranteed. Then there was the riding position. A down-turned handlebar is certainly not to everyone's taste though, admittedly, it is traditionally a part of a sports-machine specification; but here the footrests are in a normal, forward position and, if full use is to be made of the dropped bar, the resulting crouch is not the most comfortable. As for the flyscreen, while this may have its advantages when a rider is well tucked down, for normal riding it is little more than ornamental and, indeed, tends to obscure part of the speedometer dial.

The acceleration of the Ariel, as reference to the data panel will show, was pretty fantastic for a two-fifty. The standing quarter-mile in 17.6s.? That is as good as, if not better than, the average five-hundred—nor was it a fluke reading, for the figure was the average of several runs. One conclusion which could be drawn is that the engine possesses an unusually wide power band; and that was borne out by the road performance.

With most sports two-strokes the power is concentrated at the upper end of the

rev scale and, after a slow build-up, comes in almost as though the rider has been kicked in the rear. With the Sports Arrow the power build-up is more evenly spread and, as a result, there is less need to recourse to the lower gear ratios.

In illustration of this, it was quite possible to allow the machine to accelerate steadily from speeds as low as 25 m.p.h. in top though, of course, a drop into third produced a much zippier getaway. Furthermore, where time was not pressing, long, main-road hills could be climbed with top gear still engaged.

When main-road conditions allowed, many miles were covered with the speedometer needle varying between 60 and 65 m.p.h. (an electronic test proved the dial 6 per cent optimistic). Even at 60 there was plenty of urge still to come should the need arise.

Ariel steering is already a byword, and so utterly safe did the Sports Arrow feel that there was the greatest possible fun to be had from flinging the model through a twisty section of road. A further safety factor is the performance of the 6in-diameter brakes at front and rear, and the quoted figure of 30ft from 30 m.p.h. is

genuine enough. Nor are the stoppers in any way "sudden," for the machine comes to a halt smoothly and progressively.

The gear-change pedal has a light, if somewhat long movement, and ratios could be located readily. Noiseless changes, upward or downward, were child's play, although the change was found to be unusually sensitive to primary and rear-chain adjustment.

In town areas the large-capacity twin silencers earned high marks for the exhaust's quiet, droning song. When the taps were opened wide, or when the Ariel was accelerated hard, the song changed to a deeper, louder tune but this was always of an acceptable standard. Mechanical noise from the engine and transmission was at a commendably low level. An annoying clatter from below was traced to a bouncing centre stand; a change of stand spring brought little improvement. Another source of annoyance was the tool box, inset in the upper face of the "tank" pressing; access to the box itself was simple enough, but to extract the tyre pump the tool tray, held in place by a spring cross-bar, had first to be removed—and replacement of the bar was something of a fiddle. However, this small point was far out-weighed by the many practical features of the model.

Handling? Absolutely top-line—in fact there's many a *racing* machine which uses the standard Arrow beam and front fork. Suspension? Top-line again; one-up or two-up, the Sports Arrow floats over the bumpy surfaces. Speed? Near-80, if you want it; day-long cruising in the sixties, if you wish.

ARROW

Side view of the Arrow, showing the conveniently placed air filter. The kickstarter travel was very short, but it was easy to operate in practice

LEADER

Leader was supplied with a very good selection of equipment, including weather protection, panniers, mirrors, eight-day clock and winking indicators

SUPER-SPORTS

Arrow Super Sports is the same as the standard Arrow except that it has a slightly more powerful engine and a few extras such as reserve tap

The fuel tap and choke lever are quite easy to reach on the left hand side of the machine. We did not appreciate the lack of a reserve tap on this model

Rear view shows the neat appearance with the panniers which are designed for the machine. Flashing indicators worked well. Note reflectors in bumper

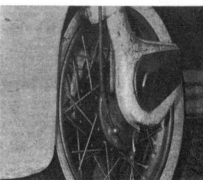

All the models have the Ariel trailing link front forks. These have nylon bushes at all pivot points to reduce wear. Front mudguard was effective

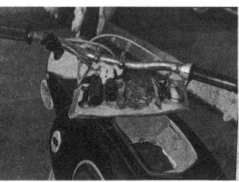

Tool compartment is in the place normally occupied by the tank. The cover is secured by an odd bar and screw arrangement but the kit is good

Dashboard was well stocked on our test model. The clock, neutral indicator, and light can be seen. The horn button was awkward to use when braking

On all the machines the seat lifts up to give access to the filler cap and battery. On the Leader the seat is lockable. Note measure in filler cap

Gear lever position was very good, but the travel was a bit too long. Ground clearance could have been better too. Panniers are Dewey Waters

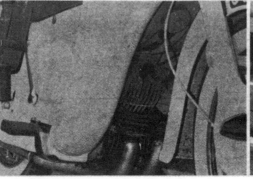

The twin-cylinder two-stroke 250 c.c. engine powers all the Ariel models and is quite smooth in operation, but lacks power lower down the rev range

Here is the result of 1,000 miles motoring in a weekend, much of the mileage being done in pouring rain. Silencing is good at exhaust end

STARTING ON THEIR TEST

HOW GOOD ARE THE ARIELS

1,000 MILES and five countries in two and a half days is not such a great achievement on a large capacity twin, but when the machines are only standard 250 c.c. two-strokes the journey becomes more of a task!

Why did we do it? Well, instead of road testing one machine over the month as we normally do, we decided to take all three Ariel models and do the 1,000 miles in only a weekend! If they could take this thrashing, they could take almost anything, and it also gave us the opportunity to compare the performances.

Above, you can see us—Weightman, Deane and Smith—left to right, setting off from London's Waterloo Road...

SOME HOURS LATER—FRENCH-GERMAN BORDER

CHECK POINTS	ARROW	LEADER	SUPER-SPORTS
Price with purchase tax	£192	£219	£206
Acceleration 0-60 mph	15 secs.	17 secs.	14 secs.
Maximum speed	76 mph	72 mph	76 mph
Fuel consumption at maximum speed	62 mpg	58 mpg	60 mpg
Fuel consumption overall	74 mpg	68 mpg	72 mpg
Braking from 30 mph	34 feet	37 feet	33 feet
Control positioning and comfort	7	8	7
Equipment	6	8	7
Ease of starting	8	7	8
Engine smoothness and quietness	8	7	7
Gearbox and clutch operation	9	7	9
Road holding	8	7	8
Braking efficiency	7	9	7
Lighting efficiency	8	8	8
Overall finish	8	8	8
General performance and reliability			
TOTAL POINTS (out of 100)	77	76	76

Briefly our trip was as follows. We left Mercury house at 5 p.m. on Friday, 28th September, in order to be at Southend Airport at 7 p.m. British United Air Ferries (now incorporating Silver City Airways) had our machines loaded on to the Bristol Freighter with very little bother and we were airborne by 8 p.m.

We landed at Calais, saw the machines unloaded, went through the customs and were away by 9.15 p.m. The heavy rain and driving winds which we had experienced all the way to Southend persisted in France, and we had to resign ourselves to a thoroughly wet trip. This, coupled with driving on the right a g a i n s t oncoming headlights, made the first fifty miles pretty miserable. However, we had little time to think about our comfort, or lack of it, because we had a pretty tight schedule to keep to.

As the machines were not fully run in, having only covered about 800 miles, we did not go above sixty on this first night. Even so, by midnight we had crossed the northern part of France into Belgium and were heading rapidly for the Dutch border. We had experienced all sorts of roads from motorways to the infamous Belgian Pavé, and one corner in particular gave us a nasty moment, because the surface changed from concrete to cobblestones half way round. If anyone had been watching, they would not have thought much of the driving of the three mad Englishmen with one riding up the pavement and two in the gutter!

We now made what turned out to be a serious mistake. The route which had been provided for us by the A.A. took us well into Holland, but we thought we would do better to get to the south as soon as possible, particularly as this might take us away from the rain. So we left the planned route to strike out across country on what appeared to be a main road. To cut a long story short we travelled for about a hundred miles on this alternative route, without finding a single petrol station open. We ended up in a small town at 3 a.m. on Saturday with two machines on reserve and the other out of fuel. We slept in the main square until dawn !

At 7 a.m. the first garage opened and we filled up and were away again. It had now stopped raining and the sun even shone now and again—so the journey was that much more pleasant. We rode all day Saturday until 5 p.m., by which time we had passed through Luxembourg and on into the German town of Saarbrücken. Here we retired for 12 hours well earned rest.

At 9 a.m. the following morning we had left our " hotel " at which we were unable to obtain breakfast ! We therefore stopped at a small garage and cafe outside the town for all six of us to take on fuel. The bikes had Shell petroil mix whilst the riders consumed numerous delicious frankfurters. We then staggered down the road to the customs point shown in the photograph overleaf.

Flat out to Le Touquet

The sun was shining brilliantly at 10 a.m. and as the machines had now covered 1,300 miles, we decided to drive them flat out from now on. This was just as well, because we had about 450 miles to go to Le Touquet and we had to be there by 8 a.m. the following morning ! Just to make the whole thing completely ridiculous we had decided to try and make Le Touquet by 7 p.m. the same evening in case we were able to get an earlier flight due to cancellations. This certainly gave us a chance to try the Ariels' all-out capabilities, as we had to keep each throttle against its stop for virtually a hundred miles at a time.

Despite the rain which started again in the late afternoon we made Le Touquet by 7.15 having covered much of the way slip streaming each other in order to increase maximum speed, and covering the last 30 miles in pouring rain at almost the same speed as in the dry ! If only we had the roads to do this in England ! As it turned out we were unable to get an earlier flight and we therefore went for a good meal and another well deserved night's rest in Le Touquet town.

At 8 a.m. on Monday morning we presented ourselves at the airport and by 9.30 or so we had been taken over to Lydd. By mid-day we were back in the office feeling completely worn out, but having covered over 1,000 miles and visited five countries in two and a half days —and we didn't get a single stamp on our passports to prove it !

This marathon j o u r n e y was far tougher than our ordinary road tests as the machines were often running for hours non-stop and yet the only trouble we had was one overheated plug. Considering that the machines were not " nursed " at all after the first 800 miles, it is amazing that one of them did not seize—however, there was no sign of this from any of them.

The comparison figures for the three models are given in the chart above and surprisingly enough the Standard Arrow seems to be the best of the bunch, and yet the cheapest. Its performance, fuel consumption, gear change and braking were all better than the other two and the engine was much smoother as well. It is interesting to note these points as the machines were absolutely standard. Some of the detail design features are shown in the pictures opposite, and you can also see the dirt you can pick up in a week-end.

Quite apart from achieving our object of covering the 1,000 m i l e s and thoroughly testing the Ariel models we also proved that it is well worth while flying to the Continent for a week-end and not terribly expensive.

46

WATCH LEN MOSS OF ARIEL SERVICE DEPT. STRIPPING AN
ARROW

SINCE the first models in the Ariel Leader and Arrow range appeared over three years ago, they have never ceased to gain in popularity. Sales have gone up and up until now, these lively 250 c.c. two-stroke twins are the choice of a vast cross-section of motorcyclists. One of the reasons for their popularity is the fact that all maintenance is extremely simple and can be carried out by the average rider.

For example the engine is suspended from the box-section frame by two large lugs and can be easily and quickly removed by disconnecting all cables and electrical leads, the rear brake rod and swinging arm and four easily accessible bolts.

As the Arrow has a two-stroke motor it is not difficult to strip and overleaf MM shows just how to do it. The same procedure applies to the Leader and Super Arrow models. Nothing tricky is involved and the job may be done by anyone with a reasonable set of tools and average mechanical knowledge.

As a two-stroke the Ariel obviously needs decarbonising more often than its four-stroke rivals but, as can be seen, it is a simple job to lift the barrel and head and clean them out. Some special tools are necessary if a complete strip-down is attempted, and these are all obtainable from the Ariel Service Dept., at Small Heath, Birmingham.

1 Once heads are removed barrels can be eased off. Make sure pistons are steadied or damage may easily result

2 When removing piston do not hammer out gudgeon pin. Warming piston will facilitate removal if pin is stiff

3 Part snap-connectors on low-tension leads and remove the contact-breaker cover. This is held by three screws

7 Drain oil, remove screws and chaincase pulls off. Do not prise apart or faces may get damaged causing oil to leak

8 Undo the nut on the crankshaft with large box-spanner. Note tab-washer. An Ariel tool clamps the flywheel firm

9 Work now starts on the clutch. Using preferably a socket or box spanner undo the three nuts in the centre

13 Off comes the nut and out comes the clutch centre as it is pulled from its splined shaft. Watch the rollers!

14 At this time it is a good idea to check the shock-absorber rubbers in the centre for signs of deterioration

15 Another special tool comes into play in pulling off the flywheel. Contact breaker cam must be replaced on shaft

 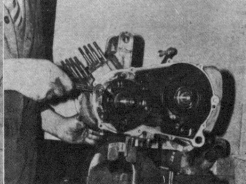 

19 Undoing centre bolt will pull rotor from end of crankshaft. This is one more item that is keyed in position

20 Now any correct-sized spanner can be used to undo the nuts which secure the crankcase cover plate in place

21 Before using the special Ariel tool to pull out the plate from crankcase be sure to replace contact-breaker cam

Complete contact-breaker assembly is simply removed after undoing the two screws holding it to the chaincase

5 Contact-breaker cam is next to come off. Undo screw in centre. Note that the cam is keyed to the crankshaft.

6 The primary chain tensioner must be removed prior to any attempt being made to take off the alloy chaincase

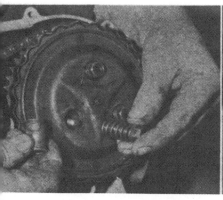

When the nuts are undone remove cups but then replace springs and nuts as this prevents pegs from falling out

11 Clutch plates will then slide out. Check the friction inserts for wear and teeth for signs of burring, etc.

12 A special tool is needed to remove clutch centre nut. It holds clutch rigid while box spanner does the job

Now the clutch, flywheel and primary chain all pull off together. Have something ready to catch the rollers !

17 Over to the other side where the cover to the alternator can be taken off after three screws are undone

18 Next thing to come off is the stator plate. This unit is secured to the main assembly by three nuts only

The same tool is used to pull out this part from the opposite side of the motor. Again utilise the contact-breaker cam

23 Another special tool to part flywheels. Large plug holds flywheels still and spanner turns shaft through centre

24 This parts the wheels and so allows the crankshaft assemblies of each cylinder to be pulled out of the case

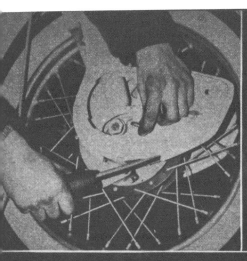

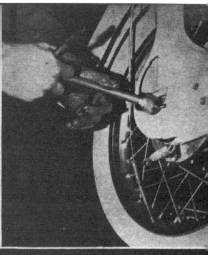

1 Obviously the first step is to remove the front wheel. Lever up arm with screwdriver and place peg (from tool kit) in its hole

2 The pegs hold the dampers in the compressed position. Next you undo the brake anchor arm and slacken the pinch bolt at bottom

3 Undo the wheel spindle nut w a box spanner. The spindle is the "knock-out" type and a b with a hammer will remove

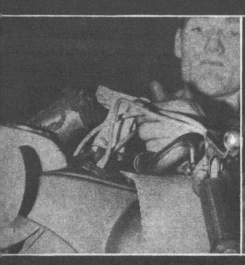
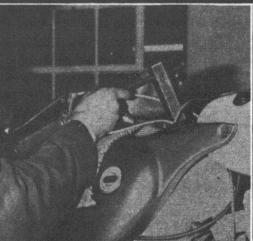

5 Now take a soft-headed mallet and tap the underneath of the bottom handlebar mounting bracket. This will remove it from its splines

6 Removing the handlebar bracket from the splines reveals the nut at the top of the forks stem. Undo it with a large box spanner

7 When you are undoing the top make sure that you support forks, as once nut is comple off forks will drop straight

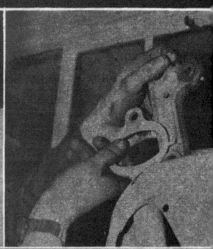

9 That was the first of the only three bolts which have to be undone. The next one is the bolt at the front of the swinging link

10 Undoing the bolt at the front of the short swinging arm will enable you to push it backwards and undo nut at bottom of the damper unit

11 Now all the nuts in actual fo are undone and they can be ta apart. First of all you pull the actual short pivoting arm u

With the wheel out, the next step is to remove the fork unit from the frame. Start off by taking out the handlebars. Lay them on tank

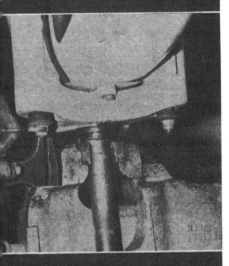

8 Now the fork strip can start in earnest. Put forks upside down in vice and undo the nut which holds the top of the suspension unit

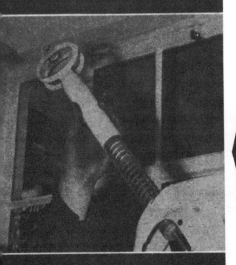

12 Last thing to be removed before strip is finished is the damper unit. This type is unique to the Ariel lightweight motorcycle range

number six in the series

JOHN SIDEBOTHAM SHOWS HOW TO STRIP

ARIEL
LEADING LINK FORKS

IT says "Arrow 200" on the tank badge. But cover up the badge and there is no difference whatever in appearance between this bike and the two-fifty. What's more, you would have a job to find much of a difference on the road. It's an Arrow all right, *bless* its willing little heart. They've underbored the cylinders a little, that's all, to give 199 cc capacity instead of the 247 cc of old. But don't let the bike hear you say that. The way it performs, it thinks it is still a two-fifty!

There was certainly nothing phoney about that 70-plus top speed (rider lying flat, of course) for it was recorded electronically. Nor was there anything phoney about the way the Ariel would hold a 60 mph cruising speed for as long as traffic conditions would permit.

As for hill-climbability—well, this was the identical machine with which John Ebbrell conquered Wrynose, Hard Knott and all those other one-in-what-have-you Lakeland passes, back in mid-August. After that demonstration, anything the Midlands could offer was laughed off in, at the least, second gear.

199 cc ARIEL ARROW 200

ROAD TESTS OF NEW MODELS

Big advantage of a two-hundred, as against a two-fifty, comes in more favourable insurance rates. So where's the catch? Answer is that the little Arrow tends to be rather more of a top-end performer than big sister, and takes a shade longer to reach the higher altitudes of the speedometer dial.

It is only a relative matter, though, for the power unit chuckles with enegry while response to the throttle is both eager and immediate. Besides, a standing-start figure of 21s from a two-hundred is good going.

First thing you notice as you straddle an Arrow is its low build. That's a confidence-breeding feature from the start. And there's nothing

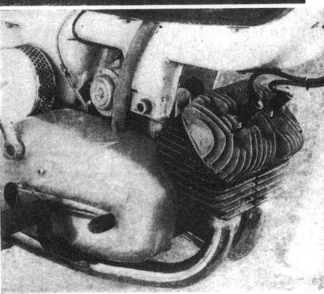

below: Bob Currie samples the 199 cc Ariel. Right: Externally, the engine is identical to the two-fifty

cramped about the riding position, with plenty of room on the seat for the pillion passenger to make himself comfortable.

This is but the beginning, for only when the model is on the move can the beautifully balanced feel of the Arrow be appreciated. All the weight seems in exactly the right place, and the whole machine gives the most satisfying impression of being solidly built.

Lay it into a bend—better still, a series of bends—and the superb handling becomes evident. Arrows always do steer well (ask any owner) so all that need be said here is that the 199 cc version upholds family honour.

Only one slight crib—on a tight, bumpy corner, it is possible to ground the centre

Frame, fork and mudguards are finished in the standard ivory, while chaincase and tank can be either aircraft blue or British racing green

SPECIFICATION
and Performance Data

ENGINE: Ariel 199 cc (48.5 x 54mm) two-stroke twin. Separate iron cylinders and light-alloy heads. Roller big-end bearings. Crankshaft supported in **three ball bearings.** Compression ratio, 9.5 to 1. Petroil lubrication: mixture ratio, 32 to 1.
CARBURETTOR: Amal Monobloc, $\frac{11}{16}$in-diameter choke. Rod-operated strangler. Mesh-type air filter.
IGNITION and LIGHTING: Lucas 50-watt RM18 alternator. Coil ignition. Lucas 13-amp-hour battery. 6in-diameter headlamp with 30/24-watt main bulb.
TRANSMISSION: Four-speed gear box in unit with engine. Ratios: 19.8, 11.5, 8.15 and 6.2 to 1. Three-plate clutch operating in oil. Primary chain $\frac{3}{8}$ x 0.225in, in oilbath case; rear chain $\frac{1}{2}$ x 0.305in in pressed-steel case. Engine rpm at 30 mph in top gear, 2,800.

FUEL CAPACITY: 3 gallons.
TYRES: Dunlop 3.25 x 16in, ribbed front, studded rear.
BRAKES: Both 6in diameter x $1\frac{1}{8}$in wide.
SUSPENSION: Ariel trailing-link front fork, hydraulically damped. Pivoted rear fork controlled by Armstrong spring-damper units.
WHEELBASE: 51in. Ground clearance, 5in. Seat height, 28$\frac{1}{2}$in. All unladen.
WEIGHT: 291 lb, including approx half a gallon of petroil.
PRICE: £187 10s 4d, including British purchase tax. Rear carrier, £1 15s 10d extra.
ROAD TAX: £2 5s a year.
MAKERS: Ariel Motors, Ltd, Armoury Road, Small Heath, Birmingham, 11.

PERFORMANCE DATA
(Obtained at the Motor Industry Research Association proving ground, Lindley.)
MEAN MAXIMUM SPEEDS: Bottom, 30 mph; second, 46 mph; third, 59 mph; top, 71 mph.
HIGHEST ONE-WAY SPEED: 74 mph (conditions, light side wind, 14-stone rider wearing trials jacket and overboots).
MEAN ACCELERATION:

	10-30 mph	20-40 mph	30-50 mph
Bottom	5s	—	—
Second	7.2s	7s	—
Third	—	10.8s	11.2s
Top	—	20.2s	18.8s

Mean speed at end of quarter-mile from rest, 58 mph.
Mean time to cover standing quarter-mile, 21s.
FUEL CONSUMPTION: At 30 mph, 93 mpg; at 40 mph, 85 mpg; at 50 mph, 69 mpg; at 60 mph, 58 mpg.
BRAKING: From 30 mph to rest, 32ft (surface, dry tarmac).
TURNING CIRCLE: 12ft 9in.
MINIMUM NON-SNATCH SPEED IN TOP GEAR: 16 mph.
WEIGHT PER CC: 1.46 lb.

---

stand just a little too easily

Starting from cold involved flooding the float chamber liberally, pulling out the strangler rod to the full, giving a couple of exploratory prods of the starter pedal then switching on the ignition. Next kick and away went the engine every time.

With the engine really hot, though, starting could be rather temperamental at times.

Exhaust noise is extremely well subdued and at a steady 30 mph in town it was no more than a whisper. Hard acceleration in the intermediate gears changed the note to a surprisingly deep zoom which, however, remained entirely inoffensive. **Mechanical and transmission noises were so slight as to be almost unnoticeable.**

Controls were pleasant to operate in the main, though the change down from second to bottom gear was a trifle harsh and clunky; in all other respects the gear pedal required only light foot movement, with the location of neutral providing no difficulties whatever.

As with any other Arrow, the two-hundred has a recess in the top of the dummy tank pressing (the real tank, of course, is within the frame beam, with the filler cap under the lift-up seat); in the recess lives quite a comprehensive tool kit.

The tool tray is itself held in place by a spring-steel strap located in slots; remove this, lift out the tray and access is given to a cubby hole within the pressing. The

The push-in petroil filler cap and battery are located under the seat

spring strap was just as tiresome to get back into place as on other examples of the make tested.

That's a minor point, paling into insignificance when weighed against the "plus" qualities of the model. **Excellent lighting, for example—much better than might have been expected from a 6in-diameter headlamp. Brakes, fore and aft,** which are potent yet smooth in action. And a roll-feet centre stand requiring no effort at all to bring into use.

The test model had the usual ivory-painted frame, fork and mudguard, but with the chaincase and upper works an eye-catching aircraft blue.

If you prefer it, there's an equally attractive alternative of British racing green.

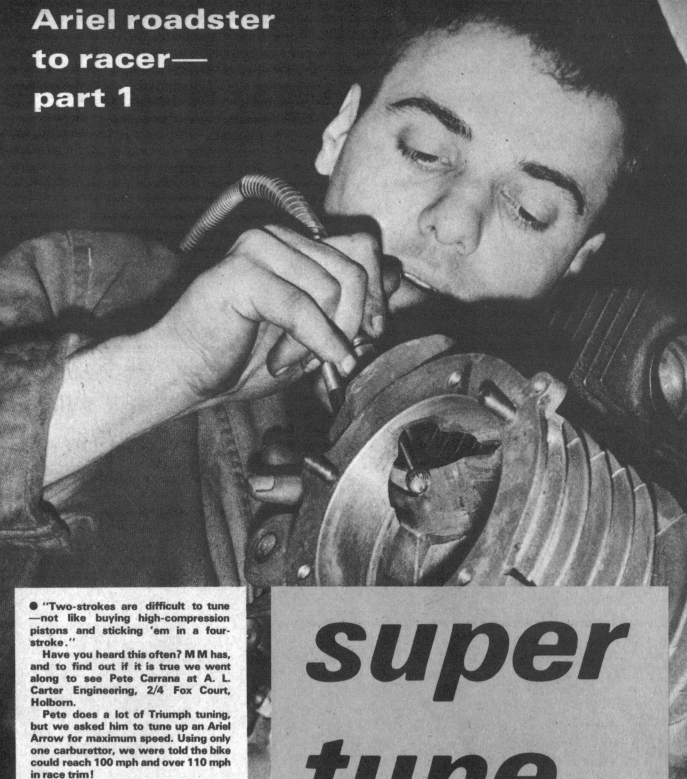

Ariel roadster to racer— part 1

super tune

Ian Speller goes to A. L. Carter to get 100 mph from MM's Ariel

● "Two-strokes are difficult to tune —not like buying high-compression pistons and sticking 'em in a four-'stroke."

Have you heard this often? M M has, and to find out if it is true we went along to see Pete Carrana at A. L. Carter Engineering, 2/4 Fox Court, Holborn.

Pete does a lot of Triumph tuning, but we asked him to tune up an Ariel Arrow for maximum speed. Using only one carburettor, we were told the bike could reach 100 mph and over 110 mph in race trim!

When we realised the potential of the bike we decided to convert the entire machine for racing, and next month we will show how to alter the rest of the machine.

Any stage of this tuning can be applied to a straight road bike if you want a few more knots—or just a bit of extra zip. Few special parts are needed and you can tailor cost to your pocket.

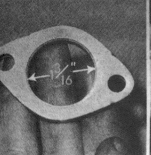

Make up this template from with the centre hole the diameter as carburettor

2. Fit the template on the inlet flange. There will be a step of alloy all round the inside

3. Carefully file or cut away the alloy until port matches the template shape exactly

4. Measure $\frac{7}{8}$ in. down from the barrel face and scribe a line. Cut the port down to this line

Central vane in inlet port be given a knife-edge in direction of the gas flow

6. Inlet ports should look like this! They are matched to the ports in the barrel spigots

7. Metal on barrel spigot is cut away between the dotted lines to give better timings

8. The exhaust port in bore can have its rough edges smoothed away with a curved riffler file

Push your Ariel to over 100 mph by following these tuning details

The tuning falls into three main categories: barrels, crankshaft and crankcase. Starting with the inlet port in the crankcase, it must be opened up to the size of carburettor which is to be used—the best size being 1$\frac{3}{16}$ in.—at the flange.

To open up the mouth of the port, it is useful to make up a template with a centre hole of 1$\frac{3}{16}$ in. which can be placed against the inlet, and the "step" of alloy can then be cut away. This leaves the correct size port and, more important, it ensures that it is central between the carb studs.

The port must now be flowed out to the two ports which mate up against the spigots of the barrels. The ports must be smooth and of equal capacity—cutting one port more than the other will cause a bias.

The inlet ports, where they breathe into the crankcase through the spigots, can be opened but, for the sake of convenience, the ports in the spigots should be done first. When they are done, they can be fitted to the crankcase and a scriber used to match up the ports.

Without doubt, the most important port alteration is to open the inlet ports in the barrel spigots. They should be cut down so that their lower edge is 0·875 in. below the face of the barrel. This gives the optimum timing with a single carburettor of 147 deg.

The ports must not be widened and on no account should the central vane be removed. If it is, the rings will catch in the port and break. The vanes can be shaped slightly so that they are angled with the gas flow. A knife-edge can be given to the vanes on the outside of the spigot (this reduces resistance to the gas flow).

Once these ports have been cut, the barrels can be slipped into the crankcase and the ports there can be matched up. All the rough edges must be removed from the spigot ports, but the basic shape must not be altered.

The transfer ports in the spigots are only "windows" in their standard form but, by cutting down, the metal between

them and the bottom of the spigot can be removed. The transfers need not be widened but the performance is improved by this deepening. Again all the rough edges can be filed away.

With the barrels in the crankcase (for all these operations the cases must be empty) the crankcase casting can be matched up with the improved transfer ports by cutting away some of the alloy and giving it a smooth line.

The barrels are fitted to the crankcase so that the transfer ports between the two can be matched up. This is achieved by opening up the entry into the barrels—do not alter the ports exit from the crankcase casting.

The transfer ports in the barrels can be polished and flowed and they can be given a radius where they breathe into the bore. This all helps the gas flow.

The exhaust ports are left with the same timing and shape as standard, but they will benefit from being polished. To remove some of the really rough edges, it is necessary to use curved riffler files, as the port is such an awkward shape.

Piston modifications

During all these modifications, the work should be kept as clean as possible and free from swarf—especially the threads in the exhaust ports.

9. With a piston in the spigot, match the ports and then file to give a knife edge to both

10. The transfer ports in barrel should be filed until they are exactly the same as in crankcase

11. This is a 12:1 cylinder head. The squish shape and central plug are good design

12. Thin alloy discs will over the holes in flywhee increase the primary compres

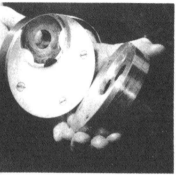

13. Thick alloy pads increase the compression in crankcase. Note the screws have been locked

14. This finely polished rod has not been reshaped but it has been checked for cracks

15. Solid alloy plugs can be used to fill the holes. These are pressed in very tightly

16. The much-diminished between the con-rod and flywheels increases compres

The pistons are next for the treatment —they should be placed in the bores at bdc and the transfer ports in the pistons matched up with the ports in the spigots. When they are matched (by cutting the piston ports), a smooth, flowing line must be given so that the gas flows easily from under the piston into the transfer port. This is done by giving a knife-edge to the piston and spigot so that, at bdc, no step can be felt between the two. No other modifications are necessary to the pistons, apart from knowing that the gudgeon pins must be a light push-fit at 75 deg. C.

The late type of cylinder heads are the only ones which are any good for high-speed work. Their compression ratio is 10:1, but it can be brought up to 12:1 by machining 0·055 away at 2·125 dia. and then the joint face can be machined so that it mates up at the 2·125 in. dia.

All 10:1 heads have central plugs, so this is a mod. which is saved.

Padding flywheels

Attention is now turned to the flywheels. These must be dismantled, by pressing the crankpins out, before any work can be done.

Once apart, the most important mod. is to fill in the holes in the wheels which are there to decrease the primary compression—filling them raises the compression in the crankcase again. The holes can be plugged with solid alloy, cut to shape and pressed in (with an interference fit), or with thin discs which are slightly wider than the holes. In this case the holes have to be recessed to take the discs, which are then locked in with grub screws or sealant.

Slightly more difficult to make, but very worthwhile, are compression pads fitted in pairs between the flywheels. These bump up the compression yet again. When making these, clearance has to be allowed for the con-rod and for the big-end.

Carburettor sizes

Most of the tuning can be done at home, but it is advisable to have the plugs and pads fitted by an expert who is used to doing this job.

The con-rods already have a good shape but they will benefit from being highly polished or shot peened. Sufficient room must be left around the big ends for lubrication when making up the pads.

Instead of the old $\frac{7}{8}$ in. carburettor, a $1\frac{1}{16}$ in. or a $1\frac{3}{16}$ in. carburettor or a pair of 1 in. GP's can be fitted, but for the sake of cost alone it is best to use the single $1\frac{3}{16}$ in. Amal Monobloc. A main-jet size is difficult to quote, but between 470 and 500 is about right with the other modi-

fications. The throttle slide should be a $3\frac{1}{2}$. If the GP's are used, the main jets will be between 180 and 240, with slides 6 to 8.

All the timings and dimensions given in this article will work best with the $1\frac{3}{16}$ in. carb, but the smaller one can be used with a reduction in the size of the inlet port to $1\frac{1}{16}$ in.

All through the motor, new bearings and oil seals should be fitted; it's a waste of time tuning to have all the work ruined by a bearing failure soon after completion. A safe maximum of 8,500 rpm is right but will vary depending on the age and condition of the motor.

The external flywheel can be dispensed with, as it is not necessary.

Experimenting with the ignition timing can be restricted to within 1 deg. of the standard settings—but for most cases the normal setting will do. The correct gap of 14—16 thou must be kept for maximum performance.

The fuel used when the motor has been hotted up is a premium petrol (minimum octane rating of 96) with a 20:1 mixture of 20 grade castor-based oil.

The gearing is a problem with the Arrow. Ariel do not make close-ratio gears or alternative engine sprockets. There is, however, a 45-tooth rear-wheel sprocket which can be used to raise the overall ratios.

FRAME FIT-OUT

N SPELLER CARRIES OUT THE
COND STAGE OF THE CONVERSION—
OWING COMPLETION OF CYCLE PARTS

ARIEL RACER PART 2

● Tearing into a corner at over 90 mph, a bike has to handle and brake without fault. Making a road bike do this is a long job and requires patience.

MM tuned up the Ariel Arrow motor last month and then we had to make the cycle parts work like a racer as well.

Starting with the wheels, we fitted alloy rims and racing tyres. The hubs had new bearings fitted and the brake shoes were soled with racing linings.

Proprietary items took care of most of the difficult items, leaving us to make only a few things like rear-brake linkage, gear-lever, mudguards and odd brackets.

Tackling one job at a time and never starting on another until the previous one was finished, we completed the bike in a couple of weeks.

When all the final adjustments have been made and the bike is run in, we hope to take the bike to Brands Hatch or Snetterton and bring back a track report.

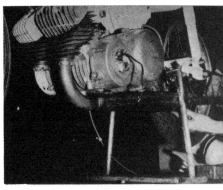

One-piece works expansion boxes are essential if the motor is to give maximum power. Brackets have to be made up to support the boxes at the rear tailpipe.

Converting a road bike into a full-blown racer can be difficult, but with the Ariel Arrow it is fairly straightforward.

There are, on the market, many items which can be bolted straight on and require no modifications. Buying all of these parts would be expensive but if you stick to the essentials the total cost will be reasonable.

We decided to use only one carburettor, not only because it makes tuning easier but also because the existing engine mounts can be used. With the twin carb. layout, the front engine mounting has to be cut away and new supports made up.

The engine then fitted into the frame in the same way as a standard motor. We obviously checked all the bolts and their threads.

The swinging-arm fork fits through the rear end of the engine and as the bike must handle perfectly, we renewed the bushes. This is not an easy job and it is best to let a dealer handle it for you.

Only work needed on the frame is removing the rear mudguard section, which unbolts. As a matter of course we stripped the steering-head bearings and replaced them with new parts. The bike had done a large mileage and these parts were well worn.

Foam rubber is very useful—we glued some on to the top of the frame to mount the petrol tank and some in the battery carrier. This cuts out a lot of frame vibration to these parts.

Electrical work

Wiring up the motor was very simple. As in most racers, the system is one without any recharging device. This means that the battery is the sole source of energy and has to be charged between meetings. The generator was not refitted to the engine and so saved a lot of weight.

The twin coils were kept in their place inside the frame—they are out of the way and protected from dirt and water. The appearance of the bike would be improved if we could keep the wiring out of sight, we decided, so we planned to run it inside the frame. The ignition switch was fitted through a hole in the frame near the coils. The wires from it ran on one side to the switch terminals of the coils and on the other side to the battery.

The contact breaker terminals of the coils were connected to their respective points with a couple of wires which emerged above the nearside front engine mount. Where it was possible, snap connectors were used and all other connections were soldered direct.

Several different types of exhaust are available for the Arrow, and as it is difficult to calculate the measurements needed to make up the correct size, we used a proprietary pair. The type we used are the works ones and sell at about £10.

We found that it was necessary to cut the rear-brake spindle brackets away from the engine in order to get the exhausts high enough. They are angled to give good ground clearance.

Bolt-on goodies

The problem of fitting a petrol tank was overcome by obtaining a Fi-glass special from the factory in Edenbridge, Kent. This new unit comprises a tank and seat and costs £11 10s. 0d. A matching fairing was also obtained in the same colour, and from the same factory—cost £16. That price also included the screen and fittings.

A rev-meter was necessary, so we got one from D M S Ltd, of 1 Wordsworth Road, N.16. It cost £10 and was complete with drive box, cable, rubber mounting and an adaptor. It bolts straight on to the contact breaker cover.

Clip-on handlebars are always a problem with bikes, such as the Arrow, which have trailing-link forks. Fortunately, Bill Selby of 179 Sepulchre Gate, Doncaster, sells special bars for 50s. 0d. which fit the Arrow and give a "clip-on" position.

Wheel alterations

Alloy rims and racing tyres were necessary if the bike was to stand any chance in a competition.

We had the wheels rebuilt with 18 in. Dunlop alloy rims onto the existing hubs. The front rim was a WM1 section and the rear a WM2. The tyres fitted were both Dunlop and were a matched pair of "sticky" triangulars. The front was 2·75″ × 18″ and the rear 3·00″ × 18″. We were advised not to fit security bolts.

The Arrow is fitted with 16 in. rims normally, but the extra size does not cause any problems.

The foot controls were possibly the most difficult items to make up. While Messrs. Monty and Dudley-Ward of 45 Hampton Rd, Twickenham, Middlesex, make rear-seat rests for road-going Arrows, which are very good, they were not quite far enough back for racing.

The gear lever was not too bad—we reversed the existing lever—bent it to shape and then drilled it and put a peg through.

The rear brake was really a swine! We fixed a strip of steel between the stays which normally hold the chaincase and pivoted the brake lever there. As the rear pillion foot-rest arm was now being used as the rider's foot-rest, the brake pedal came just behind the primary chaincase. The handbrake cable from a Morris Minor served as a cable for our stopper and was fitted via various brackets. This brake used more time than any other part.

Instant clip-ons are provided by these bars. They can be fitted instead of the usual clip-ons if you don't want to cut fork shrouds away on tele-fork machines.

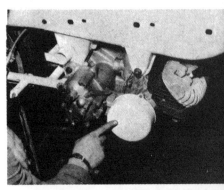

The generator cover has been replaced after having been stove-enamelled with the frame. The generator has been discarded as it is not required with the new system.

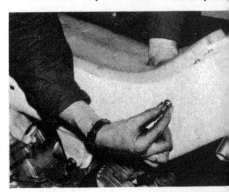

The ignition switch was mounted through the hole in the side of the frame. This put all the wires out of sight and also kept the switch and petrol tap on same side.

Petrol tank and racing seat in one unit. This is made by Fi-glass and fits onto the frame without having to make up any special brackets. Elastics will hold tank on

A complete rev-counter kit which fits on without any mods is made by D M S. The rubber-mounted head will fit the headlamp brackets on ordinary road-going Ariels

A fairing is important for high-speed work. This streamlined one matches the Fi-glass tank and seat and is made by the same firm. Two brackets hold it and they are supplied

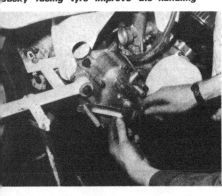

The only standard item in this wheel is the hub—and that has racing brakes in it! A Dunlop alloy rim coupled with a Dunlop sticky racing tyre improve the handling

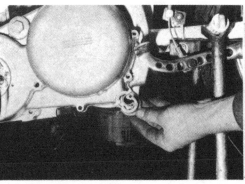

The classic Dunlop rear triangular tyre is used on all serious racing bikes. This is not recommended for road bikes, though, as it is soft and wears out very quickly

Rear-brake controls will have to be a home-made job. The various arrangements are too numerous to explain. This sort of set-up gives smooth action and good control

A reversed gear-lever is necessary. We used the old lever and by cutting and bending it we made a useful shape. A bolt was fitted to act as the actual pedal

These lugs used to support the cross-over rear-brake spindle. Unfortunately, they get in the way of the expansion boxes and so it was necessary to cut them away

The existing petrol tap from the old tank will fit into the thread of the new one. This pull-push type is not very good and the racing style of lever tap would be best

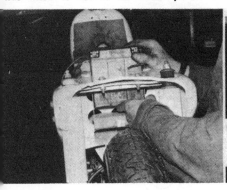

Power for the ignition comes from the battery. We mounted it in the original carrier, under the seat. The carrier had foam rubber stuck onto it to cut vibration

Many forms of carburation can be used on the Arrow. This $1\frac{3}{16}$ in. Amal Monobloc is quite simple to tune as long as you have some idea of jet sizes to start off with

The other popular way of feeding the motor is to use the Wal Phillips fuel injector. There is plenty of room to fit the instrument and the tuning is quite easy

ARIEL ARROW

RIDERS' REPORTS

NUMBER TWELVE

Collated by MIKE EVANS

WHY did the Ariels go out of production? That is the question on the lips of all contributors to this biggest-ever riders' report.

Who can really say—except Ariels themselves? The Arrow is not perfect, but it was far ahead of its day when introduced in 1959 and it is still very advanced. This is because it was a new idea in motor cycles. Appearance is unorthodox; so much, in fact, that this is probably the very reason for the marque's untimely demise.

Unorthodox or not, praise is not in short supply. " The Arrow serves two purposes absolutely ideally. It is a perfect learner's machine, with absolutely impeccable handling and a marvellous bike for a two-stroke fanatic to tune cheaply and effectively to semi-racing specification."

That hails from John Lavender of Langley, Bucks. Christopher Longstaff, of Harrogate, sends his " compliments to the chef for cooking up a real hot-pot of power and reliability."

The outstanding thing about this report is the number of contributors. Usually we receive about 100 letters—this one brought in 140! Not bad going out of 17,000 Arrows produced between December 1959 and January this year.

When the Arrow was released in late 1959 it was hailed as a sporty variant of the scintillating Leader design. It is certainly unusual, as this drawing clearly shows. The pressed-steel beam frame incorporates the petrol tank, while the dummy fuel tank is used as a tools and parcels locker

Between them, our Arrow owners have clocked up 1½ million miles. Average age of machinery is four years for the standard model and three years for the sports. The sportier types, at 20 years old, work out two years younger than the standard Arrow owners.

In both cases, however, experience of motor cycling amounts to four years.

Here, then, is your report on a machine that will certainly be very much lamented for many a year to come.

Performance

"ALTHOUGH my Arrow was four years old, it could still out-accelerate most of my mates' more modern two-fifties, and I was never left behind at traffic lights. I managed to get 85 mph when tanking—aided by only a light tail wind."

When Duncan Currie lays emphasis on acceleration in this quote he is speaking for all our contributors.

New for 1961 was this central sparking-plug arrangement; previously the plugs were mounted towards the front of the heads. At the same time the compression ratio was raised from 8.25 to 10 to 1

The Arrow, in sports or standard trim, is definitely quick off the mark.

For an untuned two-stroke twin, the Ariels also have a fair top speed, judging from all accounts. Consensus of opinion points a steady speedo needle at 77 mph. That's the figure returned by owners of standard machines; their sportier colleagues say 81 mph.

Riders of the sports version report a slightly less flexible engine. This is borne out by the lower mark in the table.

On one point all are agreed—this Ariel power unit needs to be buzzed for best effect. Low-revs power is not over-impressive. Nevertheless, revving high is no disadvantage with such a smooth goer.

A mark of 80 per cent for both sports and standard versions adds weight to the words of praise from many readers. Coupled with this good performance, however, is excessive smoke from the exhausts. A smoke screen has always been regarded as the hallmark of the Ariel two-strokes ever since the Leader was introduced in 1958. Correspondents say that the Arrow is no exception.

While the majority are unable to cure this smoking—and its attendant oil-besplattered rear end—one or two, including Nigel Songhurst of RAF

Honington, Suffolk, seem to have overcome the problem.

"The only time the exhaust smokes is when I'm doing a lot of town riding. But five minutes of open-throttle riding soon clears this."

Perhaps all our readers are not aware that Ariels recommend a leaner oil ratio for all models than formerly, 32 to 1?

Fuel Consumption

NOBODY expects a high-performance two-stroke twin to be ultra-economical. Indeed, one would assume the exact opposite. Therefore it is surprising that both Arrows come out of the stew pot as creditably as they do.

The figure decided on by reporters is 66 mpg. A few are down in the lower forties—but others manage miraculous nineties and hundreds.

Starting

WITH marks around the mid-sixties it is obvious that these two-strokes are not the world's best starters. Comments in letters show that the Arrow can be temperamental.

Says David Evans of Sutton-in-Ashfield, an old friend from the Norton Jubilee report, "Cold starting requires a knack which I have now acquired. But I don't know what it is.

"As far as I know, I use the same technique as I did when I had to give up to 39 kicks to get it to fire!"

Well in command of the situation is Keith Spiers of Doncaster: "Starting is first-class if you follow the instruction book. You have to flood the carburettor and depress the kick-starter twice; then switch on the ignition and the engine normally starts first go."

But even he has to add the proviso that his machine "can sometimes be temperamental."

Handling

SOME of our reporters swallowed a dictionary for breakfast, it would appear, if all the superlatives are to be believed.

All round, the Arrow shows a proud face to the world when the question of handling crops up. Listen to 21-year-old Robin Baker of Mill Hill: "I have hurled it through 60- and 70 mph bends with fairing, stand and footrest all on the road; changed line, snicked down a gear, braked, accelerated, all over drain covers and potholes. *Never a twitch in protest.*"

"Handling is surely the highlight of this amiable two-fifty," weighs in 18-year-old Paul Heath of Coventry.

Amid his praise, however, a Yorkshire reader voices a universal complaint: "It handles as well at 75 mph as at 5 mph. *But because the centre stand is so low, it scrapes the ground easily.*"

That stand position is slated by almost everyone. Many, too, would prefer to see adjustable rear-suspension units to cope more effectively with the extra weight of a passenger.

SPECIFICATION

ENGINE: Ariel 247 cc (54 x 54mm) two-stroke twin. Separate iron cylinders and light-alloy heads. Roller big-end bearings. Crankshaft supported in three ball bearings. Compression ratio, 10 to 1. Petroil lubrication.

CARBURETTOR: Amal Monobloc with ⅞in choke (sports, 1¹⁄₁₆in). Rod-operated strangler. Mesh-type air filter.

TRANSMISSION: Four-speed, foot-change gear box in unit with engine. Ratios: bottom, 19; second, 11; third, 7.8; top, 5.9 to 1. Three-plate clutch operating in oil. Primary chain ⅜ x 0.225in in oil-bath case; rear chain ½ x 0.305in in pressed-steel case. Engine rpm at 30 mph in top gear, 2,600.

ELECTRICAL EQUIPMENT: Lucas 50-watt RM18 alternator. Coil ignition. Lucas 13-ampere-hour battery. 6in diameter headlamp with 30/24-watt main bulb.

TYRES: Dunlop 3.25 x 16in; studded rear, ribbed front.

BRAKES: 6in diameter x 1⅛in wide, front and rear.

SUSPENSION: Ariel trailing-link front fork, hydraulically damped. Pivoted rear fork controlled by two Armstrong spring-and-hydraulic units.

DIMENSIONS: Wheelbase, 51in; ground clearance, 5in. Seat height, 28½in. All unladen.

WEIGHT: 305 lb, including approximately one gallon of petroil.

ROAD TAX: £4 a year.

MAKERS: Ariel Motors, Ltd., Armoury Road, Small Heath, Birmingham, 11.
This specification applies equally to the sports and standard Arrows. While technically the same as that of the ordinary Arrow, the engine of the sports model had the larger-choke carburettor and different porting.

HOW MUCH YOU PAY (prices quoted are fair secondhand figures for machines in average condition): Standard Arrow.—1960, £70; 1961, £85; 1962, £100; 1963, £120, 1964, £140. Sports Arrow.—1961, £87; 1962, £107; 1963, £127; 1964, £150.

Braking

THIS is where Ariel designers go and bury their heads under the drawing board. With the average mark working out at just under 60 per cent, the brakes leave a lot to be desired.

"The brakes are useless," exclaims knowledgeable Ron Herring, responsible for the preparation of the ex-Dickie Dale Arrow and of the Herman Meier Arrows, one of which Mike O'Rourke rode so successfully in the T.T. He *should* know.

Civil servant Colin Roberts of Oswestry is of the opinion that the brakes were a manufacturers' joke!

More objective comment comes from A. A. Gosling of Crowthorne, Berkshire: "The rear brake is adequate—progressive and smooth. But the front stopper is definitely not good enough for solo use, let alone for passenger carrying."

As usual, though, there is the odd opposite comment. Graham Findlay, a 19-year-old chef of Seaford, enthuses that his machines will stop on a sixpence and still give threepence change!

Transmission

"THE gear change is appalling." "The gear box is completely out of keeping with the sporting nature of the machine." Just two of the many such comments.

Proof in triplicate comes from Jim Baxter, 19, of Ashton-under-Lyne: "I have ridden three different Arrows and the most outstanding fault on all is the rough gear box. Changing down causes a noisy grind."

Hugh Ruddle of Swindon waxes very eloquent about the transmission: "The clutch takes up the drive smoothly and seldom needs adjustment. The gear box is another story, however.

"I don't like the long lever and changes from third to second or second to first are normally noisy and grating, whatever technique is used. It is necessary to push the pedal to the limit when changing up, otherwise neutral can be found.

"To change down the foot has to be hooked right under the lever in order to exert enough pressure."

No outstanding criticisms are levelled at the chain department; everything seems to be in order. The main point of note, however, is, again, a

Handling is a strong point with the Arrow, as Vic Willoughby discovered when he sampled this standard machine. Nevertheless, many reporters complain strongly of the too-easy-to-ground centre stand

criticism of the gear box.

Bottom is generally thought to be too low for normal use. Second has to be selected almost immediately the clutch has been engaged after making a start.

Gold and cream (previously gold and blue) hallmark the sports models—nicknamed Golden Arrows. Unorthodox lines, true, but the Arrow's design is one that grows on you

Riding Comfort

OKAY here. No reporter is really slating. One or two would prefer more padding.

James Whitebread of Penge took to sticking foam rubber in the seat of his overcoat.

Several owners of sports Arrows voice a preference for more rearward footrests.

helpful estimation of the average life of parts over a period of 35,000 miles.

Plugs were renewed every 8,000 miles (this is slightly better than average since the Arrow has a reputation as a plug chewer), tyres at 30,000 (a bit optimistic, really), rear chain at 9,000, brake linings and piston rings at 20,000 and rear sprocket at 25,000.

Spare electrical switches should *always* be carried, he recommends!

Service

Few are over-impressed with the factory spares situation. The low marks of 58 and 54 per cent are proof enough. But really big moans are few and far between.

Dealers come out of the report more creditably, however, and the majority of reporters find that Ariel spares are readily available—although it may mean a visit to several dealers.

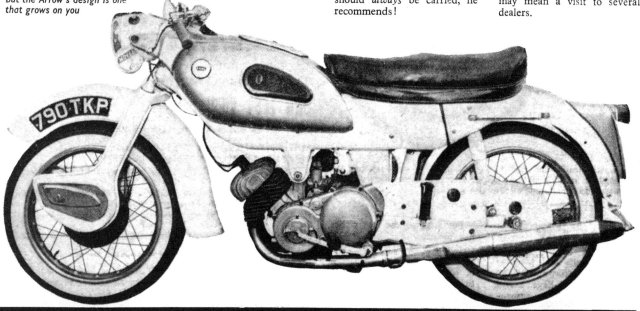

Electrics

IF reporters are satisfied with their electrics, their appreciation is grudging. Many think the sparks and lighting departments could be improved, but, of course, there is no chance of that, now that Ariels are no longer in production.

Lighting is adequate, it appears. However, a rather flimsy contact-breaker unit and a vulnerable stop-light switch form the basis of most grouses.

Detail Finish

FINISH is not considered outstanding. Stories of thin paintwork and quick rusting in inaccessible regions are common.

With a layout such as that of the Arrow it seems that a coat of underseal for out-of-sight parts would not have come amiss.

Chromium plating is voted average.

Reliability

YOU will see from the marks table that the sports Arrow receives a mark 15-per-cent down on the creditable 92 per cent of the standard Arrow. The reason for this isn't apparent from letters. Indeed, the general tendency is for the Ariels to be shown up as thoroughly reliable.

"One of the things which really endeared me to this machine was its absolute and utter reliability. I did 30,000 miles with nothing more than routine replacements." So says James Unsworth, 37, of York.

Roy Graham of Smethwick, a 23-year-old electrical draughtsman, gives a very

At 35,000 miles he found it necessary to replace the main bearings, big ends, small ends, primary chain, clutch plates and gear-box sprocket.

At this time the wear on the cylinder bore was found to be less than one thou!

Some owners are perpetually seizing their Arrows. In most cases, however, clues point to carelessness such as incorrect carburettor settings or throttle manipulation.

Some people, I am convinced, imagine that you can descend the St Bernard Pass on a two-stroke with the throttle shut and the engine turning over at six-and-a-half.

PERCENTAGE VOTE	Arrow Standard	Arrow Sports
Acceleration ..	91	96
Flexibility ..	74	68
Smoothness ..	80	80
Starting	66	68
Oil Tightness ..	90	85
Reliability ..	92	77
Clutch ..	82	83
Gear Box ..	54	50
Delivery Tune* ..	80	43
Accessibility ..	64	63
Handling ..	95	93
Suspension (front)	86	92
Suspension (rear)	72	71
Smoothness of Controls ..	73	80
Riding Position ..	78	73
Brakes	58	60
Mudguarding ..	89	85
Workmanship ..	71	65
Quality of Finish	58	65
Lighting ..	79	77
Horn	26	24
Other Electrics ..	65	64
Tool Kit	62	71
Spares from Factory ..	58	54
Spares from Dealer ..	73	73
OVERALL MARK	73	71
GOOD BUY? (PER CENT YES)	94	90
WOULD YOU BUY ANOTHER? (PER CENT YES)	73	77

YOUR VIEW AT A GLANCE

■ **After sending in their reports, readers were asked to complete a questionnaire in which they answered specific questions according to the formula good, middling or poor.**

In calculating these figures we have allowed two points for good and one point for middling. Poor got nothing.

The marks on the right are given as percentages of the total possible marks.

Secondhand machines not taken into account.

63

This massive trailing-link front fork contributes in no small measure to the excellent handling characteristics. Very generous mudguarding is another welcome feature of all Ariel two-strokes

ments and the jet nuts cannot be removed without first detaching the carburettor from the engine."

Removing the throttle slide in order to fit a new cable is an annoying task because of the proximity of the frame.

Although it is possible to do the job with the carb in place, several readers find the best scheme is to remove it.

On the other hand, one experienced motor cyclist, George Temple, of Colchester, reports outstanding accessibility.

It is, he says, perhaps the easiest of modern engines to

check, one minute; contact-breaker check, 2m; cylinder-head removal, 2m; rear-wheel removal, 4m.

Overall View

"A BRILLIANT concept originally, but somewhat marred by a lack of subsequent development to eliminate the few bugs it had. Given such development (and, for many, a four-stroke engine) it would have been one of the great bikes of all time—and a complete answer to foreign competition."

OUR TEST VIEW

Ariel Arrow Super Sports, 12 April 1962

HIGHEST ONE-WAY SPEED: 81 mph.
MEAN MAXIMUM SPEED: 78 mph.
STANDING QUARTER-MILE: 17.6s with terminal speed of 70 mph.
FUEL CONSUMPTION: At 30 mph, 108 mpg; at 40 mph, 82 mpg; at 50 mph, 74 mpg; at 60 mph, 56 mpg.
BRAKING: From 30 mph to rest, 30ft (surface, dry asphalt).

Accessibility

LOW marks and plaintive cries from correspondents go together here. Says David Evans: "Removing a suspended engine such as the Ariel's would seem to be simple. But such is not the case."

For instance, the rear wheel has to come out before the engine can be removed. And *when* the engine is out there is very little of the machine that has not been dismantled!

"Access to the carburettor is very tricky," he continues. "A double-jointed hand is needed to make routine adjust-

work on and "it is certainly one of the very few which are better left in the frame, making a special jig unnecessary."

The fairest conclusion seems to be that while there are undoubtedly some bad points, the Arrow is reasonably easy to work on.

An Ariel Owners' Club member gives some specimen times for minor jobs: battery

Left: Oddest thing for the Arrow rider is to look at the handlebar layout and see how the headlamp points straight ahead at all times. Below: Surprise for the uniniated is the dry petrol tank—it holds tools and, below the tray, small parcels

This is just the wording of one reporter; yet at the same time it represents the views of practically every one of our 140 contributors.

"Why, oh why, have Ariels stopped making one of the best bikes in the country," cries 21-year-old Peter Beardmore of Cheadle, Staffs.

Another glowing testimony comes our way from Robin Baker: "I am very fond of my *barra* and intend keeping it for years. It is brilliantly conceived and designed, and well made. It is reliable and has character.

"The lack of real effort to sell, or make it saleable, abroad, and its recent demise, are a fitting funeral dirge for an industry with vast potential that is just crumbling through mediocrity into oblivion."

A bit strong, true enough, but Arrow owners *do* feel strongly about this.

It is a machine that handles excellently, that goes well and that is reliable. Yet it is no longer possible to buy it new. It has gone the way of the Vincent, the Rudge, the Sunbeam and the Douglas.

Gone, but certainly not forgotten.

Last word to Alan Archer of Carlisle: "THE ARROW WILL BECOME IMMORTALIZED LIKE THE VINNIE."

||||||||||||||||||||||||||||||||||||||||||||||||||||||||||||||||||||

NEXT ONE ◀

IT'S back to Woolwich for our next-but-one Riders' Report. Subjects for the scrutiny will be AJS and Matchless two-fifties. All models since the unit-construction design was introduced in mid-1958 are eligible.

But don't forget that the BMW test is on the boil at the moment—and it will be next in line of publication. All Bee-Em flat twins (not the two-fifty single, note) produced since January 1960 are eligible.

Send your reports to "Motor Cycle," Dorset House, Stamford Street, London, SE1.

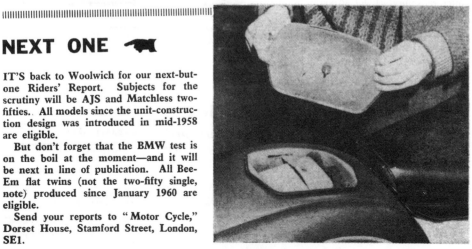

THE UNIQUE
ARIEL DESIGN

PLUS EXTRA SPEED AND POWER!

The Ariel design is something new in motorcycling—a design that is far ahead. Here is a light rigid chassis designed as the perfect basis for first-class suspension, hairline steering, brilliant handling and road-holding qualities. An Ariel is designed, in fact, *to be the finest possible two-wheeled vehicle.* And in the Arrow Super Sports—the luxury version of the Ariel Arrow—you get that unique design with the added speed and power of a high-performance engine.

The Ariel three—the Arrow, the Arrow Super Sports, and the luxurious Ariel Leader (all with a complete range of designed accessories) — give you a new standard of motorcycling.

ARROW SUPER SPORTS

THE ARIEL LEADER
£219.12.0 (inc. p.t.)

THE ARIEL ARROW
£192.0.0 (inc. p.t.)

THE ARIEL ARROW SUPER SPORTS
£206.8.0 (inc. p.t.)

ARIEL
TOMORROW'S DESIGN — TODAY

YOU SAVE ON INSURANCE!

ARIEL MOTORS LTD
ARMOURY ROAD, BIRMINGHAM, 11
Please send me your latest catalogue, and details of the special money-saving "Clearway" Insurance rates available to Ariel owners.

NAME
(Block letters, please)

ADDRESS

S-MM-71

Tick if under 16 ☐

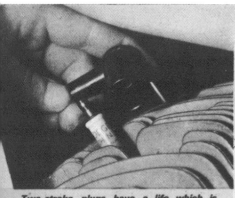

Two-stroke plugs have a life which is considerably shorter than a four-stroke due to higher running temperature and twice as many sparks per revolution. It is wise to change them every 5,000 miles

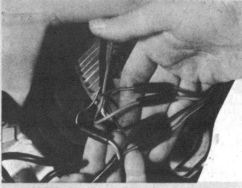

A flickering ammeter or fluctuating lamp will indicate loose snap connectors. On the Ariels they are open to the elements and it is wise to push them firmly home and then fix them with adhesive tape

Timing is of utmost importance on the two stroke. The bulb and battery method recommended. An alternative is a feeler gauge (1½ thou) which should just be gripped by points with the timing key inserted

Early model Arrows and Leaders had the 8:1 domed cylinder heads. The 10:1 high compression heads give up to 10 mph more, plus better acceleration and fuel consumption. A pair of h.c. heads, £3 4s. 0d.

Air filters can be washed according to the handbook, but a new unit only costs 5/– and it is cheaper in the long run. Also, it is wise to change element every 5,000 miles or fuel consumption will increase

Silencer baffles should be removed ever 1,000 miles for cleaning. If left, carbo will glue them firmly in place and th only way to remove them will be a solu tion of caustic soda poured into silence

Rapid primary chain wear will take place if the correct SAE 20 oil level is not maintained. Also, the wet-plate clutch will give trouble if allowed to run dry. Check the oil level in chaincase weekly

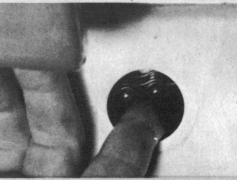

The rear chain should have ½ in. slack with the machine on the road. The chain should be oiled weekly as the automatic oiler is not efficient and rapid wear sets in if the chain is allowed to run dry

A juddering front brake can be due to faulty or dusty lining, but a difficul to-diagnose fault is this worn brake pla bush. This allows twisting movement the plate and juddering. Renew for 2,

Silentbloc bushes on the rear swing arm wear out at between 10 to 15,000 miles. For a 15/– deposit, tools can be hired to remove and replace the bushes and regain perfect handling with new bushes for 5/–

A front wheel wobble causing very poor handling may not necessarily be due to worn bearings or steering head. The wheel spindle itself may be worn on this lipped shoulder. Cure? New spindle and bearing

Grounding centre stands and bottomin rear suspension units can be cured b fitting auxiliary springs—15/– a pa Hold damper in vice and unscrew top cove clockwise to expose main spring benea

JIM CALVERT OF WRITERS SHOWS HOW TO GET THE BEST FROM YOUR

ARIEL ARROW

● Within three years of being voted the "Machine of the Year", the unique Ariel two-stroke twins fell from favour and production of this superb lightweight was abandoned. Thousands of owners were amazed at this decision as the Ariel two-stroke 250 has much to recommend its continued production.

It has a performance equal to that of most other 250s and can be tuned to better most, as its seventh place in the Lightweight T.T. proved, while it is also reliable, has good roadholding and reasonable economy.

Fortunately, Ariel owners are not being abandoned when it comes to the supply of spares and service. Writers, of Kennington Lane, Kennington, London, S.E.11, are one of a few dealers able to provide a first-class Ariel spares service.

Jim Calvert, manager of Writers, showed MM over the main stores and we were surprised to find a stock of Ariel spares dating back to the four-stroke era.

An example of trouble encountered with two-stroke Ariels is the excessive, high-pitched rattle which is usually accompanied with an extra high fuel consumption.

The fault? Sticking piston rings. These become gummed in their grooves by sticky oil deposits.

The cure is to remove the cylinder head and barrel to expose the piston, then remove the rings and scrape the grooves clean with an old broken part of a ring.

The Honda hub was a tight squeeze in the forks and involved removing metal from the hub flanges and the inside of shrouds

To locate the Honda brake plate, the Ariel torque arm was bolted to a new bracket welded to the nearside fork shroud

The works exhaust system is carried by long steel tubes bolted to rear frame. The tube ends were filled to prevent fractures

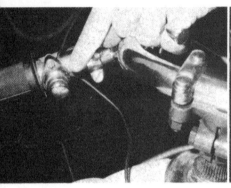

Instead of using the clutch for changes at speed, this "kill" button earths the ignition for a second—revs drop slightly

A spacer is needed to take up the end-float on shaft instead of the rotor. The rubber tube holds fairing in place

The rear sets were difficult to make. Ours are carried on an alloy plate. The tube in the pivot is a home-made grease nipple

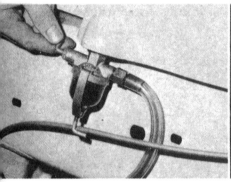

Ian Speller tries out M M

Superlative braking, fier

good handling soon showe

mechanical modificatio

To cope with the vast amount of fuel and oil used, we fitted a Wipac filter. Filtrate oil causes petrol to go black

An alloy adaptor carries Tiger Cub rear sprockets. A wide range of gearing is possible with this £5 adaptor

▶ With a shriek like a scalded cat, the two-stroke twin 250 motor burst into life. M M's Ariel Arrow racer was back on the track after a winter season in the workshops.

The racer is a bike we converted last year from an ordinary roadster. The motor was extensively tuned and runs at 12 : 1 compression ratio. Handling proved a bit of a problem, and the braking was definitely not up to the 100 mph performance we were squeezing out of the motor at the end of last season.

During the winter we concentrated on fitting a Honda front wheel with racing linings, plus new suspension units. Another problem with the Arrow is the scarcity of close-ratio gears, and even worse, the difficulty of changing the overall ratios.

No alternative rear wheel sprockets are available, and we eventually fitted an adaptor made by Geo. Todd Engineering, Falfield, Via Wooton-under-Edge, Gloucestershire. This allowed us to fit Tiger Cub sprockets, which are fairly plentiful.

Out on the track at Brands Hatch, the motor ran well after we had jetted up to 560 on the single Amal 1$\frac{3}{16}$ in. carb. Nearly 9,000 rpm was available which gives just under 110 mph equivalent.

The rear brake proved to be a bit spongy, even with its race linings, but it worked fairly well. The front brake was very powerful and only two fingers were needed to bring the bike to a tyre-screeching halt.

The general "feel" of the bike was improved just by fitting the Amal alloy racing levers. These spring back faster than steel ones and give a feeling of quality.

The Ariel is quite a large machine for a 250 and so the 7R fairing proved to be

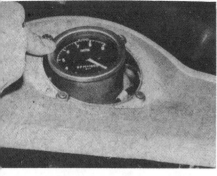

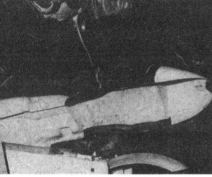

e rev-counter was supplied by D M S
d fits into the fairing shelf. It is
rried in rubber to prevent vibration

o change the battery, the one-piece
eat and tank is lifted off. The battery
carried in its original frame position

iel Arrow racer.

celeration and

mselves. Follow these

improve your Arrow

ARIEL ACTION

just the right size. The rider can tuck well in with plenty of room to move about.

The triangular Dunlop tyres were brand new and they were not fully run-in before the test ended, so we could not corner as fast as we would have liked.

The Arrow handles rather like a Greeves Silverstone, and a loose style of riding is necessary. Hanging out on the corners is essential.

Generally, the bike can be compared to a Silverstone in everything but the brakes—the Arrow brakes are much better!

The smart appearance of the test Leader belies the fact that it is five years old. Two of the "optional extras" already on the bike are shown—panniers and flashers

The fuel tank is hidden away under the seat. It holds two gallons, which is enough for a journey of 150 miles or more. There is room for a few tools here if luggage is carried

This is the trailing link fork which contributes so much to Leader's handling. Brake plate and anchor arms are all fully floating as the wheel moves up and down, not front forks

JEFF HUTCHINSON KEEP
Look

SECONDHAND
MOTORCYCLE MECHANICS ROAD TEST No. 125

Vehicle	'Ariel Leader (1961)'
Price now	S/H £79
Engine	249cc twin cylinder 2-stroke (54 mm x 54 mm)
Gearbox	Unit Construction 4 speed
Final drive	Chain (½ in pitch)

GENERAL INFORMATION

Weight	320 lb
Saddle height	30 ins
Turning circle	16 ft
Is toolbox lockable	Yes
Is steering lockable	Yes
Fuel tank capacity	2 gallons
Reserve capacity	½ gallon
Oil tank capacity	nil
Gearbox capacity	1 pint
Fuel specified	20:1 Petroil
Overall consumption	80 m.p.g.
Braking from 30 mph	42 ft
Acceleration 0-50 mph	15 secs

SPEEDS IN GEARS

(chart showing mph 10–110 vs GEAR 1 2 3 4 5 6)

EQUIPMENT SUPPLIED

STANDARD FITTINGS
Headlamp trimmer, lifting handle, pillion footrests

OPTIONAL EXTRAS
Flashing Indicators
Panniers, rear carrier

SPARES PRICES

Engine gasket set	8s 6d
Set valves & guides	
Piston with rings	£1-13s-0d Exchange
Set of clutch plates	17s-6d
Silencer	£3-2s-0d
Pr Exchange brake shoes	17s 6d

▶ **Mourned by the many, the Ariel two-stroke twins ended their short six-year heyday two years ago —and we want to add our names to the long list of unhappy enthusiasts.**

The 250 cc Ariel Leader we tested was picked from three similarly clean models at Elite Motors, of Tooting.

Testing the bike in all weather conditions proved that the machine is still a successful example of a motorcycle with scooter-style weather protection. The screen and stylish leg shields gave the rider almost complete protection from the elements, and it was possible to ride right through a shower and not get wet.

For a touring bike the compression ratio is very high—10:1, but this does not affect tractability and smoothness in any way, and it gives the demure Leader a sporting punch in the acceleration department. Top speeds in the gears were: first—25 mph, second—40 mph, third—55 mph, top—68 mph. Vibration from the

engine was never bad and the only time that it began to be noticeable was when a gear change was necessary.

The gearbox behaved perfectly throughout the test with a crisp lever movement that made for positive changes. First and second were grouped fairly closely, but there was a noticeable jump between second and third which in turn was fairly close to top.

Handling is a bonus point with the Leader and Arrow—it is perfect. This is due mainly to the excellent trailing link forks and a very low centre of gravity.

One bad point, though, was the centre stand, which grounded all too readily and although the contact was not enough to unsaddle the rider, it was rather unnerving.

Brakes were up to the job, but only just. Most of the load was taken by the back brake, whilst the front one felt very spongy.

Lights were good enough for fast touring

at night, the headlight being surprisingly powerful for a 6 v. unit. Another point with the headlight is that the rider had to get used to turning corners almost blindly, because the light turns with the bike itself and not with the front forks. The neat "trimmer" lever sticking up on the instrument panel adjusts the beam height whilst running. This is handy when carrying pillion passengers or heavy baggage, because the headlight can be trimmed according to the weight carried.

The flashing indicators were good for night riding, but on sunny days it was advisable to revert to hand signals as the flashers were difficult to see.

The test Leader was fitted with several extras including rear carrier and panniers, mirrors and a screen extension.

The rear carrier and panniers proved useful on more than one occasion. The beauty of the Leader is that you can ride it anywhere and put all the kit you usually carry about in the panniers and "tank" compartment and lock them up.

The windscreen extension could be easily adjusted whilst riding and this was useful in the rain.

The side panels can be removed easily to give access to the engine. The sparking plugs could be inspected without disturbing the panels. These are situated the two legshields, behind the front mudguard.

Putting the machine on its stand was an extremely simple operation as there is a built-in handle under the seat. This handle, coupled with the easy roll-on stand, made parking the Leader a pleasure.

The bike never felt as though it weighed the 320 lb. stated by the makers, either on the stand or whilst riding. It made an ideal commuting machine as it was so easy to manoeuvre through heavy traffic.

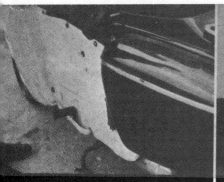

lifting handle saves many a broken seat p. It just slides away when not in use. leg shields proved exceptionally protec—even come under rider's feet at front

The choke and petrol tap are extended to protrude through the side panels. The panels themselves are easily removed for any adjustments to be made on engine or carb

The Leader's dash layout is effective. The headlight trimmer was very handy at night especially when picking up a 'passenger. Badge can be replaced with eight-day clock

NE DRY IN DIRTY WEATHER ON THIS '61 MOUNT—AND SAYS

at the Leader!

The fuel consumption figures for the test are based on a short run of 120 miles, and we really expected, as the bike was five years old, that the figures would have been rather lower than the recorded 80 mpg.

Throughout the entire test, this five-year-old 250 proved itself well worth the £79 asked for it by Elite Motors.

USED BIKE TEST

Before you can remove the primary case, you must take out this nylon peg which operates the chain tensioner inside the case

Some special tools; Bearing dr⸱ with oil seal attachment (centre flywheel/end cover puller (lef⸱ and head and flywheel Allen ke⸱

The left-hand cover has no spacer. Tap oil seals in with a light hammer, add grease to protect them during first hour's running

End covers should slide on easil⸱ but withdrawal demands the u⸱ of this tool. Never try to or knock covers from crankca⸱

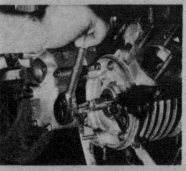

Tighten, but don't over-tighten the screws and bolts on end covers. Nuts have shakeproof washers, which must be renewed

Flywheel goes on next. Make su⸱ the taper is clean and keyw⸱ undamaged before attempting fit it. The taper holds the . ⸱

As rotor nut tightens, insert feeler gauges between c/shaft and case —there should not be less than 8 thou clearance when tight

If you retained your own sh⸱ there should be no need to shi⸱ Now the stator can be fitte⸱ Check that rotor is running tru⸱

PETE CARRANA SHOWS HOW TO REBUILD THE ARIEL
LEADER

▶ The Ariel Leader and Arrow are basically the same; the only difference being that the Arrow was the sporting version of this popular two-stroke twin.

Many people feel that if development had continued on these machines and a decent frame had been fitted without all that ghastly panelling we might have had a respectable challenger to the Japanese two-strokes of today, but that's the way it goes . . .

One good thing about Leaders, etc., is that a complete overhaul can be carried out with the engine in the frame.

Being a two-stroke, crankcase compression is important, so all oil seals must be replaced and extra special care taken not to damage them when fitting the right hand flywheel. And when putting end covers on tempor-

arily to enable crankshaft to be tightened up, leave the seals out until you refit the covers permanently.

It is important to get, where possible, a reground crankshaft —not a service exchange unit. The reason for this is that all of these crankshafts are set up individually for their respective crankcases. If you get a crankshaft which was made for another Ariel, you will have the added bother of shimming. It can be done, but it's better to keep your own crank.

A. L. Carter Ltd, of 7 Chiswick High Road, London, W.4, where we watched Pete Carrana do this rebuild offer a very good crankshaft reconditioning service for these models. In fact A. L. Carter have specialised in Ariels for many years, so if you have any problems, you know where to go for service.

need to dismantle clutch, or ...ove engine from frame. Clean ...nkcases thoroughly and warm ...ring housings with blowlamp

If carburettor is left on, watch that blowlamp! Using special drift, tap main bearing into position. It must go in squarely right away

Warm end covers and use same drift to insert outer bearings. Any burrs must be removed before bearing is entered into casting

The right hand side end cover has an oil seal and spacer, plus a bearing retaining circlip that fits into a groove in housing

...portant—when joining crank-...fts, the tapers must be per-...tly smooth and clean. This is ... most important part to . . .

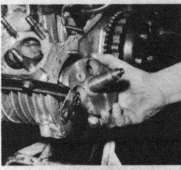

. . . remember when rebuilding the Ariel. Waggle the crankshafts in by getting conrod at TDC—yes TDC! Turn shafts until they locate

Put end covers on temporarily to tighten shafts. Tighten from right-hand side with Allen key. Should be torqued to 60 ft lbs

Having tightened crankshafts, put end covers on after fitting and greasing new gaskets. Don't for-get the grease on the oil seals

. flywheel, keys are merely ...ety measures. A strap wrench ...useful when doing up the secur-...nut. Renew the tab washer

When replacing the outer case, be very careful not to damage the oil seal as it slides over the contact breaker points cam

Check the ignition cam for wear and replace if any is apparent. Wear here can affect the timing and cause loss of performance

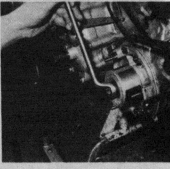

Fit and tighten rotor. Now you will see why it is best to get your crankshaft re-ground instead of a service exchange unit . . .

...rm the pistons, fit gudgeon ...s and attach to rods. Piston ...gs are fragile, so take care when ...ing the barrels over them

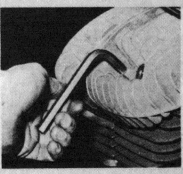

Make sure everything is turning smoothly and quietly, then fit exhaust pipes and cylinder heads. Heads are secured by Allen bolts

This air filter was in a terrible state. After an engine overhaul, you owe it to your machine to renew the filter and check carb

Maximum and minimum permissi-ble contact breaker gaps are 17 and 12 thou respectively—a satis-factory balance is necessary

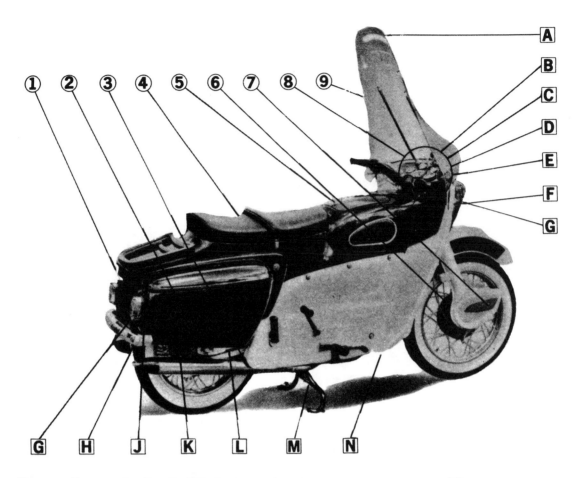

Only the LEADER has so much... offers so much

The most important thing about any motorcycle is the basic design. Ariel design is far ahead. Based on the rigid steel "chassis" that gives such a superb standard of road-holding and steering, it makes Ariel the *finest possible two-wheeled vehicle.*

But your pleasure and comfort in riding are enhanced by many thoughtful details. See what the luxurious Leader gives you as standard equipment. See the neatly designed features you can easily add, choosing just what you want. Isn't this the logical way to arrive at the perfect motorcycle for *you?*

LEADER £219.12.0   ARROW £192.0.0   ARROW SUPER SPORTS £206.8.0
Prices include purchase tax

TOMORROW'S DESIGN—TODAY!

Standard on the LEADER

1. Stoplight worked by either brake.
2. Quick-detachable wheels (complete tail unit hinges upward).
3. Totally enclosed rear chain.
4. Pull-out lifting handle.
5. Locking tank-top parcel compartment (steering and dualseat also lock).
6. Full-width hubs.
7. Nylon bushes on front and rear suspension pivots, no greasing needed.
8. Instrument panel with ammeter and trip speedometer.
9. Windscreen.

And other features that are often extras on other makes.

Designed accessories you can fit

A. Slotted windscreen extension.

B. Neutral gear indicator light.

C. Parking lamp (low consumption).

D. Plug-in inspection lamp.

E. 8-day clock.

F. Rear-view mirrors (pair).

G. Flashing trafficators.

H. Chrome rear fender with reflectors.

J. Carrier.

K. Locking pannier cases (also lift-out zip bags to fit).

L. Supplementary heavyweight rear springs.

M. Prop stand.

N. Detachable front stand.

A wide choice of useful items! All of them fit right and look right because they're Ariel designed.

ARIEL'S 250

OP BRITISH MACHINE OF THE EARLY SIXTIES.

MOTORCYCLE

SCOOTER & THREE-WHEELER

MECHANICS

THE ILLUSTRATED HOW-TO-DO-IT MAGAZINE

ENGINE ANALYSIS

No. 10

▶ When Ariel's first introduced their two-stroke twin, in the form of the Leader, it was given a fantastic reception by public and Press alike.

And it deserved it. Not only was it the only radically different design around at the time, but it was to prove smooth, reliable and powerful.

This was one of the few British bikes, since the 'thirties, to be designed as a complete unit with tradition thrown to the wind.

The engine was of fresh conception, slung *under* a pressed steel frame, the swinging arm pivoted at the rear of the gearbox and the front forks had short trailing-link suspension. Even the fuel tank wasn't in the "proper" place!

The great thing was that Ariel produced this completely new machine with a competitive selling price.

The Leader appeared in 1961 and was fitted with fully enclosed engine, legshields, screen and panniers. Then Edward Turner suggested that there was room for a sportier version and the Arrow appeared in 1962. This was virtually a Leader minus the trimmings, but later the engine was beefed up, resulting in the Sports Arrow.

Although Ariel stayed away from competitions, it was inevitable that someone would race one. O'Rourke, on the Herman Meier tuned Arrow came in seventh, the first British entrant to finish, in the 250 TT, and every race fan must have seen the Arrow that Peter Inchley spent so much time on around the short circuits.

In addition, George Brown started to take sprinting records with another Ariel.

These reliable little machines were voted machine of the year for three years running, but were finally killed off by accountants rather than any fault in the machine.

LEADER

ARROW

ARROW SPORTS

ARROW 200

lubrication
petroil, with petrol/oil ratio of 32:1, or $\frac{1}{4}$-pint oil to one gallon petrol

engine
two-stroke 180° twin with piston-controlled ports and separate crankcase induction on each cylinder

bore × stroke	54 × 54 mm
	2.125 × 2.125 in.
capacity	247 cc
	15 cu. in.
compression ratio	8.25:1
alternative ratio	10:1
	(different head)
power output	16bhp at 6400 rpm
(high-compression)	17.5 bhp at
	7000 rpm

piston:
skirt clearance .002–.0035 in.
(measured at front or rear of piston at bottom of cylinder barrel)
ring gap .070–.073 in.
rebore oversizes +.020 and .040 in.
crankshaft bearings:
the shaft is supported in three roller bearings, with double row roller bearing big-ends
ignition:
twin coil and contact breakers
contact breaker gap .014–.016 in.
timing 20 btdc
.080 in. btdc
2 mm btdc
spark plug Lodge 2HLN
plug gap .030 in.

carburettor

Type	Amal 375/33
nominal choke size	$\frac{7}{8}$ in.
main jet	140
pilot jet	30
needle jet	105
needle position	3
throttle slide	$3\frac{1}{2}$

transmission
primary drive by chain to four-speed gearbox via multiplate clutch. Final drive by chain

primary chain	single row, 70 links $\frac{3}{8}$ in. pitch, .225 in. wide
clutch	three driven plates shock absorber in clutch centre

gearbox, overall ratios:
first	19.0:1
second	11.0:1
third	7.8:1
fourth	5.9:1

internal ratios:
first	3.24:1
second	1.86:1
third	1.32:1
fourth	1.00:1
final drive	chain, 113 links $\frac{1}{2}$ in. pitch, .305 in. wide

sprocket sizes:
engine sprocket	22 teeth
clutch sprocket	50 teeth
gearbox sprocket	18 teeth
rear wheel sprocket	47 teeth

road speed at 1000 rpm in fourth gear, 11.0 mph, 17.7 kph

electrical equipment
6 volt ac/dc lighting, coil ignition.
alternator	Lucas RM 13/15 or Lucas RM 18
output	50 W
battery	6 volt, 13 amp.-hr. Lucas MLZ9E
rectifier	Lucas FSX 1849 FSX1501 or 2DS 506

(the three types may be interchanged)
coil	Lucas MA 6 (2 off)

capacities
fuel tank	2.3 gallons or, 3 gallons
primary chaincase	$\frac{3}{4}$ pint
gearbox	1 pint

The Leader and Arrow machines follow the same specification, but the Sports Arrow and the later 200 cc machines vary from this data on the following points:

Sports Arrow
compression ratio	10:1
power output	20 at 6500 rpm
carburettor	Amal 376/277
nominal choke	$\frac{11}{16}$ in.
main jet	230
pilot jet	30
needle jet	105
needle position	3
throttle slide	$3\frac{1}{2}$

200 cc engine
bore × stroke	48.5 × 54 mm
capacity	199.4 cc
compression ratio	9.5:1
power output	14 bhp at 6250 rpm
carburettor	Amal 375/57
nominal choke	$\frac{13}{16}$ in.
main jet	130
pilot jet	30
needle jet	104
	(with angled spray tube)
needle	B
needle position	3
throttle slide	$3\frac{1}{2}$

transmission:
rear chain	$\frac{1}{2}$ in. pitch
rear wheel sprocket	49 teeth

overall gear ratios:
first	19.8:1
second	11.5:1
third	8.15:1
fourth	6.2:1

road speed at 1000 rpm in top gear 10.7 mph

BARREL

PISTON

ARIEL
ENGINE
ANALYSIS

▶ **The two-fifty Ariel twins were built as an entirely new and original concept. This enabled the designers to incorporate unusual and very desirable features into the machine, one of which is the accessibility of the engine for maintenance work.**

The motor is slung under the pressed steel frame and is separate from the gearbox. This means that an entire engine overhaul can be carried out with the engine in place.

Both cylinders and heads are separate units, making a top overhaul very simple indeed, especially as there is no frame to hinder things.

The crankshaft is also built up in two halves which are secured by a bolt. This is accessible through the hollow offside crank. The bolt also acts as an extractor for the crank.

There is a point to watch when rebuilding the motor—the alignment of the primary chain.

A straight-edge should be put across the sprockets and they must not be more than 0.010 in. out of alignment (measured with a feeler gauge between the sprocket and the straight-edge). At the same time there must be at least 0.015 in. clearance between the outer crank and the crankcase wall. To maintain these clearances, the crankshaft is repositioned by fitting shims.

If the chain alignment is altered it is essential to check the crankcase clearance afterwards and vice versa.

The engine can be locked in the correct position for ignition timing by fitting a rod through the nearside cover into the flywheel. This rod should be 9/64 in. in diameter and 3 in. long. It is pushed through the top screw hole in the contact breaker cover—carry on pushing while slowly turning the engine over until the rod locates in the hole in the flywheel. At this stage upper contact breaker (for nearside cylinder) should just be opening.

When setting the contact breaker gap, it may not be possible to get equal gaps on each set of points. In this case the maximum and minimum gaps permissible are 0.017 in. and 0.012 in., respectively. Decreasing the gap on one set should increase the gap on the other, until a satisfactory balance is obtained.

The standard carburettor has an angled spray tube and is fitted with a 140 main jet. Some machines have a 170 main jet, because the spray tube is not angled. The spray tubes are interchangeable, provided that the correct main jet is also fitted.

The gearbox holds approximately one pint of SAE 30 oil, and is fitted with a level plug. It is important that the gearbox is not overfilled.

Special tools

Quite a few special tools are needed for work on the Ariel engine. There is a complete set, part number 43569, which comprises the following:

part number	tool
43540S	clutch banjo
43552S	flywheel strap spanner
43545S	extractor plate
43547S	centre screw extractor
43546S	end cover extractor
43548S	flywheel extractor
43544S	sleeve
43541S	locating plate
43542S	plug—locating plate
43551S	key—crankshaft bolt
43549S	box spanner—flywheel nut
43550S	tommy bar
43543S	sleeve
43570S	ignition timing peg
43500	combination spanner
43523	D.E. tube spanner
43524	,, ,, ,,
43525	,, ,, ,,
43501	cylinder head bolt wrench

There are also two other kits, part number 43572S for removing and replacing bearings and 43592S for fitting and extracting oil seals and bushes.

The 10 to 1 head used after 1961 has a "top hat" section and quite a wide squish band. George Todd has 12 to 1 heads available, but for racing only

A rod pushed through upper screw hole on the contact breaker cover locates in a hole in the flywheel and locks the engine in position for timing ignition

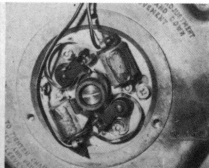

One cam operates both contact breaker points and care must be taken to get the point gaps as near as possible to being equal to get maximum performance

Barrels and heads are easy to remove as they are well clear of the frame and are made as individual parts. In fact it is possible to overhaul the engine . . .

. . . without removing it from the frame. The crankshaft is in two halves, held by a bolt which is also used as an extractor, and can be stripped as shown

One disadvantage of this engine is that it requires quite a few special tools in order to strip it down with the minimum amount of fuss

Ariel Leader

Up until the summer of 1958 Ariel Motors Limited had made their name in the motorcycling world with four-stroke machines of one, two or four cylinders. Some may have been surprised to hear that the company was set to launch a two-stroke but many people were taken aback by the audacity of the design. With a 250 two-stroke twin-cylinder engine, extensive weather protection, pressed steel frame, trailing link forks and 16 inch wheels the Ariel Leader certainly grabbed both the headlines and the attention of the motorcyclist when it was first given a public airing.

In 1954 market research had suggested to the Ariel management that a machine like the Leader would prove extremely popular. So chief designer Val Page and his team set to work the following year and within six weeks had the engine design drawn up (based on the proven German Adler), patterns made and castings completed and machined. The factory's carpenter Ted Brown had constructed a complete wooden mock-up of the unusual machine.

The first prototype was soon built and subjected to extensive testing, many miles being covered on the mountain roads of North Wales. The design proved sound and the testing helped ensure that the machine would be durable and reliable in production form.

Ariel's parent company, the BSA group, were none too enthusiastic about the new machine, first christened the Glida. But the machine went into production, although involving high tooling costs and was on sale by 1958, renamed the Leader. The magazine "Motor Cycling" said of the Leader, "surely the most advanced motorcycle to go into production." One could

Not for the fair weather rider, the Ariel Leader affords superb protection against the elements

by Don Upshaw

argue about the use of the word "advanced" it would perhaps have been more appropriate to describe the bike as being radically different if not revolutionary.

The use of a monocoque pressed steel frame was indeed very different to the tubular steel item employed on most other machines. The frame consisted of two pressings of 20 S.W.G. steel made by Homers, the Midland company who made motorcycle tanks for many manufacturers at that time. The two sections were welded together to form a boxed beam structure which offered a great deal of torsional rigidity. The engine was suspended from the frame at two points.

The engine's crankcase was not split and so a built-up 180 degree crankshaft was employed. In the Frankfurt built Adler gear couplings were used but the Leader had a bolted-up two-piece crank with a taper connection, supported by three ball-race mains with roller big-ends.

Carburation was from a single Amal Monobloc carb feeding the piston-ported motor, which had a pressure die-cast alloy head and separate cast-iron barrels inclined forward 45 degrees but with horizontal finning. The pistons in the square (54 x 54) motor gave a compression ratio of 8.25:1. Ignition was via points and coil with fixed ignition and a Lucas RM13/15 50 watt alternator on the drive-side end of the crank providing current rectified and fed to a six-volt 13 amp-hour battery.

Primary drive was via a 3/8" x 0.225" chain with a cast aluminium cover forming an oil bath. The multi-plate clutch incorporating a shock absorber had Neolangite faced plates running wet. The gearbox shell was cast integrally with the crankcase, the gears and shafts of the Burman four-speed box could be removed with the engine in situ. Overall ratios were 19.0:1, 11:1, 7.8:1 and 5.9:1. The rear drive chain (0.5 x 0.305 in) ran in a pressed steel case.

The engine was hidden from view by the leg shields extending laterally as detachable side panels and upwards into the screen. What appeared to be the fuel tank was in fact a dummy with access to parcel and sandwich space through a top panel. The petroil mixture was carried in a 2½ gallon tank mounted in the frame beam beneath the seat, hinged to give access to the filler cap. The filler cap doubled up as a measure for the two-stroke oil.

Today the use of 16 inch wheels is becoming increasingly popular though by no means universal, in 1958 such diameter wheels were extremely unusual. The Leader had them, chromium plated steel rims with 3.25 x 16 inch Dunlops with white-wall tyres available as an optional extra. Braking power was provided by full width (1 1/8 inch) six inch drums with fulcrum adjusters, both connected to switches operating the brake light.

At the rear, the swinging arm and the Armstrong oil damped shock absorbers were conventional, but the front suspension was innovative and effective. It consisted of hydraulically damped trailing forks with pressed steel stanchions in which the damper pivots were below the spindle of the 16 inch wheel. The design was notable for the way the oil damped spring units were hidden in the fork leg pressings and the heat treated die-cast alloy trailing links. The system resulted in good stability and steering at all speeds with the

The Leader's seat hinges upwards to give access to the fuel filler cap, battery and tooltray

wheelbase remaining constant, an enviable asset when braking into bends. The front wheel was shrouded by a large and valanced mudguard, large enough to accommodate the number plates on either side.

The shrouded and shielded style of the Leader afforded superb wet weather protection and at the same time measures were taken to afford a good degree of accessibility to the engine and gearbox. The side panels were retained by five coin slot headed screws but on the right, the gear lever and kick-start lever had to be removed before the panel could be taken off.

The Leader was not, by the standards of the day, an easy machine to steal. The hinged lid of the dummy tank was lockable and contained within the tank compartment was the steering lock and release for the comfortably padded dual seat. As already mentionedd, it was hinged to give access to the fuel cap, battery, tools and tyre pump.

The pressed steel instrument console houses a Smiths speedo, Britax ammeter, lights and ignition switch. The Ariel badge sits where the optional clock was housed, the trafficator lights are still defunct on Roger's bike

Unmistakable style, by virtue of its looks alone the Ariel Leader is unique

For ease of lifting the machine up on to the standard centre stand a retractable handle was provided, but a side stand could be fitted. The machine was available with a comprehensive array of optional extras so that one could buy a machine better equipped than any other in the quarter-litre class. Those options included indicators, a chromium rear bumper, attractive panniers, an inspection lamp with four foot flex, neutral indicator, eight-day clock, cast alloy rear carrier, oddometer, low-consumption parking lights, telescopic jack and prop-stand.

The Ariel Leader was one of the stars of the 1958 motorcycle show on stand 46 at Earls Court carrying a price tag of £209 11s 7d for the basic model. Despite the enthusiastic and universal accolade from the motorcycling press the Leader failed to sell in the numbers Ariel had hoped for and very few were exported. Riders found a bike with a pressed steel frame hard to swallow at that time, especially in America.

The Leader has the distinction of being the first machine to win the "Motor Cycle News" Machine of the Year title way back in 1959. The title went to the Ariel Arrow the following year, when it was introduced, being essentially a Leader without the superfluous superstructure.

In January 1961 a new model, the Sports Arrow, was added to the range and was quickly dubbed the Golden Arrow because of the gold panels of the dummy fuel tank. At first the gold paint was offset against a predominantly light grey paint job but the grey was soon changed to an ivory white. The ivory white scheme was also adopted by the Leader set against a choice of colours; seal grey, red, black or turquoise.

The cylinder heads of the two-stroke motor were redesigned with a centrally located upright position for the spark plug resulting in a more compact combustion chamber shape and raising the compression ratio to 10:1 using the same pistons. The fuel tank capacity was also increased to 2¾ gallons.

The Sports Arrow was stripped of the weather protection — leg shields windscreen and side panels — that characterised the Leader, and a smaller dummy tank was fitted. To give the Sports Arrow a more fitting image a perspex handlebar screen was fitted along with dropped handlebars and chrome plated covers on the timing side of the engine and on the front fork legs. An Amal Monobloc carb of 1 1/16 inch bore was fitted to the Sports Arrow compared to the 7/8 inch unit of the standard Arrow.

With the Sports Arrow engine producing 20 bhp at 6,650 rpm it was ten miles per hour quicker than the Leader which could reach 70 mph. It could cover a standing quarter mile in under 18 seconds, 4 seconds faster than the Leader.

In the early sixties the Sports Arrow was used in the Thruxton 500 mile race; another was used in national road race events by Peter Inchley, who was later to become the factory tester for the Villiers Starmaker.

The demand for motorcycles in general was on the decline and in 1963 the parent BSA group decided to rationalise their operations by closing Selly Oak and moving the Leader and Arrow production line to Small Heath. It has been said that orders for machines at the same time of the move numbered just 15.

In 1964 new metallic colours such as red and green were used against the ivory white which still predominated the superstructure of the Leader. The pop out handle for lifting the machine on to the centre stand was replaced by a screwed-on handle.

A number of factors bought the Leader, Arrow and Sports Arrow range to the end of the line. Burman, the company who supplied the gearbox internals, wanted to end their involvement and concentrate on parts for cars as did the manufacturers of some of the pressed steel items. Sales were still declining and a 199cc Arrow, built as an economy bike to slip inside the 200cc insurance bracket, failed to stimulate sales in 1964. Production of all the Val Page inspired two-stroke Ariels ceased the following year, although it was still possible to buy a new machine from some dealers as late as 1967.

In retrospect it was easy to state that the machines were ahead of their time, although they were a well built and engineered motorcycle, they failed to sell as expected. Perhaps they were just a touch too different for the rider of the day to swallow.

The Leader and Arrows failed to sell well abroad, notably in America where buyer resistance to a machine with a pressed steel frame was strong. Ironically it was not too many

The Adler inspired motor of a Sports Arrow with alloy head and iron barrels inclined forward 45 degrees

The Sports or Golden Arrow conceived as a more sporting stablemate for the Leader

years later that Japanese machines with pressed frames were to sell there in large numbers.

Roger Abbott, an active member of the Ariel Owners MCC, East Anglia branch, paid £300 for his Leader in August of 1982. The machine was built in May of 1958 and had worn well, but was in need of some work. The bike had been sprayed non-standard black and white so one of the first tasks was to bring it back to the original colours. Many ancillary parts needed rechroming and the wheels were rebuilt. A number of parts for the machine were obtained from Dragonfly Motorcycles of 587 High Road, Leytonstone, London E11. The right-hand half of the crank was badly scored near the central oil seal and an exchange item came from Dragonfly for £27. From the same source a new seat was obtained for £34.

The gearbox, the rest of the engine and clutch were all OK, although the clutch is now in need of some attention as it judders when pulling away from rest. The bike was originally fitted with indicators but these had been removed at some stage and replacements have so far proved elusive, nor has Roger been able to locate a rear bumper for his Leader.

Roger likes the Leader so much that he is now intent on adding a Sports Arrow to his stable. He is not a rider who is solely involved with older machines but has owned modern BMWs and Kawasakis. He reckons the Leader handles a darn sight better than the 250 Kawasaki S1 he once owned.

The machine starts easily and runs cleanly with very little vibration getting to the rider. Roger said the images in the mirrors remain clear at the 55 mph speed he normally cruises at. It is an extremely quiet machine with the long tapered silencers emitting a characteristic two-stroke haze with fuel being consumed at the rate of around 55 mpg.

The Leader's superstructure affords the rider superb protection in bad weather and Roger finds it extremely comfortable to ride even on long runs. Handling, even by todays standards, is good although though the bike dives under braking more than it should do as the front damping needs some attention. The brakes themselves are good. In 1962 "The Motor Cycle" tested an Arrow Sports and it proved capable of stopping from 30 mph in 30 feet with a ten stone rider.

Today it is rare to see a Leader, Arrow or Arrow Sports on the road, they have become collectable and therefore uncommon machines. These Ariels remain interesting examples of machines made by the British motorcycle industry in its heyday and are a case of "what might have been."

The Leader and its kin never gained universal acceptance and by the standards of the day were an oddity albeit an innovative one. Had the design been developed and refined to a more acceptable degree, it could well have been a machine capable of competing with the flood of quarter-litre Oriental two-strokes, which appeared not long after the British bike's demise.

FASTER ARROW—from page 36

Fuel

Always use premium petrol. This means that you won't be able to take advantage of most of the petroil dispensers because they usually only contain cheap petrol. Remember that if you use a self-mixing oil you need a 20:1 mixture, otherwise a 25:1. (See handbook for which is which.)

Although not recommended by the factory, many owners have improved their performance by using one or other of the special two-stroke lubricants that call for a much smaller proportion of oil to petrol, sometimes as low as 40:1, or even less.

Cycle Parts

It might seem obvious, but you are just wasting your time in tuning the engine if the cycle parts are not working freely. Take the brakes, for example— are they binding? Spin each wheel to see. And the primary chain must not be too tight.

Air Cleaner

The fabric air cleaner is designed to keep the dirt out of the engine, not the air. If it gets clogged with road dust, mud and flies, then you will suffer a dramatic loss of power.

Decokes

The first thing you have to learn when you buy an Arrow or Leader is that you must decoke the silencer more often than the engine. On no account leave the silencer more than 2,500 miles between decokes. If you do, not only will it take all the zip out of the motor, but you will find it very difficult to remove the baffles.

* * * *

All these modifications will improve your performance. There are one or two others that have been tried, but in fact have no advantage at all. For instance, this business about reversing the cylinder heads front to back. It won't do any harm, it's true, but on the other hand it won't do any good. Owners who have tried it have probably seen a very hairy Arrow on race tracks with the heads reversed—but remember that these were no ordinary heads!

Another misconception is that you can improve performance by altering the ignition timing. The truth is that you can't —get it spot on, strictly to maker's recommendations. And whilst removing the cylinder head gasket may increase the compression, the chances of power loss through leaks more than outweigh the advantages of the higher compression. In any case, you are still using the old head, without the benefit of the improved combustion chamber of the new squish heads.

One last word of reassurance. These engines are strong enough to withstand the extra stresses involved with higher performance. There is no need to fit stronger con-rods or bigger big ends— even if it were possible. We do a very big spares service for Arrows and Leaders here at Writers, and when the models were first introduced in July, 1958, we laid three big-end assemblies in stock. Nearly three years later they are still on the shelves! ●

Classic Test
250cc
Ariel
Arrow

photography Colin Curwood

Brave new concept

British motorcycle design took a major step forward with the introduction of Ariel's Leader and Arrow two-stroke twins. Jerry Clayton assesses how the package stands the test of time.

THE WAY in which this road test finally reached fruition could have been a freelance writer's dream. The circumstances in which an Ariel Arrow was finally tracked down would probably take several pages alone to explain, and that would have meant plenty of money for me. But to cut your agony short, let me simply state that for what was once such a popular machine, strangely few Arrows can be seen on British roads today when compared with such ubiquitous iron as Triumph and BSA twins.

However, at the time I was asked to find one I had by pure coincidence spent almost a week with a Golden Arrow — the sports model — that was in almost pristine condition. The bike was owned by a new motorcycling convert in South London, John Doyle, who had finally succumbed to endless years of badgering by yours truly to try two wheels. My experiences with his bike had been unusual, to say the least.

Unfortunately John, with uncharacteristic exhuberance, ran out of road — that's probably kinder than saying he was going too fast — and the bike's right hand side was badly chamfered in the process. The owner was luckier, and escaped with a chipped ankle. But with the unexpected commissioning of this test, my 'unusual experience' with the Arrow took on a new meaning — I now had to locate another one. The task wasn't to be as easy as I had expected.

For those of you who can recall, as I do, the early sixties, the fact that the Arrow is now a rarity might come as something of a shock. Certainly, I hadn't given the problem much thought while I'd been involved with John Doyle's bike. But now I followed the trail of another Arrow from the police station at Bexhill, to Mr Weston at Heathfield Motor Cycles in Sussex (they carry quite a few Ariel spares), to ex-owner Roy Lesson at Hailsham, and finally to the machine's present owner in Lower Willingdon, near Eastbourne, John Stretton. Basically original, the Stretton Arrow had inevitably suffered the rigours of 13 years of use, losing along the way its right hand engine cover, the air cleaner hose and the original seat.

Anyway, I digress, but I hope the point is made that it does seem as though there are not too many Arrows about these days — although I must admit I've noticed a few Leaders since being involved in this test venture. The Leader, a fully enclosed, touring version of the Ariel twin-cylinder two-stroke theme was launched in 1958, and was designed by Val Page, one of the most brilliant and versatile engineers in the history of British industry, who sadly died earlier this year at the age of 86.

The bike was distinctly unorthodox, for it featured trailing link front forks, and the engine was slung beneath the 20-gauge pressed-steel beam frame. The fuel tank resided under the seat and the dummy 'tank' housed a tool tray which, when removed, uncovered electrical components such as the rectifier and the coils. Honda Gold Wing, you were scooped.

The Leader had so much going for it, especially with regard to road-holding, that the next step was pure logic — a sporting version duly dubbed the Arrow by Selly Oak. Even today, that road-holding is exemplary. The 1964 Arrow I rode was suffering slightly from worn rear shock absorbers — they are not adjustable for pre-load, incidentally — and the front forks appeared to have some lateral movement probably caused by worn bushes. These faults wouldn't have been apparent when the bike was new. Even so, it was easy to appreciate why people used to get so hooked on Arrow handling. With 16-in wheels, the whole plot sits low to start with, and the centre of gravity is further kept down by the under-slung engine and the fuel housed under the seat.

The design of the beam frame is such that the loads imposed run parallel to the walls, and it has to be fairly deep near the steering head to cope with braking loads. The Ariel design gives an extremely high degree of torsional stiffness which, in all probability, would have been improved only marginally by the use of a box section swinging arm at the rear. The trailing link front forks, with dampers and springs running up inside the legs, took everything in their stride, and, at least when the units were new, fast bumpy bends would be smoothed out and the bike would remain rock steady.

But quite apart from the Ariel factory's own problems, the biggest marketing bugbear the Arrow and Leader had to overcome at that time was the motorcycling movement's peculiarly insular feelings about anything unconventional. It was therefore something of a boon to the factory when, in 1960, the government

**illustration
Bill Bennett**

restricted all learner riders to machines of 250cc or under.

Now the novice motorcyclist of those days was less set in his ways than dyed in-the-wool enthusiasts who had been nurtured on conventionally-framed four-strokes. An advertisement in the June 16, 1960, issue of *Motor Cycling* carried the kind of weight that might woo learner riders to the inherent virtues of the Arrow. Placed by the giant dealers, King's of Oxford, it announced that an Ariel Arrow 'practically the same as you can buy for £167 13s 5d (£167.67p) lapped the Isle of Man Mountain TT course at 80.17mph'. The fact that the race report in the magazine more correctly listed rider Mike O'Rourke's average *race* speed as 80.18mph during his seventh place in the 250cc Lightweight race is splitting hairs, but suffice to say that the Arrow finished ahead of NSUs, Bianchis and Ducatis. The cheers that greeted O'Rourke as he crossed the line on June 13, and again the same evening at the Villa Marina prize-giving ceremony, were just rewards for an 'underdog' ride on a roadster-based two-stroke with piston-port induction racing against specialist machinery. The Arrow had indeed arrived.

And while it couldn't be maintained

that the Herman Meier-tuned engine of O'Rourke's bike was anything like standard, it's significant that in October of that year, the compression ratio of the Arrow's 'square' 54 × 54mm engine was raised from 8.25 to 10:1. New oval con rods were fitted, and the carburettor was changed from an Amal 375/33 to a 376/277, which meant that the choke size went up from 7/8in to 1-1/16in, while the main jet was increased from 140 to 230. On paper at least, the changes gave an extra four bhp (up to 20 at 6,500rpm) at 500 fewer revs, but on the road the difference was startling. It was not

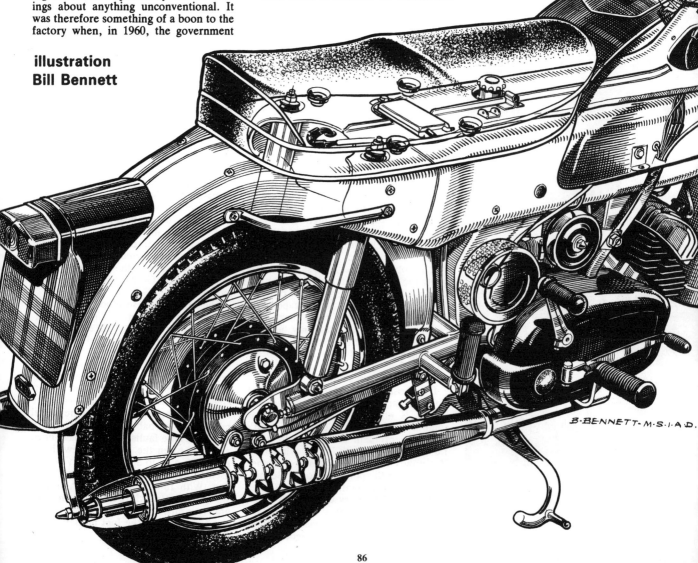

uncommon to see packs of riders mounted on Triumphs, Nortons, Ajays, Enfields and the like thundering off to their local haunts on summer evenings with, perhaps slightly behind, another couple of riders, heads down, humping along in the upper seventies with that telltale swirl of blue two-stroke haze spiralling behind. Nine times out of ten, 'L' plates would be taped over the deeply valanced front mudguards of the pursuing Arrows, indicating that their riders were fledglings learning to fly!

So, when we return to the present day and get the chance to ride a Golden Arrow, as the sports version of October 1960 eventually became, it comes as something of a shock to realise how the world has passed it by — on two counts.

Firstly, while I've stressed the qualities of the beam frame's structure and torsional ability in keeping the Arrow's wheels pointing in the same direction under varying circumstances and over differing road surfaces, no other manufacturer has taken up development in this direction.

Secondly, riding the bike today reminded me just how much sophistication the Japanese have introduced into two-strokes. The Arrow engine as ridden — and bear in mind its age and the careless treatment it may have been subjected to — was fairly noisy on John Doyle's bike. There seemed a fair amount of clatter and ignition resonance through the separate alloy cylinder heads, and the noise emitted by the exhaust was slightly coarser than expected.

Despite the bike's age it was easy enough to start, and everything in this department seemed as standard. The ignition key fits into a switch on the right of the headlamp shell, and with the fuel switched on, the choke near the petrol tap is pulled out. Only once did it over-choke in warm weather, and it was found that it would fire up even more easily with just half the choke engaged. A petroil ratio of 25:1 was used on the test machine, but, as revealed later, was probably too rich a blend.

Gear changing through a right hand lever with a one up, three down, pattern was notchy, and the operation of the three-plate clutch was deceptively stiff.

Despite the worn items on the test bike, the handling remained first rate. The only snag was a weak centre stand spring, which allowed the stand to flutter

Cutaway drawing shows the pressed-steel beam frame, and the fuel tank located beneath the seat. Entire concept of the machine represented a radical step forward in British motorcycle design. Chain was fully enclosed and lubricated from primary chaincase — features that modern bikes giving up to four times as much power could well do with.

Parallel twin engine features 'square' bore and stroke dimensions, and runs on petroil mixture.

Instrumentation was basic, consisting only of a small speedometer and an ammeter.

up and down on bumpy surfaces and make contact with the road. But the biggest snag of all, and one which I believe was also experienced when the bikes were first tested years ago, was the soggy feeling of the rather puny 6in front brake. I learned later that by slackening the fulcrum adjusting bolts and applying either the front lever or rear pedal while retightening, optimum lining area can be brought into contact with the hub. Even so, a poor front brake appears to be the norm on Arrows.

The forks are unusual in that the legs containing the dampers and their springs only extend up as far as the cup-and-cones steering head, the handlebars being mounted on the central steering column, as there is no top yoke. The rod operating the 6in rear brake emerges on the right hand side of the bike from the left foot-operated pedal. The fully enclosed rear chain is lubricated from the primary chaincase — a first rate scheme — and this is on the left, hence the brake arrangement. The rear anchor proved much harsher than the front unit in operation, incidentally.

Electrics on the Arrow were six volt, which wouldn't matter so much except that the diameter of the 24/30-watt front headlamp is only six inches, on a machine capable of reaching nearly 80 mph! Needless to say, night riding was conducted with due caution. It was at night that an indicated 50 to 55 mph in top gear was found to give the most satisfying ride. At that speed the Arrow just burbled along, with all the harshness of hard acceleration forgotten. Speeds in the gears, as indicated on the somewhat small speedometer which tended to run haywire at readings over 70 mph, were just under 20 mph in first, 40 mph in second, 55 in third, and somewhere in the upper 70s in top.

Originally fitted with Dunlop whitewall tyres, the wheels on John Doyle's bike were shod with Czechoslovakian Barums. In · contrast, John Stretton's bike was using the combination of an Avon Speedmaster and an Avon SM Mk 2. The Arrow's rear wheel is quickly detachable after attention to only three bolts, when removal leaves the chain undisturbed. Original equipment on the Golden Arrow included 'ace' bars and a flyscreen which clipped to them. The test bike had neither, being fitted with semi-straight bars and lacking the screen.

There are varying accounts of fuel consumption figures on the Ariel two-strokes, but this can probably be explained by the differing carburettor choke sizes on the early models and those on the far more popular later models that ran from 1960 until 1966, when production ceased. Some owners of Leaders claim around 80 mpg, but consumption figures closer to 50 mpg are more likely on the Arrow. With a three-gallon tank, however, this will be acceptable to most owners.

In a recent issue of *Motor Cycle News* there were just two Arrows on offer in the classified ads pages. One was a 1962 model with loads of spares that was going for £165, and the other was a 1960 version, available at £87. John Stretton paid £170 for his 1965 Arrow, and was offered £240 just a fortnight later.

Perhaps, too, modern two-stroke oils have advanced sufficiently over the years for John to mix his petroil in a 32:1 ratio quite happily. I've since discovered that even in the Leader/Arrow handbook, a ratio of 24:1 was recommended with some types of two-stroke oil, while 32:1 was advised for other lubricants.

On the question of spare parts, John Stretton needed a stator plate for his generator and got one off the shelf at John Groombridge Motorcycles in Sussex on an exchange deal! But as with most obsolete machinery, it can be wise for riders to join the appropriate owners' club. Membership of the Ariel Owners' Club costs only £2.50 a year (the secretary is John Mortimer, 75 Sebright Road, Barnet, Herts), and different officials specialise in looking after spares supplies for the various Ariel models. Engine components for the two-strokes are in reasonable supply, although items such as panels, boxes and screens for the Leader bodywork are becoming more difficult to locate. For Leader and Arrow riders in the Midlands, Bob Joyner and Son at Warley, West Midlands, is another source of parts.

There could well be a resurgence of interest in these bikes, which represent the last fling of a once great factory — apart from the disastrous Ariel-3 three-wheeled moped produced by BSA in more recent times. I didn't like at the time the bikes were being produced the use of cross-head bolts on the frame and engine, but that is personal taste. On test, I found too that the coils are not readily accessible and that to actually reach them, the headlamp has to be removed. Access to the rectifier, on the other hand, is through the aperture behind the left-hand 'tank' badge. Owners could probably do well to re-locate the coils inside the 'tank' so that they are accessible after the toolbox is removed.

I found, too, that the centre stand played havoc with the sole of my right boot as I manhandled the bike onto the stand. Even so, because it was such an unconventional model, beloved by youth a decade and a half ago, the Ariel Arrow takes on a character all its own. It won't hold a modern Yamaha or Suzuki 250 on acceleration, but just wait for the next corner to prove a point!

In Brief

250cc Ariel Arrow

Engine	two-stroke twin
Bore and stroke	54 x 54mm
Capacity	249cc
Compression ratio	8.25:1 pre-1960; 10.0:1 from 1960
Carburation	Amal 7/8in pre-1960; Amal 1.1/16in from 1960
BHP @ RPM	16 @ 7000 pre-1960; 20 @ 6500 from 1960
Primary drive	single row chain
Clutch	multi-plate, wet
Gearbox	4 speed
Electrical system	Lucas 6 volt 50 watt generator, battery and coil ignition, 6 volt lighting

DIMENSIONS

Wheelbase	51in
Seat height	30in
Overall width	27in
Ground clearance	5in
Kerb weight	296lb
Fuel capacity	3 gal

CYCLE PARTS

Tyres (original fittings)

(front)	16 x 3.25 Dunlop
(rear)	16 x 3.25 Dunlop

Brakes

(front)	6 x 1.1/8in drum
(rear)	6 x 1.1/8in drum

PERFORMANCE

Top speed	78 mph (approx.)
Standing quarter mile	19.5 sec (approx.)

Fuel consumption

(overall)	50 mpg
(ridden hard)	45 mpg

Braking distance

(from 30 mph)	41ft
(from 60 mph)	129ft
PRICE (new, 1960)	£167 13s 5d

Back To The Future

Rick Kemp *rides Ariel's designer 250 Arrow.*

At the beginning of the sixties, the Ariel Arrow was a pretty radical machine. We'd had about two years to get used to the Ariel Leader, the touring version of this bike with built-in panniers, leg shields and screen. The leader also sported some fancy features like a headlight adjuster lever, the normal method of doing this was a swift thump but the leader's upright riding position and screen prevented this. As a commuter/tourer the Leader looked fine but turning it into a sports bike was another matter. The general reaction to the Arrow at the time was similar to John McEnroe's disbelief of tennis umpires – you cannot be serious!

What Ariel had done was to strip the Leader down. Gone was the engine enclosing bodywork, panniers, legshields and screen. What remained was the dummy tank that enveloped the steering head and the rather quaint trailing link fork that looked like something off a scooter. This was really the nub of the Arrow's identity crisis, it was kind of halfway between a bike and a scooter and in those days the two definitely didn't mix. Apart from the fork, another scooter type feature was the lift-up seat for access to the petrol filler. But perhaps the biggest single drawback was the fact it was a two-stroke in an era when real men and therefore boys rode four-strokes.

But the Leader and then the Arrow were deliberate attempts by Ariel's designer Val Page to dictate a new trend. The design concept was actually the Leader and uncharitable folk might suggest that the Arrow was a slightly desperate attempt to boost Ariel's two-stroke sales as the Leader never achieved its hoped for potential.

When considering this concept we have to look at the Leader rather than the Arrow. It seems to have started with two things, full enclosure and a two-stroke twin motor. The standard tubular motorcycle frame is a rather clumsy thing to enclose so Ariel went for a pressed steel spine object which would easily accept the additional bodywork. Basically the frame is two large steel sections with a steering head tube at one end and two rear suspension mounts at the other. In between there are two hangers, one for the engine and the other for the swing arm assembly. The fuel tank is enclosed in the seat area and as a result is a rather meagre 2.3 gallons. The dummy petrol tank holds a tool tray and some of the electrical components. A relatively simple idea that worked save for the fact that Ariel didn't put much paint on the inside of the frame and if water got in it would rust in a short time.

The, trailing link fork was used for sound engineering principles, the wheelbase doesn't alter as the suspension compresses, well it does slightly in this case but it's less than ¼in.

Tastes change, the Arrow looks even better to modern eyes.

The steel fork carries the trailing link pivot at the front and coil springs with Armstrong dampers inside the 'legs' provide four inches of controlled movement. The brake torque arm is levered in such a way that the front end doesn't dip under braking, mind you the six inch drum probably wouldn't have much effect on a telescopic fork. The twin shock absorbers supporting the rear wheel also provide for four inches of travel.

Even though the motor was designed from scratch it's not as innovative as the rest of the bike. As with most two-stroke twins, the Ariel engine is two singles together. In this case it's very simple to see, two heads, separate barrels and even the crankshafts are independent but bolted together on a keyed taper. This assembly is mounted in three heavy duty ball bearings and is actually quite rigid. Each big

Cylinders are inclined at 45 degrees with deep cooling fins.

end uses a double roller bearing with the other end of the conrod having a plain bush for the floating gudgeon pin. The 50 watt alternator is driven from the right side of the crank with the engine sprocket and outrigger contact breaker assembly on the other end.

The clutch is a conventional multiplate item running in oil, three springs provide the pressure and there is a rubber shock absorber on the clutch hub. From there the drive goes into what is essentially a scaled down Burman gearbox. A fully enclosed chain transmits the power to the 16in rear wheel. That power is claimed to be 17.5hp at 7,000rpm.

For the more sporting Arrow, it was claimed that a larger carb produced another 2.5hp but the largest factor in increasing its performance was the weight loss. Getting rid of the bodywork saved 55lbs. This improved power

to weight ratio resulted in a 4.5 second benefit in standing ¼ mile times, putting it on a par with the old Honda 250 Dream.

Despite the owner's guide stating that a cold start lever is fitted so that there is no need to tickle the carb, the carb needs to be tickled for easy starting. The choke is activated by a piece of wire with a white plastic knob on the end, you simply pull it out. Once the spade ignition key is turned on you can kick away. The kick-start lever would be more at home on their four-stroke twins, it's somewhat over engin-eered, also the gearing isn't quite right for a two-stroke. Anyway, a few kicks usually has it going and like most air-cooled two-strokes you have to juggle the throttle and choke for the first couple of minutes. Choke on for too long and it will start to oil up, choke off too soon and it won't rev. The clutch is light but with a bit of snatch if you're not careful. Gear change is one up, three down and on the right hand side of course.

Changing up the box is fine but coming down is a different story. Fourth to third is fine, but when the engine is hot, third to second is a veritable nightmare of reciprocating inertia. To its credit neutral is easily found from either first or second gear but again when hot, first has to be felt in. Fortunately the motor produces a good amount of torque and throttle response is good from low revs so providing road speed is kept up, the top two gears are all that's needed. In fact, the torque characteris-tics of this motor is about the only thing that saves it because once you pass the ¾ mark on the throttle it's almost impossible to keep your feet on the footrests due to the vibration. The vibration is accompanied by the resonance of the dummy tank and in the absence of a rev counter, serves as a good indication of when to change gear. The reasons for this aren't entirely clear as the 180 degree offset on the crank pins should make it a smooth engine and mechanically it's quite quiet. Rubber mounting would have made all the difference especially as the exhaust baffle rod is bolted to the

Trailing fork works well, single-leading shoe brake doesn't.

rear mudguard.

Providing the engine is kept out of its resonant frequency it makes for a very good ride. Throttle response isn't instant but better than you'd expect from a 25-year-old bike. Vibes apart, the Arrow should be capable of 80mph but with a front brake like this one you'd only want to achieve this speed on an empty motorway. Perhaps the lack of front end dive makes the brake feel worse than it is but there isn't a lot there. The rear brake on the other hand is strong and has enough feel to be useful. This is probably helped by the short 51in wheelbase as the rider's weight is more over the back wheel and the fact that the bike doesn't pitch forward.

The surprising thing about the Arrow is that in spite of its design age it doesn't feel that dated. The way in which it handles engenders the same mental approach as a modern bike. It's low speed manoeuvrability is excellent and the 29.5in seat height combined with a 285lb dry weight makes it easy for anyone to handle. Carving through the traffic is simple but the

16in wheels make for very decisive open road riding. To lay the bike over requires quite a bit of negative input on the bars and once you're in a corner you have to keep it there, it won't stay on its own. The ground clearance is adequate at 6¼in but it's still very possible to ground the centre stand on both sides. At higher speeds the bike runs absolutely straight probably due to the large steel front mudguard which must contribute to steering inertia. Likewise through long sweepers there's no hint of wallow or weave.

The Arrow is equipped with a small flyscreen and, yes, those red grips are standard equipment. Even though the screen is handlebar mounted, the bike doesn't go fast enough for this to upset the steering. Other equipment is minimal with only a horn button and dip switch mounted on the 'bars. The lighting switch is mounted on top of the headlight shell on the other side to the ignition switch. For a 6 volt system, the Arrow has very good lights, you can actually see a pool of light in front of you on lit streets. As previously said the petrol tank is under the seat and this means that the seat has to be lifted a lot. To this end, the seat pan has four rubber feet which fit into metal cups on the frame but depends mainly on the riders weight to keep it in place. the pillion has to put up with footrests on the swingarm but does get a healthy pair of grab rails. These rails help with putting the bike on the stand, as the bodywork is smooth and there's nothing to get hold of, the Ariel also caters for left handed folk as there's a kickdown on both sides of the centre stand.

The Ariel two-strokes did sell well throughout their model life but they needed to because the idea was low cost and high production and they had to recoup their tooling costs. When the Arrow first came on market it was the cheapest 250 available but whether it actually made the company any money we don't know. Some Arrows found their way into club racing and the factory did issue a tuning sheet with information on how to improve the porting and up the compression ratio. But despite its swift looks and reputation most L riders of the day were still four-stroke mounted. With the benefit of hindsight the Arrow was obviously ahead of its time as a design idea and was executed very well given the engin-

eering of the day.

Our test bike came from A Touch of Classic in Croydon and was a spanking example creating interest wherever it went. Some younger bikers actually thought it was a new model and wondered what country it came from. I suppose it could look like a modern East European bike come to think of it . . . after all, Volkswagen Karman Ghias have made a comeback so why not the Ariel Arrow? The design appeal is about the same.

Distinctive Ariel silencer stays.

Engine

Type	Air-cooled, two-stroke twin
Capacity	247cc
Bore & Stroke	54 x 54mm
Compression ratio	10:1
Maximum Power	20hp @ 7,000rpm
Lubrication	Petroil
Carburation	1 x Amal 1¹/₁₆
Transmission	Primary chain, wet multiplate clutch, four-speed enclosed chain.
Ignition	Coil and contact breakers
Electrics	6v, 50 watt alternator

Performance

Top Speed	80mph
Fuel Consumption	80mpg

Cycle Parts/Dimensions

Suspension	
Font	Trailing link fork
Rear	Swingarm with twin units (rear)
Brakes	
Front	6in drum
Rear	6in drum
Tyres	
Front	Avon 3.25 x 16
Rear	Avon 3.25 x 16
Seat Height	29.5in
Ground Clearance	6.25in
Dry Weight	285lb
Fuel Tank	2.3 gallons
Suppliers	A Touch of Classic, 44/45 Tamworth Road, Croydon, Surrey. 01-686 4139

Contact breakers are easily got at under external cover.

The Ariel Arrow two-stroke twin formed a sound basis for racing development, and a Herman Meier-tuned version found instant success. Sadly, writes Charlie Rous, its potential was never fully exploited

Right: Michael O'Rourke guns his Ariel Arrow-based racer past White Gates, May Hill, Ramsey, in the 1961 TT

Straight as an Arrow

ARIEL were never famous in road racing, but an opportunity arose in 1960 that could have given the Selly Oak factory a chance to lead the world in racing two-stroke development ahead of the Japanese.

For that was the year when Londoner Michael O'Rourke finished seventh in the 250cc Isle of Man TT on an Ariel Arrow. Now seventh might not seem particularly remarkable, but only ultra-

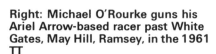

special works GP racing machines headed O'Rourke, whose bike was nothing more than a mildly-tweaked roadster.

A distinction of the 1960 TT was that the 125, 250cc and Sidecar races returned to the Mountain course that year from the shorter 10-mile Clypse circuit around Onchan, where they had been held between 1955 and 1959. So the targets for the returning 250cc

'Mountaineers' were the records set by Werner Haas in 1954 on a dohc NSU twin. He won that three-lap race at 90.88mph, with a lap record of 91.22mph.

That successful development had continued during the six-year absence from Snaefell was clearly demonstrated by the first three home in 1960. They were all much faster over five laps than the old lap record.

Gary Hocking won on an MV twin at 93.64 mph from world champion Carlo Ubbiali on an MV single (93.13 mph) and Tarquinio Provini's similar double-knocker single cylinder Morini (92.98 mph). Then came the four cylinder Hondas of Bob Brown, Kitano and Taniguchi, with O'Rourke's Ariel next—ahead of Luigi Taveri on another works MV and Perfetti on a works Bianchi.

A further feature of O'Rourke's remarkable ride was that, although his 80.21 mph speed was well below that of the leaders, it was nonetheless the fastest-ever TT performance by a British 250cc machine.

That Ariel Arrow racer was the work of German-born Herman Meier who at that period, 25 years ago, was best described as a part-time two-stroke enthusiast, rather than a full-time engineer. Herman came to England from Bremen in 1949 and worked for several years in the South London motorcycle shop of Norton's triple Senior TT winner Harold Daniell—where Michael O'Rourke was also employed.

Amid that 100 per cent Bracebridge

George Brown gets his Ariel Arrow sprinter cleanly off the line during his record spree at Thurleigh in September 1961

It is interesting to compare George Brown's Ariel Arrow sprinter of 1961 (left) with Herman Meier's racer of the same period, the latter's fuel capacity boosted to six gallons by the addition of a second tank

Street atmosphere, it was amazing that Herman retained his extreme interest in two-stroke power, for that was the era when four-strokes were supreme, and nobody other than German engineers visualised the eventual superiority of two-stroke combustion. Herman Meier was one of them.

Michael O'Rourke was also a highly-experienced and capable rider. He began racing when Brands Hatch was still a grass track in 1947 and, after RAF service, was a short circuit star of the early fifties. He raced regularly at the TT from 1950, and in 1957 became the first rider to gain three replicas in one year.

Recalling the Ariel Arrow racer, Michael, now 53 and a test engineer with Castrol at Bracknell, Berkshire, told me of how he and Herman anticipated it.

'We planned and spoke about developing a 250 two-stroke for ages; but there was no suitable basic design to work from until the Ariel twin came along,' said Michael. 'My brother Terry had bought one of the first Leader touring models, and despite all the tinwork—legshields, pannier boxes and massive windscreen, it was light, steered superbly and the engine was full of life. It was obviously the perfect basis for a nice little racer, and Herman agreed.'

But they were not alone in appreciating the potential of the Val Page design. Ariel themselves realised the limited appeal of the Leader's touring specification, and widened this by introducing the stripped-for-action Arrow sportster and subsequent Golden Arrow which helped allay the high tooling costs of the original design, with its pressed steel frame and front forks.

The success of the three models with the public was marked by them winning the Motor Cycle News Machine of the Year award in 1959 (Leader); 1960 (Arrow) and 1961 (Golden Arrow).

'When Herman got in touch with the factory', said Michael, 'he discovered that an experimental engine had already been converted to take twin carburettors. Sammy Miller was there, of course, along with Peter Inchley and Clive Bennett in the experimental department, and they got up to all sorts of tricks.'

'Herman didn't buy a machine. Ariel

It was during 1960 that Herman Meier first started playing around with the Ariel Arrow as the basis for a serious racer. Here, he poses with his first slightly-chopped machine

sold it to him bit-by-bit as he converted it. The amazing thing about that bike was that it was almost entirely standard. The only special parts were Herman's squish cylinder heads with central plugs, which replaced the standard hemispherical heads with offset plugs.

'The crankcase was standard except for being welded and re-machined to take two carbs (the original single carb was a ⅞in bore Amal Monobloc; the racer was fitted with a pair of 1-3/32in bore Amal GPs). The crankshaft, pistons, bearings, ignition and clutch were all standard. Only the con-rods were altered from their original H-section to an oval section.

'Herman knew exactly what he wanted to do, I remember one night he sat down and filled two sheets of paper with figures and equations to work out the size and shape of the exhausts. And when the pipes were made, they worked.'

'Herman knew exactly what that bike would do at each stage of its development, and it did just that. It was not fitted with a rev-counter; I just revved it until it peaked,' said Michael.

'At its first testing, with standard barrels, the engine peaked at about 7,500. But by TT time, and with streamlining, it was up to about 8,500—around 115-120mph. But the bike was also very light, not much more than 200lb, which helped acceleration and its standard brakes.'

'The only disadvantage was with the four-speed gearbox. Five or six gears would have been better, but that was impossible. Herman was able to improve the ratios a bit, but the snag we could not overcome at the time was a wide gap between second and third. Even so, the spread of power, from about 5,000, pulled it through.

'The most amazing thing about that bike was its utter reliability,' Michael said. 'It was air-cooled with standard finning, but still ran very cool, and never gave a sign of seizing. My fastest lap in the TT was the last one, at 85 mph, and when the engine was stripped, it was perfect.'

After the 1960 race, Meier said there was still a great more to come from the Ariel twin, but little if anything more was achieved, for he subsequently left England for Spain where he became development engineer at the Lube factory, and the Arrow racer was sold to Syd Lawton.

'We had another bike for the 1961 TT,' said Michael, 'but it didn't compare with the first one, and it packed up.'

Several private racing efforts were made with the 250 Ariel two-stroke twin with varying degrees of success. Notable, of course, was Peter Inchley who worked for the factory, and the record breaker of George Brown which also had works support.

Among George's successes was a British national record of 14.32 sec. for the standing quarter-mile and 126.64 mph for the flying quarter-mile, when his 186lb bike was fitted with full streamlining and running on alcohol fuel.

Why BSA—the parent company of Ariel—failed to exploit this obvious racing potential is another of those mysteries of the British industry that will never become known.

But in 1960, the BSA empire was still the biggest motorcycle producer in the world, Japan had scarcely arrived where two-stroke development was concerned and Britain did have the brains...

Herman Meier subsequently returned to this country to become involved in the development of the Royal Enfield racer of the mid-1970s, but after that he went to America to work on outboard boat engines.

BACK IN THE SMOKE

ALAN McGUIRE STOPPED SMOKING WHEN HE SOLD HIS FIRST ARIEL TWO-STROKE BUT THE HABIT WAS TOO STRONG. A CAUTIONARY TALE FOR MOTORCYCLE ADDICTS EVERYWHERE

For months I had been looking for a reasonable Ariel Arrow or Leader as a restoration project and I finally spotted a 1965 Arrow Sports for sale at a South London address. My reasons for wanting this particular machine were quite simple: it was the first bike I had ever owned (a Leader, back in 1964, registration number 376 FKD). I worked for our local dealer, Jack Frodsham Ltd, at the time and, as they have recently closed, the memories of this era are particularly strong for me.

> TO MY SURPRISE THE ENGINE RAN SMOOTHLY, THE CLUTCH FREE, THE GEARBOX SMOOTH AND ALL THE ELECTRICS FUNCTIONED

In those days we supplied all makes of British machines, from AMC to Velocette, and all models from Ariel Pixie to Triumph Bonneville. I worked in the parts department of the dealership with Terry Nicholl — still a friend — and Bernard Webb. For me those were the best days of motorcycling; no fancy high tech, high revving machines totally enclosed in bodywork, almost impossible to maintain but rather bikes with real character and, being British, oil leaks!

The Arrow Sports was 99.9% complete, with only the small perspex flyscreen missing. Paintwork was reasonable but the chrome, as you would expect on a 22-year-old, was tatty. Once I had it back at my house I put in some

Alan McGuire's **Ariel Arrow** came in a very complete state, with only the flyscreen missing - note the other trim and paintwork details. **Restoration** started with the taking of lots of reference photos. **After the engine** has been dropped out, dummy tank and mudguards are removed to reveal stark and simple spine frame. **Clever design** allows support systems to be kept out of sight and protected. **Steering stem** arrangement looks odd even now. The bike ran reasonably and could have been used like this but Alan decided to give it back its **dignity**

BACK IN THE
SMOKE

fuel, charged up the battery and hoped it would run OK. Although I'd heard the engine running when I went to see it, I had not roadtested the bike, having no helmet or insurance cover with me. The engine fired after a couple of kicks and, donning my Belsataff jacket and brand new FM Grand Prix helmet (red, white and blue colour scheme, of course) I went for a spin.

To my surprise everything seemed to work alright. The engine ran smoothly, just a slight small end rattle on the right cylinder. The clutch was free, gearbox smooth, brakes operated properly and all the electrics functioned. As the bike had only 1463 miles on the clock I was a little suspicious; on checking the MoT slip, the mileage figure stated only 60 miles fewer. Could it be genuine?

IT WAS STILL ON THE ORIGINAL PISTONS

Back at the house, I took a good number of photographs of the bike to help with the restoration work, concentrating especially on wiring routes, cable routes, the position of rubber seals and so on as I had no manual to work from. Once the film was developed and printed I could set to work stripping the bike.

I started on what I considered a logical sequence, removing the cables, mudguards, dummy tank/headlamp and wiring, leaving the wheels and handlebars until last so that the machine was still movable. As it turned out I was able to remove most components before the wheels were removed. Having sorted the painted parts from mechanical and chrome parts, I took them to Warrington Shotblasting for attention, together with the cylinder barrels. They did an excellent job of shot, bead and sand-blasting these items and also primed the various pieces, except cylinders, of course, for respraying in the two-tone paint scheme.

Whilst these parts were away I worked on the engine unit. When I removed the heads and barrels, I was very surprised to find it still on its original Ariel standard size pistons, with very little carbon deposit on them or the heads.

I slackened off and removed the primary chain tensioner, then the chain case

cover, revealing flywheel and three-plate clutch arrangement. All was fairly clean and very little wear was apparent on the clutch plates when I removed them from the chainwheel assembly. The primary

chain tensioner pad also had few signs of wear on it, so it began to seem likely that the Arrow really had done only 1463 miles. In the end it turned out to be a genuine one-owner-from-new, very

When **Val Page** designed Ariel's two-stroke range he was intent on making as modern a machine as possible, and the Arrow lives up to that brief. The **engine dimensions** of 54 x 54mm are shared by many modern two-stroke racers, though the power output of 20bhp at 6,500rpm has been improved on. A **pressed-steel box spine frame** built on the same basic principles as the Ariel's features on Norton's new Commander and Interpol models. Stresses caused by cornering and suspension movements run along the walls. Because of the Ariel frame's very large cross section it was extremely resistant to twisting forces. The motor ran when **Alan McGuire** bought the bike, though there was evidence of small end wear; **the gearbox**, built in unit, worked smoothly enough to need no attention - a good job since the owner admits to cowardice in the face of pinions! **Pistons** were still on the original size and their crowns and the cylinder heads showed little sign of wear or carbon. The **primary chain tensioner pad** and the **three-plate clutch** were similarly unworn. Alan's bike turned out to be a **genuine low mileage** example - 1463 miles from new. A find like this is good fortune indeed for the restorer, but poses the question of just **how far to restore**

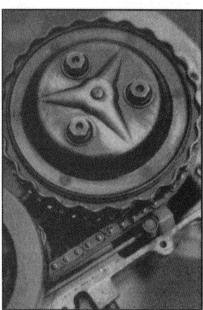

low mileage example.

Being a coward as regards the mysteries of gearboxes I did not strip this part. It had worked well during my brief run, all four gears were smoothly engaged

and there were no strange noises coming from it.

Having now got most bits apart, I started to compile a list of the parts required — gaskets, cables, small end

bushes, replacement seat, exhausts, silencers, rims and other little bits, but where to get them I did not know. A letter was sent to the Ariel Owners Club and I must say their archivist was a great

BACK IN THE
SMOKE

help. Parts were then ordered from Draganfly Motorcycles and I arranged to go down to see them early in February. Sadly one or two bits were on back order — rims, seat and pipes — but as these were not yet desperate, I was able to do quite a bit of work without them.

The only strange thing on the engine side of it was the use of a 375 carb instead of a 376/277. Obtaining the latter provided great fun, especially getting the larger choke assembly. After attending various autojumbles a friend, Ian Jones of Llandudno, found a carb minus choke at Mochdre, North Wales. The choke was eventually found on a complete bike, offered for sale at Tatton Park vintage transport show. I bought it for £3, taken off the bike, and I extend my sympathies to the person who bought the rest of this machine at the Northern Show in Bolton.

AMONGST THE NEW SPARES WAS A CHOKE ASSEMBLY, LABELLED IN MY OWN HANDWRITING

I heard locally of some spares at Colin Rides, Widnes, phoned him and arranged a visit. He has quite a number of British bikes and some spares and could supply me with a pair of exhaust pipes, a pair of cylinder heads, all new, a spare primary cover, toolbox lid and clip. There was also very special find for me for amongst his bits was a 375/060 choke assembly, not what I wanted initially but on closer inspection it had fastened to it a handwritten price tag of 13/3d in my own writing from the days at Jack Frodsham's!

Draganfly Motorcycles, Bungay, Suffolk — spares, alloy polishing, chrome plating and help;

Warrington Shotblasting, Athlone Road, Warrington — blasting and priming;

Eric Whitfield Ltd, Penketh — respraying cycle parts;

Bill Pope Ltd, Winwick Road, Warrington — small ends, wheelbuilding, MoT;

Sid's Place, Radcliffe, Manchester — Arrow manual;

Mates — Geoff Kelly, Alan Wilcox, Terry Nicholls, Ian Jones;

Special thanks to *George Thornton* for colour photography.

Pressed steel front forks conceal spring/damper units for the trailing link mechanism. Box design gives great strength while the link counteracts dive under braking; front brake has a floating anchorage

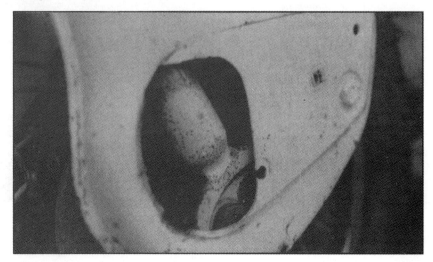

BACK IN THE SMOKE

PART TWO

ALAN McGUIRE TAKES UP THE TALE OF HIS ARIEL ARROW RESTORATION. LAST MONTH WE LEFT HIM WITH A REMINDER OF HIS LONG LOST YOUTH. NOW, READ ON ...

With all the engine parts now back in my possession, work was started on rebuilding the unit. First of all the small end bushes needed refitting and reaming. The only name I could think of for this work was Eric, chief mechanic at Bill Pope Ltd in Warrington, our local Suzuki dealer. I've known Eric for years and to my knowledge he is the only motorcycle mechanic in our area who had ever worked on Ariels in their heyday; his skill and knowledge is terrific.

This job done, the engine was reassembled with new gaskets, main bearings and crankcase seals, the clutch and

---

THE ENGINE WAS REASSEMBLED WITH NEW GASKETS, MAIN BEARINGS AND CRANKCASE SEALS

---

primary drive refitted and the cover put back on.

I then got in contact with Draganfly again: still no rims, though the seat was in stock and arrived in the post a few days later. I tried locally for rims, and finally obtained them from Birmingham. The six inch brake drums were bead-blasted and repainted gloss black and the alloy brake plates polished by Draganfly, who also supplied new spokes. Having got all the bits together, I went to see Eric to get them built up, again a first rate job. I later fitted a new rear brake assembly after discovering that the orig-

inal shoes offered hardly any braking at all.

So we now came to the respraying. It had not been done sooner as I did not want it getting chipped or scratched in the small shed I had at my disposal for the rebuild. This work was carried out by Eric Whitfield Motor Body Repairers of Penketh, nearby. The colours were

COLOURS WERE TOYOTA 073 WHITE AND VOLKSWAGEN HELLAS GOLD

matched very closely by P&M Auto Panels of Warrington and for the reference of any other Arrow restorers the colours were Toyota 073 white and Volkswagen Hellas Gold 98C. After a couple of weeks, all cycle parts were back in my possession and assembly could commence.

Reassembling the Arrow proved snag-free, thanks to a works manual; being constructed on simple principles has advantages besides strength - and note the depth of the steering head. Alan McGuire has seen 75mph and over 150mpg; handling and performance is all he hoped for!

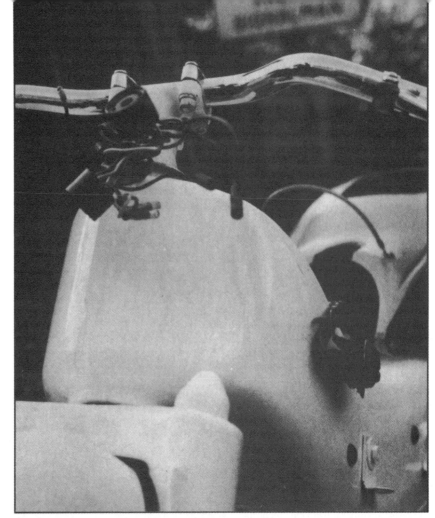

BACK IN THE
SMOKE

I had obtained a workshop manual which I could photocopy, thanks to my mate Geoff Kelly who borrowed it from Sid's Place of Radcliffe, and I just followed the assembly order to the letter. As you would expect, no snags were encountered as care was taken so as not to damage paintwork, nuts and bolts, etc. New headstock roller bearings were fitted as a matter of course, and all other

The engine had proved to be in good condition but Alan played safe and replaced the little end bushes and main bearings. Crankcase seals should always be replaced on a two-stroke, as should gaskets on any motor; smart finish to the outer cover is correct. Once a flyscreen had been found and fitted, the simple front end layout was complete; wiring the switches is easy thanks to socket connections - in fact all the wiring is easy if the loom is threaded through the frame before the fuel tank is fitted. New silencers and wheel rims really set off the paintwork and polished brake backplate.

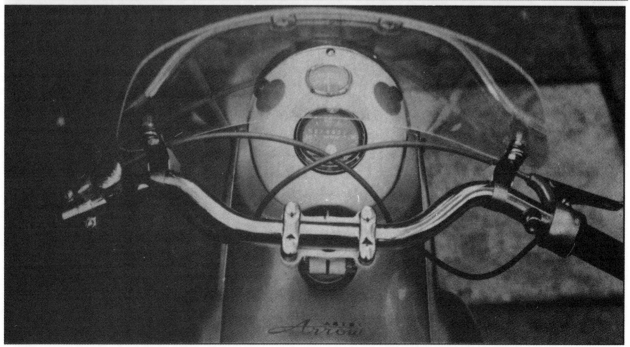

bearings and felt seals greased as per manufacturer's instructions.

The wiring went together easily, the electrical system being built with twin coils and twin points. The coils are mounted within the box section frame just behind the headstock and in front of the fuel tank - a pig to get at! The points are mounted on the left side of the engine under a chrome plate on the clutch cover. The worst part of this lot to fit is the wiring, as a section of it passes through a small hole on the side of the frame alongside the tank. If you make the mistake of fitting the fuel tank first it is impossible to get this wiring in place.

Instrumentation consists of a speedo, ammeter and two Lucas switches, light and ignition, all mounted in the headlamp shell. The switches are of the plug and socket type, very easy to connect, and I encountered no problems during the refitting of these items. A number of wires are carried down a PVC tube on the right hand side of the bike to the alternator assembly, and the speedo cable is also passed through this conduit.

I had decided to fit the 375 carb whilst running the bike in, to stop me getting power crazy, and if all went well for a couple of months, replace it with the 376 version.

My holidays were getting close and I wanted the Arrow running before I went away. This was managed with two

weeks to spare and I went round the block on it. There was a problem with the gears, changing either way being noisy. This was eventually traced to a Leader clutch cable being supplied instead of an Arrow one - it's about an inch longer and I could get no adjustment on the clutch after taking up all the slack in the cable.

The holiday was now upon me so I contacted my mate Terry Nicholls, to ask if he would set it up while I was away, and this he did. On Saturday September 3rd the bike was taken to Bill Pope's for an MOT, which it passed, and the following Monday it was taxed and insured

---

MY ARROW IS NOT CONCOURS, NOR IS IT MEANT TO BE - I BUILT IT TO REPRESENT AN AVERAGE MACHINE OF THE 1960S

---

ready for road use.

During the miles I have done since, various comments have been passed on its appearance, most of which were kind, although one bloke had the nerve to ask if it was a Japanese engine! My Arrow is not concours, nor is it meant to be - I rebuilt it to represent a machine of the

1960s as produced by a major manufacturer of the time.

Since running in I have taken it up to 75mph on the small carb and attained a range of over 150 miles on two gallons of fuel - not quite the "What shall it be? 100mph or 100mpg?" claimed in Ariel's advertising, but good enough. One day I'll get around to following Barry Hickmott's advice on tuning the engine and then we'll really see what it can do.

Thanks to:
Draganfly Motorcycles , The Old Town Maltings, Broad Street, Bungay, Suffolk NR35 1EE (0986 4798) - spares, alloy polishing, chrome plating and help

Colin Rides Motorcycles, 189 Albert Road, Widnes, Cheshire WA8 6LQ (051 424 7486);

Warrington Shotblasting, Athlone Road, Warrington - blasting and priming;

Eric Whitfield Ltd, Penketh - respraying cycle parts;

Bill Pope Ltd, Winwick Road, Warrington - fitting small ends, wheelbuilding, MoT;

Sid's Place, 90 Church Street, Radcliffe, Manchester (061 723 5827) - Arrow manual;

Mates - Geoff Kelly, Alan Wilcox, Terry Nicholls, Ian Jones;

Special thanks to *George Thornton* for colour photography.

A polished performance

John Ascroft and the Leader he had to restore twice

John Ascroft's Ariel Leader won the Classic Bike of the Year award at the very first *Classic Bike* Show at Belle Vue in 1980. Since then, the classic motorcycling scene has expanded and changed incredibly.

John's seen changes in his own life, too: he's been divorced, moved house and become engaged to marry again. And he's bought a modern machine. But the Leader, which went on to win countless other concours trophies, has been kept continuously taxed for road use.

'Winning that first show changed my life,' says the 44-year-old driving instructor, who now lives in St Helens, Merseyside. 'I've met Geoff Duke, Mike Hailwood and Lord Hesketh through my bike. For pleasure, it has been the best investment of my life.'

John's enthusiasm for his machine — which draws a crowd wherever it goes — fizzles and explodes. Don't approach unless you want to know about Ariel's Leader! If you do, then this could be the best example of the futuristic all-enclosed 250cc two-stroke twin made at Selly Oak from 1958 to 1965 that you can study.

It's not just mere originality that makes it hard for concours judges to resist. What probably wins John most points is the range of authentic catalogued Ariel optional extras fitted to the Leader. Varied and sophisticated compared to those for

Ten years at the top of the concours scene
Mick Duckworth

other British machines of the time they include:

● Pannier cases containing soft bags
● Rear view mirrors
● Flashing indicators
● Smiths eight-day clock
● Rear fender
● Waterproof PVC seat cover
● Parking lamp, neutral indicator lamp and inspection lamp
● Propstand and telescopic front stand
● Luggage carrier with two straps

Also available for showing with the machine are a workshop manual still in its box, the machine's guarantee, owner's handbook, service card and care leaflet, the pad provided for cleaning whitewalled tyres and a copy of the Highway Code.

After its dramatic Manchester show debut, the Ariel went on to win major awards at Bristol, the Festival of 1000 Bikes, the National Motorcycle Museum Annual Assembly, Plymouth British Bike Show, and the TT British Rally.

But before you dismiss John Ascroft as some namby-pamby trailer-and-polish-tin specialist you should know the background to the Leader's success.

In the seventies, John was living in Haydock. He became friendly with neighbour and motorcycle enthusiast David Houghton, and got interested in his racing activities with a 1967 Velocette Thruxton.

This led to him seeking a machine for himself and an Ariel Leader was his first choice for nostalgic and practical reasons.

'I passed my test on a Leader when I was sixteen,' he says. 'And I went on holiday to Cornwall on it along with other lads on Leaders and a 250cc AJS. I never had a machine that was so reliable, and it seemed to handle better than the bigger bikes everyone wanted in those days.' He did eventually own a 650cc BSA Rocket twin, but as a man of short stature he always found it big and heavy.

The Leader he was looking for turned up in Rugby. It needed restoration, but priced at about £250 it looked attractive to John, especially with its distinctive registration mark 11 AWK.

He fixed on the coming Belle Vue event (a show for classic motorcycles was a bold new concept then) as a target date for showing his renovated Ariel to the world.

'As soon as I got the MoT certificate I went for a weekend trip to Wales,' John says. 'Then, on the following weekend I

Left: centrestand lifting handle is instantly retractable

Right: rare rear fender was bought for £1 at an autojumble

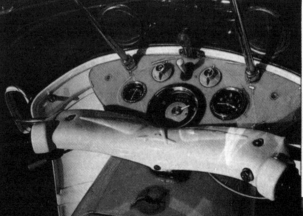

Above: dashboard extras include parking light and clock

Left: tools, fuel and inspection lamp are under seat

Right: whitewall tyres are a concours clincher

A polished performance

was hit by a car.' The accident meant hospitalisation followed by a spell in a wheelchair for John, and the Ariel was badly smashed up.

Despite the disablement caused by a leg broken in four places, John started restoring all over again. Fortunately he was able to count on help from his friend Dave Tyrer, whose reward came in accepting the Belle Vue Show award on John's behalf. Back on his feet, John had taken a holiday in the USA causing him to miss the show.

'When I got home and went into the garage I saw the trophy left on the seat of the bike. There were tears in my eyes,' John recalls.

He's aware that the Leader is a potentially controversial choice for overall

'I didn't get knocked off and injured by not riding'

winner at a major show. Just as they did in the sixties, a lot of motorcyclists view the enclosed Ariel as a bland, tinny machine, lacking the charisma of a cammy single or a lusty twin with its large-capacity engine on display.

But John points out that his machine stands as a record of Britain's most advanced design thinking of the fifties. He appreciates the practicality of its weathershielding, the logic of carrying fuel low under the seat, and the sense of an engine that can have its bottom-end overhauled whilst still bolted in the chassis.

'Look how solid that 20-gauge front mudguard is,' John enthuses. 'If you feel underneath, it has channels to drain water away — how much would it cost today?' He can point to the excellent centre-stand lifting handle, too. Twist the knob just below the seat on the left and it pops out to form a useful grabbing point, then stows away just as easily.

But the main fascination has to be the wealth of unusual details, like the early form of indicator flasher knob (also used in Reliant cars) mounted, albeit rather inconveniently, under the left handlebar. The various extras are rarely seen together on one machine — and their presence on this example testify to John's tireless searches.

One thing he thought he'd never find was the elongated rubber grommet atop the dashboard. It surrounds the lever which allows instant re-aligning of the headlamp when a passenger's weight lowers the machine's rear end. Patient combing through those endless boxes of small bits and pieces at autojumbles eventually turned one up. 'You can bodge something similar up — but it'll never look the same as the real thing,' he says.

The rear fender, surely one of the most non-essential options ever sold for a British motorcycle, is not exactly common. John spotted his jutting from a carton in acres of jumble at Beaulieu and got it for £1. The little lenses for the neutral indicator and flasher repeater lights on a dashboard bristling with gadgets are also hard to find. John gleefully produced screw top jars full of the orange and white plastic mouldings to show he has a lifetime supply of them for himself, and a few other Leader owners.

Many bits and pieces have been offered to John by admirers of his Leader: that's how he got the mint-condition manual. At that first show, *Classic Bike's* photographer Ian Buckden offered an eight-day clock he happened to have. John had it attended to by a clock repairer, noting that the CL code on its face marks it out as a

The only accessory John doesn't have is the executive case to fit the luggage rack

genuine Leader accessory: MG cars used a similar Smiths instrument but it has a different code.

Also fitted since the '80 show are the whitewall tyres. A striking original feature of the Leader, with black treaded portions coated onto white carcases during manufacture, these followed trends in the American automotive market, which the machine was aimed at without success.

John now has his Leader's 16in wheels shod with authentic items. The ribbed front cover, found at a Bolton Autojumble, should be good for a few years yet, but the quicker-wearing rear tyre may have passed its final MoT, John estimates.

For those whose favourite cry is: 'That's not original' here are some pointers. Front number plates were a stick-on type, not screwed-on. John has recently found a template to make some of the original sort up. The rear brake pedal should be painted, not plated. The seat should be red, to match the upper bodywork, but John prefers black. He also took a slight liberty with paintwork, using the Cherokee Red and Ivory scheme from the 1964 Ariel bro-

HOWEVER original, unusual or historic a machine is, to meet the extremely high standards prevailing in today's concours competitions it has to be presented in a clean and attractive condition.

What's John Ascroft's secret in achieving that dazzling finish? For heavy duty alloy refurbishment he recommends Hermetite Ali Clean, and Solvol Autosol polish for keeping chromium and bare metal's sparkle. He keeps an eye on the paintwork, using touch-up when necessary, and occasionally cuts it back with Brasso or T-Cut then shines up with Turtle Wax polish. He also swears by Armor All protectant for general beauty treatment.

chure. His machine dates from at least three years earlier, when the lower portion would have been in Admirality Grey.

Despite this, the Ariel is extraordinarily rich in genuine factory components, compared with the average restored classic. John is not an engineer, and doesn't have much in the way of workshop facilities, so parts haven't been specially made. Except for the exhaust downpipes, which are pattern parts, he can't think of anything else that isn't Ariel. Many spares came from 2M, whose stock has since been absorbed by Draganfly Motorcycles (0986 4798), and he's also benefitted from the services of Magpie Motorcycles, Manchester's Ariel two-stroke Mecca (061-881 0157), and Colin Rides Motorcycles in Widnes (051-424 7486).

Technical advice has come from a friend, John Shaw, who was formerly on the staff of Cundalls, a main Ariel agent in Liverpool. John Ascroft has always seen the simplicity of the Leader's 54 x 54mm two-stroke, four-speed unit construction engine as a virtue. He recently replaced the bottom-end oil seals — done over a weekend — and is now on plus-0.020 in cylinder bores.

Looking at the paintwork shows that the cellulose applied by a small Haydock company over ten years ago is standing up

John and the Leader on the road. Its main use is for trips from Merseyside to Wales

well, though a close check will show a little damage inflicted by the Isle of Man Steam Packet Company on a TT trip. Another blemish John pointed out is slight marking of the right-hand silencer, caused by battery acid spillage after his accident.

He admits that making good the crash damage in 1980 and his determination to go for an ultimate specification nearly ruined him financially. He also suggests that his pre-occupation with the Ariel contributed to the breakdown of his first marriage. But so far he has resisted offers for the registration number, even through the toughest times. Its desirability stems from the fact that by placing a fastener between the 1s, it could be made to spell HAWK: with offers exceeding £2,000, no-one could blame him for taking the cash.

John senses some disapproval for his increased use of a trailer for getting the Ariel to shows outside his home county. 'There's a lot of cattiness on the concours scene,' he says. 'But I don't hide it when I trail. What I dislike are people who pretend to have ridden to an event, when they

have taken their bike off a trailer nearby.'

He has two other forceful points to make on the subject. 'I didn't get knocked off and injured by not riding. And, if you don't take your wife and family along to shows, you'll end up divorced.' He's determined that his hobby won't come between him and his wife-to-be Sue.

In fact, until John was invited back to the *Classic Bike* Show's tenth anniversary this year, he had stopped showing the Leader for more than a year. 'I'd done the rounds and people had seen a lot of the machine,' he says. About 18 months ago he bought a modern 125cc Aprilia — with an enclosed two-stroke engine.

There's another Ariel project on the way, however. Parts amassing in John's garage for an Arrow racer include a period Fi-glass fairing and a pair of exhaust expansion boxes. And he never tires of collecting information relating to Selly Oak two-strokes. John can even tell you which sixties' feature films to watch for brief glimpses of Arrows and Leaders!

'We've been through so much together,' he says of his pride and joy since 1979. 'But winning awards is just the icing on the cake. The real satisfaction comes from meeting so many people and hearing them say about the Leader "How nice to see one of these again" □

Ariel leader — as interpreted free hand by Roger Cramp.

A cat amongst the pigeons?

John Ruth tries out a two stroke that just makes the Vintage club's eligibility limit. Pictures by John Downs.

ARIEL ARROW/ LEADER

UNTIL a few seasons ago, the vintage racing scene was all but dominated by four strokes. The exception was the idiosyncratic Scott marque which often proved successful when matched with the talents of Messrs Moss, Pierce and Williams.

More than once they proved to be the fly in the Poppet valve brigade's ointment but this situation would soon have changed if the Vintage club's minimum 25-year rule had allowed in a new wave of

A cat amongst the pigeons?

Snail cams replace original thread studs allowing more accurate wheel alignment, while interchangeable rear wheel sprockets are a must for precise gearing for each circuit.

machinery with every succeeding year. The foreign invasion of the early 60's would soon have occurred in vintage racing!

The very thought of Hondas, Suzukis, Yamahas and the odd Italian filling the grids was unthinkable for the VMCC so it was voted to keep the cut-off date at 1958 and stave off such an onslaught.

So the four stroke stalwarts once again rested easy, confident that the sight and sound of the dreaded two strokes had been nipped in the bud. Indeed, general consensus of vintage racing opinion was summed up by one South East London member who said he had nothing against two strokes being allowed in the paddock as long as they didn't start them up!

He had not reckoned, however, on the humble proprietary

Four speed Burman box is Achillies heel of power unit and restricts further development.

Villiers engines, Greeves, James or the revolutionary Val Page designed Ariel Leader. All had first arrived on the scene in 1958 and as such were perfectly eligible under the new 1958 rule.

The original Ariel Leader, with fully enclosed engine and weather protective panels, could hardly be described as a racer, but with everything removed

things looked a little different — although the only section resembling a conventional tubular frame was the rear swinging arm and spoked wheels.

Ariel themselves realised this and launched the Arrow in late 1959 with a more sporty and conventional look — but the petrol tank still remained under

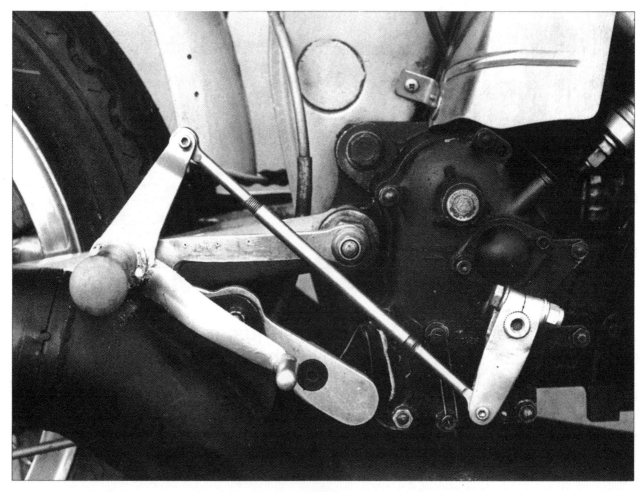

Twin expansion chambers exit through original tail pipe silencers. Girling gas units replace original Armstrongs.

the dual seat and heavily valanced mudguards were still fitted.

It was in 1959 that Hermann Meier and Mike O'Rouke produced their own development of the Leader, aided and abetted by Ariel's managing director Ken Whistance. He supplied a rolling chassis and a set of specially made twin carburettor crankcases, the result being O'Rouke's seventh place in the 1960 Lightweight TT at 80.18mph. (See Summer, 1989, *Classic Racer*).

Ariel produced their own version for 1961, but with little success, and other notables flirted with the little two stroke twin. Bill Boddice coupled two together in his outfit to make what must have been one of the first two stroke, four cylinder in-line racing sidecars — which he raced at Brands Hatch over Christmas, 1960 (the first road race meeting I ever attended).

George Brown also sprinted one in the mid-1960s and it was the memory of this that tempted Roger Cramp, for many years a VMCC racer and tuner, to return to the scene. He and David Wakeling decided to join forces and develop a racing Ariel Leader for the lightweight vintage class, Dave preparing the bike while Roger concentrated on the power source.

WITH no special twin carburettor crankcases available Roger's initial development work had to be restricted to the original single inlet cases. The induction tract is cast into the main support, from which the power unit is hung from the pressed steel frame member — unlike the

Meier/O'Rouke Arrow unit which was modified to hang from the cylinder heads.

By the end of the Arrow's first season in 1988, Roger had managed to wring out 28.2bhp at 8500rpm for rider Ian Austin who achieved several 'first under the linen' results. However, he did once manage to throw the Arrow up the road while

heading for a certain win on the last lap. Luckily, only dented pride and a dented machine was the outcome.

Cramp, being a perfectionist, felt that further development was restricted by the single carburettor so in the off-season he went to work on a twin carb version in search of the elusive 31bhp that Meier had produced in 1960.

The lack of special crankcases meant Roger had to modify the originals. This he did by milling off the casting back to where the single inlet orifice merged into two. Then he mounted a plate from which the engine could be suspended — before relieving the plate to form part of the induction tract and allow the twin Amal 10TT carbs to be mounted at the required position.

Cramp favoured his own twin carb set-up for two reasons; it gave a sturdier location to that of Meier's, which stressed the cylinder base flange and separate cylinder heads;

Ariel leader trailing link forks remain as standard — unlike the Huntmaster. Brake laced into an 18″ rim which allows the fitment of decent rubber.

A cat amongst the pigeons?

Power unit is now suspended from angular bracket mounted across cut back induction tracts, while twin Amal 10TT carbs and power jets can clearly be seen along with flexibly mounted expansion chambers.

diversant/convergent resonant type, incorporating the original Ariel Leader's tail pipes and silencers.

Electronic ignition replaces the original points system. The Burman C/R four speed gearbox and Ariel clutch are both as fitted originally, although C/R clusters for Arrows are now practically unobtainable.

Cycle parts are virtually standard with 18in rims replacing the 17in originals. The short trailing-link forks remain standard but an Ariel Huntmaster front brake replaces the original — keeping within VMCC rules requiring all external parts to be from the same make of machine.

The pressed steel frame looks (and is) quite substantial, contributing more than a little to the all-up weight of 255lbs, but the fuel tank now lives between the rider's knees and not under the seat. Tank, seat and all other pressed steel work was fabricated by Wakeling — and a nice job he's made of it too.

The swinging arm has been strengthened around the swinging arm pivot point and snail cams replace threaded studs for ease of wheel alignment.

The Ariel parallel twin with distinctive horizontal finning is inclined forward at 45 degrees. Bore and stroke is a square 54 x 54mm and Cramp is currently running a compression ratio of 7.5:1 measured from above the exhaust ports.

He now reports a healthy 30bhp at 8000rpm at the gearbox sprocket — which means there probably more in the engine than meets the eye. But, as he says, it all boils down to basic two stroke theory. (Something the four stroke brigade consider a black art.)

secondly, it also made removing the heads and barrels an easier job in the paddock.

AND that proved convenient at our test session at Mallory when David Wakeling's son Dean returned from a few warm-up laps to find that the nearside head gasket had blown necessitating removal of the left side head only. This turned out to be as simple a job as the development team had predicted.

While they swarmed over the bike, my over-the-shoulder observations evinced one or two visible modifications to the power unit.

The twin Amals are fed from a single remote Amal float mounted between the carburettors. A power-jet type system is also fitted to help keep the mixture consistent at long throttle openings, the jets being mounted on the bottom of the bell mouths. (More than this Roger wasn't divulging, other than it was his own design.)

The exhaust system, also designed and developed by Roger, is of

ANYWAY, time to fire it up. This turned out to be an art in itself. It involved running the equivalent of an Olympic 100 metres time before dropping the clutch and pushing until it burst into life. Roger did this successfully and all seemed well until it came to my turn.

"No need to pull back on compression, just run as fast as you can and drop the clutch," were the last instructions as I shot off along the Mallory paddock, pushing like crazy. At last the Ariel wheezed into life, only to die again as I failed to catch the engine's revs, leaving me wheezing breathlessly instead.

Still, things went better on the second attempt and eventually

both bike and rider (running hot and sweetly) trundled out onto the circuit.

PULLING away from scratch involved lots of clutch slip to get into the rev band, starting at about 6500. Then there's a 3000rpm rev band within which the C/R cluster which provides perfect service, upward and downward changes falling within the power band.

Negotiating the Mallory hairpin was another matter altogether. Copious amounts of clutch slip were needed to sustain momentum no matter which line was used. It was soon apparent that the only way to ride this bike is flat against the stop, keeping the motor buzzing within its (by two stroke standards) wide power band.

Cramp aptly described the close ratio Burman gearbox as 'a typically vintage unit providing positive selection of the gears, but requiring a slow, purposeful movement of the reversed lever'. I would second that opinion. Even so, I only mis-selected once in my haste, knocking her into top on the exit from Gerrards.

Handling-wise the Ariel has a soft comfortable feel to it. The high-backed racing seat gives good support and the short trailing link forks soaks up bumps — but the Leader had a tendency to wallow initially on the approach to faster corners. This was not excessive though.

In fact the adhesion problem lay at the other end. Although the Avon Roadrunner 90/90 F2 on the front end performed adequately, the matching 100/90 rear felt uneasy and could be made to let go quite easily. Getting down to a bit of short circuit scratching, I had a couple of hairy moments on the fast right hand dive into The Esses.

But with daylight fast expiring there was no time to experiment with tyre pressures or pre-load settings on the Girling gas damped rear shocks. This could well improve things.

There was plenty of ground clearance with the footrest and ace handlebar configuration being just about right — but the single bicycle-type headstock and splined handlebar location initially felt a bit strange.

Lack of setting-up time meant carburation changes could not be tried. This was unfortunate. Although the Ariel twin accelerated briskly and cleanly out of most corners, by the exit of Gerrards it began to feel woolly and flat at 8000rpm in third. This cleared on the back straight and Roger afterwards suspected fuel starvation — a problem they have experienced in the past, and the reason for the power-jet device.

The four speed transmission now holds back further development. It needs the optimum in final drive gear ratios matched to mixture settings to achieve good results. Unfortunately six speed C/R clusters for Ariel Burman gearboxes were only a pipedream in 1959.

However, who can tell if the engineering talents of Roger Cramp, David Wakeling and son Dean can come up trumps? Indeed, the 'formula cosmetic' approach employed in vintage club racing tends to be the norm rather than the exception, so if Triumph Tiger 70s, Scotts, and three wheeled Morgans can sport more than their original number of ratios, a six speed stroker twin could become a reality in Vintage club racing.

Now that would really put the cat amongst the pigeons...

Above: JR gets down to some serious scratching.

Dean Wakeling gives the Ariel an airing.

1958 ARIEL LEADER

Engine: 250cc parallel twin cylinder, inclined forward at 45 degrees. **Bore and stroke:** 54 x 54mm. **Compression ratio:** 7.5:1 above exhaust ports. **Carburation:** Twin Amal 10TT carbs with remote float chamber. **Fuel:** Petroil 16:1 mix. Oil Castrol R40. **Exhausts:** Divergent/convergent resonant type with tailpipe silencers. **Power:** 30.3bhp at 8,000rpm at rear wheel. **Power band:** 6000 — 9500rpm. **Gearbox:** Four speed close ratio. One down, three up. **Frame:** Pressed steel. **Suspension:** Short trailing links (front), swing arm, reinforced Girling (rear). **Brakes:** Ariel Huntmaster twin front, standard Leader rear. **Tank/seat:** Aluminium, custom built. **Tyres:** Avon Roadrunner F2 90/90 H18 (front), Avon Roadrunner R2 100/90 H18 (rear). **Weight:** 255lbs dry.

A POLICEMAN'S LOT

Policemen on motorcycles vary from lordly beings mounted on expensive BMWs to objects of pity and derision puttering by on miniscule Honda twins. It was ever thus. A copper's lot might include riding a rorty Triumph twin capable of 120mph or a near-silent side-valve Velocette with the searing acceleration of an electric milk float.

'Hey, Noddy! Where's Big Ears?' we used to yell.

In between these extremes you can probably recall seeing the constabulary on a bewildering variety of powered two-wheelers. For despite the popularity of Triumph twins and the Velocette LE with the UK's many police forces, cost-cutting led to some strange experiments.

How else does one explain the serious weirdness of a West Mercia law-enforcer on a 250cc DMW Deemster? This two-stroke, a child of the union between a motorcycle and a scooter, also appealed briefly to the Pembrokeshire police in the early1960s, but that Force re-equipped with Ariel Leaders.

On paper, the innovative 250cc twin Ariel made an ideal police mobile. Another scooter-motorcycle cross, it has 16in diameter wheels that are too large for a scooter, but small for a motorcycle. A weather-cheating fairing and clear plastic windscreen are attached to the Leader's pressed steel body shell, along with a dummy fuel tank that serves as a luggage compartment. Optional equipment included everything

Can be a very happy one with an ex-constabulary Ariel Leader 250cc twin
Peter Watson

the touring motorcyclist could desire, from a pair of steel luggage panniers to flashing indicators and a clock.

Among the Ariel twin's few drawbacks are limited ground clearance, marginal brakes — a common flaw on British-

Roger James prepares to smoke out those villains on his ex-Sheffield police two-stroke

made two-strokes — and its engine type. Then as now, the mechanical simplicity of a high-performance two-stroke must be balanced against its requirement for spot-on ignition timing and an annoying tendency to sulk when asked to start.

Today we rely on electronic ignition and electric starter motors — not to mention improved spark plugs and semi-synthetic oils — for reliable starting. In the 1960s we made do with strong calf muscles, spare plugs and loud curses.

Ariel was to develop its police business despite the public prejudice against foully-smoking 'stinkwheels' that pre-dated the 1958-65 Leader by 40 years. The Birmingham company sold 31 British police forces 320 Leaders and Arrows — the latter being a stripped-down sports version of the 250cc twin — between 1961 and 1965.

I'm indebted for this statistical information to Keith Bragg, who wrote a carefully researched article for the Ariel Owners Club magazine *Cheval de Fer* entitled *Two-stroke Motorcycles and the Police*. Keith is restoring an ex-Shropshire police Arrow. But his friend and fellow club member Roger James beat him to the finish with a 1963 Leader that was once the pride of the police garage in the city of Sheffield.

After owning the remains of the ivory and black twin for 14 years, and collecting special police equipment for over two years, Roger completed the restoration in just ten weeks. This included painting all the metalwork with aerosols 'in order to retain control' of the restoration rather than save money. He was therefore able to take the Leader ▶

Police radio equipment plus civilian extras on Leader make a superb patrol package

a high-output alternator but has a Pye M200 radio, supplied by Metropolitan Police officer Harry Harris. The large public address speaker came from Derbyshire's police HQ at Ripley.

How dependable was the Leader as a police patrol machine? The Northumberland constabulary kept its Ariel two-strokes on the road for more than six years. Roger James owned his first example in 1969, when he was 17 and a naval rating. 'It was my only form of transport and I ran backwards and forwards on it from Devonport, Portsmouth and Chatham to my home in Walsall. It was completely reliable,' Roger said. He cruises at just under 60mph.

As a former organiser of the Ariel club's two-stroke parts scheme and the owner of two Ariel Arrows and a 1960 civilian Leader, Roger James knows the breed through to every bone and sinew. Never rebuild an engine without having the crankshaft reconditioned, he advises. That's £200 well spent. And it's vital to ensure that the flywheels are perfectly aligned.

The art of ignition timing is covered in the Leader's workshop manual. I'd fit an electronic system and spend the time saved building an Airfix kit of the Arrow.

Civilian or police, the all-enclosed Leader exerts a strange fascination. 'As a schoolboy I knew the Leader was the bike for me long before I'd ever tried one,' said Roger. 'It was the visual image it created. The Leader seems to have everything you'd ever want in a motorcycle.' ⑬

A POLICEMAN'S LOT

to the Ariel club's major UK rally in 1991 and come away with the Two-Stroke Cup.

'I'd been telling people about the Leader for years without restoring it,' he said. 'I believe it's the only one built up as a police bike in the country, but I'd like to be proved wrong.'

Police Constable James has been issued with a bicycle for his role as one of Derbyshire's community policemen. Yet after watching him ride his recently-restored Leader for half a day I became convinced that this quietly-spoken, reserved man must spend his working life aboard a police BMW. Not so; he has never been a police motorcyclist. Roger's machine control at low speeds is so complete it looks uncanny.

I'd come quietly if I was nicked by PC James.

Some police machines were always bought as civilian models and modified locally to meet the requirements, prejudices and pockets of local Forces. But Ariel's Leader package for the police usually included most of the standard civilian options plus a fire extinguisher, heavy-duty springs on the twin Armstrong shock absorbers at the rear, a strengthened lifting handle to raise the machine on to its centre stand, a high-output alternator, an extra battery in one pannier, Cossor radio telephone, an aerial mount and a large PA speaker on a bar clamped across the right-hand legshield.

Obsolete police equipment is very hard to acquire, even for serving officers. A machine's Cossor 105 radio set — mounted in the dummy fuel tank with the hand-set on a glass fibre trim panel — had to be handed in before a Pye Westminster unit was issued to replace it. So Roger's Leader is not only devoid of panniers and

GOING for G

Bert Page's golden Ariel Arrow scooped gold in the Classic Bike readers' restoration competition at this year's CB International Stafford Show. Here he reveals how it was achieved/Val Ward

NOTHING was left to chance when Bert Page decided to renovate his 1962 Ariel Arrow Super Sports. The machine's one previous owner had been meticulous about logging every service chore. This inspired Bert and his restoration was also fastidious. At the Stafford show this year the Ariel deservedly won the CB readers' restoration competition.

Bert only had to correct a crankshaft fault to get the Arrow back on the road after he acquired the 'bike six years ago. He thinks the machine stood idle for ten years after its first owner realised repairs were beyond him. Bert estimates that when the two-stroke twin passed to him it had done just 11,000 miles in 16 years.

'The Swindon Motor

Company sold the new machine in July 1962 to Robert Taylor who lived locally. When I first saw the Ariel in non-running condition, Mr Taylor produced a full maintenance record,' says Bert. 'He still had the origi-

nal documentation. He kept everything, including the proper handlebar and flyscreen with all the fittings.

'The first owner preferred to use the Ariel without its flyscreen, so removed it early in the machine's life. All I've done is put the screen back on. It appears to be brand-new.'

Dent-free original bodywork and good chrome in places eased the restoration of Bert Page's award-winning Arrow

OLD

With the crankshaft repaired, Bert used the Ariel for short journeys and rode it on many runs organised by the Ariel OMCC and the Vintage MCC. Then the little learner bike broke down during a coast-to-coast run in Yeovil last year. Bert lost all the oil from the gearbox when the core plug dropped out. With temperatures in the eighties, the 'box seized.

Bert stripped it on the spot but saw the damage was a workshop job, and the Ariel had to be trailered home to Swindon. This was to be the start of his quest ⟫⟫➤

Period promotional leaflets proclaim the Super Sports Arrow as the most glamorous sporting twin ever designed, with youth built into every line

930 AHR

GOING for GOLD

continued

for gold, although restoration originally began because Bert wanted the Arrow back on the road for the 1994 coast-to-coast run.

A transmission overhaul revealed the gearbox mainshaft seized on the final drive bush. He fitted new parts, junked a worn second cog and made sure the new core plug was a perfect fit in the gearbox body. Several clutch plates were renewed, along with the primary chain, which was fitted with new neoprene-faced tensioning blade.

The engine was rebored and fitted with plus 20 thou pistons and rings which Bert acquired with the 'bike. He referred constantly to Ariel's own rider's maintenance handbook and the official factory workshop manual for guidance during the rebuild: 'They are excellent, and give all the information and advice anybody could wish for.'

Bert concluded the machine had led an easy life in Mr Taylor's ownership. 'As renovation work progressed, I found many signs that this Ariel had been well treated

Handling is first class but six inch front brake isn't. Supple suspension is master of all road surfaces

'Dipswitch apart, it is to authentic Ariel specification'

the lift-up dualseat which was mint, with no trace of deformed foam filling. Bert did not have to touch either base or cover.

He decided to replace the entire exhaust system with parts from Armours, but prefers the quieter exhaust note of genuine Ariel baffles, and needed to grind down the old baffles to fit the new pipes. Both Jones wheel rims were removed because the chrome had faded. In their place are new Radaellis.

Bert could not obtain new whitewall tyres, so he has used detachable white Atlas circular trims. These are designed to be trapped between rim and tyre, and have been teamed with the new 16in paired Avons to create a whitewall appearance. The old brake linings were good and went back in, but both wheel hubs were given new bearings.

'I think Ariels could have made a better job of the paintwork,' says Bert. 'Some areas of the main frame were just left in primer when these machines came out of the factory.

'And because the rear mudguard is short, road filth gets thrown off the back tyre up into the frame and starts corrosion of the metal. I was lucky — this frame was okay.'

He gives full credit to a good friend for the new paintjob on the Arrow. 'His work is superb. I matched pristine original cycle parts in ivory and gold to Opel White and Renault Gold — that just required a slight tinting to be spot-on. My friend used two-pack kits. The finish is brilliant,' says Bert.

This project avoided many pitfalls because the Arrow was never messed about or robbed of parts. Genuine chrome gearbox covers and rear chaincase tops and bottoms are becoming scarce, although Bert says Draganfly and the Ariel OMCC, of which he's Swindon secretary, can help.

'I think a lot of gearbox covers were just taken off if they got damaged, and the problem with rear chaincase bottoms is they rot. Draganfly can supply the chaincase in fibreglass, and the Ariel Club people are trying to get steel gear covers made again,' says Bert.

He put an Ariel OMCC transfer on the Arrow's rear mudguard in gratitude for the Club's spares scheme. The spares peo-

Distinctive silencer stays would normally be covered in soot. Modern oils prevent this

before I got it,' he says, adding 'I believe he just used it for commuting and on short trips in the Swindon area. I'd guess it had never done a really long journey all the time he ran it.'

This was confirmed by the condition of

ple supplied new authentic tank badges, air filter and correct script style Ariel Arrow transfer for the top of the dummy fuel tank.

'I must thank John Ellis and his wife Sandy for their help,' says Bert. 'John is our Swindon chairman and he does very good work helping Ariel two-stroke owners'.

Many auxiliary items on the Ariel required careful work and Bert lost count of the hours he spent on fiddly, time-consuming jobs in his cold workshop last winter. He says the hardest job was refitting black slotted beading round the front fork's mount for the valanced mudguard.

Smiths speedo reads up to the ton, but seventy would be nearer the mark

Flight of the Arrow: Ariel two-stroke development

Ariel introduced the 247cc Leader in 1958 and produced the last one in 1965. The 247cc Arrow, which was made from 1960 to '64 was basically a stripped Leader, shorn of handlebar fairing/screen, legshields and body panels. Both use the same twin two-stroke engine with 54 x 54mm bore and stroke and bolted-up four-speed Burman gearbox suspended from a beam-type frame using edge-welded, box-shaped steel pressings.

Suspension for both comprise Ariel's own unique trailing-link front forks and a conventional rear swinging-arm pivoted from the gearbox shell. Armstrong hydraulic-spring units control movement of both wheels, which carry 3.25 x 16in tyres, and six-inch sls full-width brakes. Some machines have alloy hubs, others cast-iron. Wheels are quickly detachable.

The petroil-lubricated engine uses separate conrod-crank assemblies pulled together by a central bolt and locknut. The built-up three bearing crankshaft has four self-adjusting rubber oil seals. The crankshaft drives a Lucas generator on the offside, with twin contact-breakers mounted outboard of the primary drive chaincase on the nearside. Running in oil in the chaincase, a single-row endless primary chain, with externally-adjustable tensioner below the bottom rim, drives an Ariel patent-

Ariel Leader sports body panels and large screen

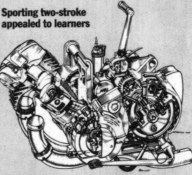

Sporting two-stroke appealed to learners

ed three-plate wet-type clutch fitted with rubber shock absorbers.

Early Leader and Arrow cylinder heads give 8.25:1 compression ratio; later heads were restyled with 10:1 ratio and central plugs. Carburation was by a single ⅞in Amal Monobloc with cold-starting device and cartridge element air filter.

This Arrow Super Sports, made from 1961-65, has 10:1 heads, a 1¹⁄₁₆in Monobloc and a claimed 20bhp @ 6600rpm — 3.5bhp up on other models. An improved torque reaction linkage for the front brake was carried over from later versions of the Leader and standard Arrow.

The Super Sports has the same general lines and dummy fuel tank. Concealed in the main frame is a three-gallon fuel tank as fitted to late-model Arrows and all Leaders. Super Sports models were finished in ivory and gold and were fitted with drop 'bars, ball-end levers flyscreen and folding kickstarter. Ariel claimed that its Super Sports would cover 78-80mph and average 70-75mpg. All had whitewall tyres.

For one year only, 1964-65, a sleeved down 199cc Arrow power unit, with 48.5 x 54mm dimensions, 9.5:1 compression ratio, ¹³⁄₁₆in Monobloc and a claimed 14bhp at 6250rpm, was teamed with the standard Arrow's cycle parts to beat an insurance barrier for young riders.

'The mudguard is in two parts, and you have to hold everything in position and press the beading back into place at the same time. Fortunately the complete fork and steering stem assembly was off the main frame when I started the job, but it still took up most of one evening,' he grins.

Bert's bike retains its original wiring loom. The six-volt electrical system was sound and intact, complete with headlamp-mounted Lucas ammeter, with separate switches for ignition and lights nearby. He doesn't like Ariel's choice of black moulded dipswitch and uses a chrome pattern switch for better appearance.

Outwardly everything else is ex-factory specification, including red HT leads and red handlebar grips. Faithful reproductions of the silver-grey sheathed cables Ariel used were also obtained.

Various secondary fittings, nuts, bolts and screws in a cadmium finish were freshly zinc plated since Bert prefers it, saying zinc's easier to have done than cadmium now and looks very similar. Clamps for the clutch and front brake levers on the 'bars had a distinctive silver-grey finish originally and these, with correct ball-ended blades, were specified for the rebuild.

He dismantled two old Lucas horns and

used the best bits to make a good one which was then zinc plated. No welding was called for, and front and rear light assemblies are the originals, suitably refinished. The headlamp rim polished up to as-new condition.

Bert took a lot of trouble to achieve a really convincing, one hundred per cent accurate cosmetic appearance. So he obtained new aluminium kneepad trims, new rubbers for footrests, kickstart and gear levers and new white moulded covers for the upper suspension unit mounts on the front forks.

He spent a long time using a friend's facilities to beadblast the Ariel's alu- ➤➤➤

GOING for GOLD

continued

Stick-on number plate numerals are correct for period. Dummy tank conceals toolbox. Trailing link front forks work well

minium cylinder heads back to the authentic shade of silver, and has improvised his own pullers and presses to strip and rebuild the crankshaft. He fitted new end-plate seals.

Every part of the machine's suspension was still sound, but Bert stripped it to the last nut and bolt for a thorough clean-out and respray.

Ariel man Bert Page has good reason to smile. He scooped gold with his Arrow

'Dipswitch apart, I believe that in outward appearance this Arrow is exactly to authentic Ariel specification in every way,' says Bert, who added a new £12 six-volt Japanese battery 'only because it is hidden away out of sight under the seat in a frame compartment.'

He adds, 'I estimate all the pretty work cost £500. Another couple of hundred went on the engine. I think anybody should be able to get a complete Leader or Arrow today for around £800. I know a bloke who spent £3000 on a professional company's renovation of a Leader, but there's no need for such expense if you do most of the work yourself.'

On the road, sweet power delivery allows the rider to exploit the Arrow's steering and roadholding qualities.

Starting is prompt from cold. Ariel's choke device is a foolproof induction shutter that can be fully opened up after a few seconds running. Disengaging the clutch produces jangling noises from the transmission and the first big let down is the gear change action.

A long-travel gear lever clashes with the bike's racy image. Upward changes are accompanied by loud grating sounds, although the clutch lifted cleanly. The Burman four-speeder is really poor, it's ratios no help when accelerating hard.

Exceptional suspension masters all surfaces. The Arrow's simple and smooth set-up keeps the wheel base constant and helps the bike float over the worst obstacles — a perfect ally to superb line-holding. Nothing deflects the sportster from its intended course, although poor ground clearance limits the press-on rider.

Rear wheel braking is adequate, but the six inch front unit is frail. A sudden need to pull up becomes heavy drama.

Bursts of acceleration make the cylinder barrels resonate loudly because finning lacks ties and rubbers to damp out vibration. Oil smoke from the silencers is tolerable thanks to modern lubricants which permit a leaned out petroil mixture.

So much about the Ariel keeps it attractive today. Another 10mph or so at the top end, plus a crisp and accurate five-speed 'box would ensure the necessary all round performance to make the Arrow a sound proposition for daily use. First priority, however, is improved braking. Learners on this sports twin must have suffered a baptism of fire. Low slung weight helps the Super Sports live up to its name, but the front brake is less than ideal for eager first-time bikers ◉

Parts and services

Exhaust pipes, silencers Armour Motor Products (0202 519409)

Tank badges, air filter, transfers Ariel OMCC John Ellis (0285 861510)

Paint Tony Edginton (0793 611653)

Whitewall trims Bravado Automotive (0932 858248)

Wheelbuilding Charlie's Motorcycles (0272 511019)

Fork top shrouds, tank trims Draganfly Motorcycles (0986 894798)

Paint Sunbase (0793 511203)

Chrome plating S & T (0454 313162)

Zinc plating Swindon tools and fasteners Ltd (0793 488822)

Foot rubbers Jim Hunter Engineering, 2671 Stratford Road, Hockley Heath, Solihull, W Midlands B94 5NH (all enquiries asked to write)

Control cables JJ Cables, care of J & P Engineering (0926 651470)

Seals, bearings Thamesdown Bearings, Swindon (0793 724554)

LAST GASP

Steve Wilson Rides Ariel's smaller Arrow

I had the Honda in my sights, and wound up the Ariel as hard as I dared. Agonizingly slowly the gap between us closed, the 2-stroke twin working hard in 3rd, and I took the rice-burner just before the bend ... finally getting past this 50cc Honda Express and its gallant skirted lady rider, as 30mph came up slowly on the Arrow's clock.

It was the only overtaking I did that day. This lovingly-restored rarity may have been in faultless nick, but its performance was, ah, underwhelming.

Fletching the Arrow

The 200 Arrow was a product of convenience made in 1964-65, six years after the Ariel marque had turned over their entire production to Leader and Arrow variants of their innovative beam-framed 250 2-stroke twin. When sales of these had sagged, Ariel were grudgingly moved in with their parent BSA

company at Small Heath. And in the grim market of the early Sixties, chasing a £12 loophole in the cheap insurance sector, that was where the square-engined 250 got its 54mm bore sleeved down to 48.5mm, to create the Arrow 200.

Different heads and barrels, gearing lowered by adding two extra teeth to the 250's 47-tooth rear sprocket, a smaller, 13/16ths inch Monobloc carb, a '200' tank badge and a £10 cheaper purchase price – that was about it for changes from the stock Arrow. Oh yes, and the enclosed rear chaincase on the 200 was also finished in the primary colour of the two-tone paint schemes, rather than the usual contrasting Ivory. Not many people know that. The primary colours for the Arrow 200 were either good old British Racing Green, or as with Mike Portsmouth's example seen here, Aircraft Blue.

Mike bought the test bike, a 1964 model, from dealer Bill Little (01666-860577). It's

actually the second example of the little Arrow which Mike has acquired, the earlier one being in rougher condition; it was a one-owner-and-a-dealer bike, the dealer having believed it to be a Golden Arrow. Mr Hawkins, the Ariel Owners Club archivist, was particularly pleased to confirm that it had actually begun life as a 200, since of the 884 smaller models which had been built, only 34 had survived on the Club records. Mike is currently restoring this first 200, despite the fact that it's identical to the test bike, right down to the ivory and blue finish. 'When people come out of the beer tent and see the two, they'll think they're seeing double,' he laughs. This bike had been fitted with 250 barrels and gearing. Then it turned out that the test machine, despite still being registered as a 200, had also been so converted. After my ride on the 200, I think I understand why.

The Owners Club provided excellent back-up during the rebuild, which after ☞

119

Left: *Tester Wilson, shaken — but refusing to be stirred — by the smart but small Arrow 200.*
Far right: *Ariel rear carrier and cantilevered silencers.*
Above: *The Arrow scoot did however have its good points: neat underseat area, for example, which holds fuel tank and cap, plus battery.*

complete dismantling took Mike around six months. Club man Mick Taylour had passed a brand new pair of 200 barrels for Mike to the Club 2-stroke spares specialist John Ellis; the heads had to be secondhand, but brand new pistons were sourced via *Old Bike Mart.* Many phone calls to John Ellis accompanied the rebuild, and John's 'Two-Stroke Technicalities' information sheets, which go out with the Club magazine, also proved helpful. 'There's quite a lot to know, with these bikes,' says Mike.

On the cycle side, replacements were required for the Arrow's rear quarter-mud-guard, and for the dummy fuel tank and headlamp shell, both of which were in poor order and had holes drilled in them, possibly for indicators. Mike believes that the missing

section of mudguard may have accounted for the machine's perfect condition behind the engine and under the seat, as oil had thus been able to get sprayed on there to preserve things! All these bits were sourced secondhand from specialist David Pool at Magpie Motors (0161-881-0157), who advertises in the Club magazine. The other major item needed was the correct round-section swinging arm, as the bike had been fitted with a pre-'61 D-section type. Mike found a brand new round one, still in its wrappings.

New 49-tooth rear sprockets, as well as invaluable workshop manuals and parts books, plus much else, came from Ariel gurus Draganfly Motors (01986-894798) who were also very helpful with advice — 'I must have

been there ten times,' says Mike. It was the jaunting involved in sourcing parts, tyres, paintwork and chrome which helped push the cost of the project to 'more than I'll ever see back on it,' Mike admits. But the result is certainly very smart.

One element in this is the grey lacquered timing side cowling, which on the Arrows conceals seperate covers over the off-side mounted alternator and the gearbox. John Ellis had a batch made up, since these outer covers frequently used to go missing. Mike explains why. 'You have to remove the kickstart pedal, gear lever and right footrest to pull away the cover and work on the timing side. So kids used to leave them off.' Tyres for the Ariel's 16 inch wheels can be a problem, but Mike found some at Vintage Tyre Schemes (01926-817207) though inevitably this involved a trip to rural Gwent. Once there, V.T.S. proprietor Joyce Cobbing told them to stay where they were, and went off across the yard on a little electric cart to wherever the tyres were kept. She returned with a Cheng Shin 3.25x16 ribbed front and an Italian C.E.A.T. 3.25x16 rear, though she said that from then on she would only be stocking fronts, as she had been stuck with too many rears — a curious reversal of the usual pattern of wear, and hence sales.

Chroming meant another excursion, to the MFS Polishing and Plating Co. (01487-711103) in Ramsey, north of Cambridge, 'down a dirty old track in a converted barn'

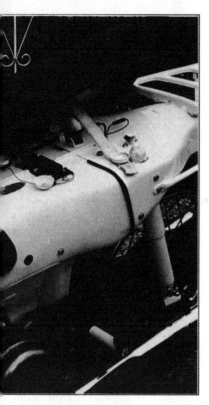

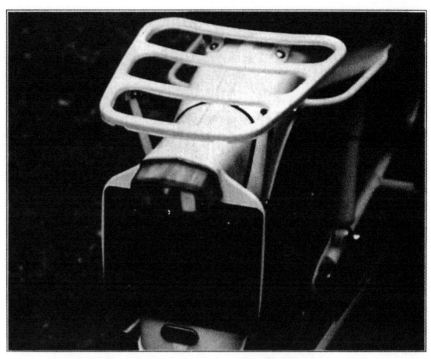

– but worth it, Mike reckons, for the quality of work. Paintwork was done closer to Mike's Oxfordshire home, by Classic Refurbishings at Witney (01993-708788). They are vintage car specialists and the Arrow was the first bike they had tackled – at one point they couldn't tell the front from the back! Although they lost the battery carrier, they soon found it again, and Mike is very happy with the result of their work. It was extremely hard to get definite information on a good equivalent for the Ariel 2-strokes' base Ivory colour, but help came from John Ellis' wife Sandy (whose Leader I tested in *CBG* 41). Sandy told Mike decisively that the closest available was a Rover white, an ICI paint coded P030-3738. It certainly looks right.

Meanwhile the engine was being meticulously put together by retired motorcycle mechanic Charles Hurst. Mr Hurst had worked all his life at an Oxford bike shop, 'mostly on Bantams, so he's quite good on 2-strokes,' Mike confirms. Mr Hurst only does occassional work but if any readers would like to check out the possibility, contact me via *CBG*. Likewise for Les Leach, another Ariel friend of Mike's who assembled and installed the gearbox and clutch with its secondhand plates from Draganfly. After that, Mike says, 'everything went together without too much of a struggle.'

Release?

After I had admired the Arrow's appearance – the deep blue and white finish seems appropriately ... sensible for a restricted model, and the smartness takes away from the unpanelled 2-stroke's fundamental oddity – it was time to unclip the seat and check the petrol level via the filler cap to the tank which is located under there. The seat arrangement is one of the Arrow's better design features,

with clips on either side, and then the seat is easy to prop up on a wire bracket hinge which is loose enough not to snap with use, while the seat itself is also held on by a strap of woven nylon fabric. The top of the battery is also visible under the seat, though like most batteries hidden away in slots, Mike confirms that it's awkward to remove for checking, etc.

There was at least a gallon of fuel in the 2.8 gallon tank, which was going to be OK – even the Sports 250 was good for around 70mpg overall. Mike runs a 4-star and modern 2-stroke oil mix at a fairly lean 30:1 ratio (although not as lean as the 40:1 dared by the Ellises). Mike's choice seems to eliminate most of the spiral smoking contrails usually associated with these models; the only time I spotted any smoke to the stern was when pulling away from a standstill.

Despite a bent wire choke lever (not available on the fully panelled Leader), starting proved problematic – 'I've found starting is a knack – they're easy to flood,' Mike admits, and cold starting is proverbially poor because of these models' butterfly choke lever not inducing enough mixture into the engine. In the end we gave up and push-started it, which is easy to do. Just as well, since even after the engine was fully warmed up, after a stop I had to bump-start it again.

Moving off in first, amazement at its agonisingly low ratio, with forward movement

Moving off, amazement at its agonisingly low ratio, with forward movement only just discernible, was immediately replaced by dismay ...

only just discernible, was immediately replaced by dismay at the tick-tocky, uncertain feeling to the front end, which was accentuated by the Arrow's notably narrow handlebars. Old bike problems sometimes seem like London buses – after a long absence, the same ones then come along together. I hadn't had the steering head blues for years, until the 600 Matchless I'd tested the previous month; now here they were again.

As speed (slowly) gathered, the problem went off, but to me the front end would continue to feel a little uncomfortably unpredictable, and with damp roads, this inhibited cornering. After a while I realized that the leading link front forks were coping very well with surface irregularities, steering true, so the problem definitely seemed to lie in the head bearings – perhaps a tad overtightened when Mike had replaced them?

Speed will get you out of most things, as they say, if you can just hang on, and in mild desperation, winding the plot up once in second revealed a power step and some definite forward movement. Speed would have been useful, as with all the Ariel 2-strokes, to scrub out a rather uncertain feel when cornering slowly, but ... the engine was newly rebuilt, with only 400 miles on it, and I'd said I would keep it to 50 and not wind it on. So I was left to contemplate the forked stick which is the Arrow 200 a machine 🏍

with the 278lbs dry weight of a stock Arrow, but with power, despite its 10:1 compression ratio, reduced to just 14bhp – that's 3.5 less than a stock Arrow, and a full six horses less than the Sports 'Golden' Arrow. A late model 175 BSA Bantam puts out roughly the same power, but weighs some 60lbs less, and while no zipgun, accelerates noticeably better than the Arrow 200.

And is also a deal less fussy. The standard Leaders and Arrows have a narrow enough power band, but the 200's lack of poke and different gearing have reduced this to miniscule. First gear as mentioned is even less useable than the 250's, and while the latter's gap between second and third has been improved upon, the yawp has moved up to a black hole between 3rd and top.

It's no good changing up to top at 30; the engine goes completely flat on you and there's a long, long wait to get out of this. You have to hold on in third till as close to 40 as you can stand before upshifting.

Peaky, peaky, peaky, and then you discover that 40 is also the optimum cruising speed. I did take it up to 50 once for form's sake, but it was a prolonged experience which severely depleted the balance of mechanical sympathy. Testers in 1964 achieved 71mph on an Arrow 200, and they have my profound respect. It's possible of course that had the 200 engine been a little looser, and not on loan, one could have adopted the traditional 2-stroke

> *Peaky, peaky, peaky, and then you discover that forty is also the optimum cruising speed ...*

solution to all this – ie. revved the nuts off it through the gears and got some sort of result. But not that day.

Trundling gloomily round a ring road with Sunday drivers up my cantilevered tailpipes, I reminded myself of a couple of this Arrow's virtues. The gearchange and clutch were the lightest and nicest I had ever encountered on any Burman box; Les Leach had done a fine job. Sadly even that couldn't undo the inherent defects of the CP box, and after the engine had warmed up I experienced a couple of the customary false neutrals, naturally when I least needed them, while changing down (and hoping for engine braking) halfway into sharp bends.

Out in the country, after fifteen miles or so I realized that the bike was comfortable, with well-matched, well-tuned suspension and a good full-size seat. There was a factory luggage rack fitted, and the mudguarding was excellent too, with no spatter reaching the boots. The kindest you could say about the 200 was that it might have made a reasonable commuter. You could burble along comfortably at 40, except it wasn't a burble but a harsh, quite rorty exhaust note which I caught the gist of particularly when turning my head to glance behind; the Arrow wasn't fitted with a mirror.

But then a bend would approach, you'd slow down a little – no, no, I don't think so. Never lose revs or speed! was the golden rule with the 200 – it took so long to get them back again. Charging into bends at full tilt was the way to go, but as mentioned, I didn't feel too comfortable bend-swinging on this Ariel, although Mike thinks it corners nicely so perhaps it's an acquired taste. Roadholding from the Oriental front tyre seemed fine, as did the rear, until the one time it was suddenly and unexpectedly knocked off line by a raised manhole cover.

The Ariel 2-strokes' 6 inch brakes, especially at the front, are known weak spots, but low speeds and good engine braking had kept the spotlight off this until I was trickling up the side of a traffic tailback and reached for the front anchor to trim progress. The lever came most of the way back to the bars, but we kept on going. Time for a swift downchange.

The 200 ticked over well and the lights seemed adequate, but when I passed a group of friends outside their house and laid on the horn repeatedly, the pitiful cheeps which emerged totally failed to attract their attention. Very Sixties Lucas. Incidentally Mike does know that the hooter itself should be black, not chrome.

Mike is a nice man and I tried to like the 200, but as we hauled it back onto its rather awkward centrestand (chipped already, a living argument against the silly fashion from those days of painting working parts white), I have to say that while I was grateful to a meticulous restorer for the ride, what I chiefly felt was relief that it was over.

Conclusion

While the Arrow 200 represents an interesting footnote historically to the Ariel story, and even if you're into British 2-strokes, practical considerations would recommend the robustness of a Bantam or Villiers 197 single, or the smoother, torquier Villiers 2T twin, rather than this, for me, charmless machine. In fact this undergunned bike calls to mind an old story about another Last Arrow.

It seems that as Robin Hood lay on his bed mortally wounded, he gasped, 'Bring me my mighty longbow. I shall let fly one last winged shaft, and where it falls to earth, there shall you lay me to my long rest.' Choking back the tears, friends brought him his bow, and with the last of his strength, slowly, agonisingly, Robin drew back the bowstring a final time, and as he loosed the last arrow, fell back dead.

So they did as he'd told them, and buried him on top of the wardrobe...

Facing page: Mike Portsmouth and his well-restored Ariel Arrow 200.
Above: Smart lacquered timing side cover, often discarded, comes from Ariel Owners Club scheme.
Below left: Tank badge is one of few distinguishing marks to tell Arrow 200 from the stock 250.
Below: Arrow's dummy tank holds a useful parcel compartment. Seat is comfortable too.

FULLY LOADED

All 15 optional extras on Phil Morris's 1963 Leader. George May analyses the Ariel that pre-dates the car world's mania for factory extras

Optional extras: how about this lot?(Top) Inspection lamp, seat cover and elastic ties for luggage carrier. (Middle) Eight day Smiths clock right of the 80mph speedometer, parking lamp behind screen. (Bottom) Lockable panniers with inner soft bags.

How does it feel to own every stamp in the Stanley Gibbons catalogue, or every model car Matchbox ever made? If it feels good, take a look at this Ariel Leader.

In his meticulous restoration of a machine he originally owned as his first motorcycle in 1969, Phil Morris has incorporated every one of the Leader's 15 optional extras. The car world would call it fully loaded.

The options are: lockable panniers complete with inner bags Phil had reproduced, rear luggage rack with elastic ties, seat cover, screen extension, side stand, mirrors, decorative chrome rear bumper, eight day Smiths clock to the right of the 80mph speedometer, neutral indicator light, trip meter, parking lamp behind the screen, hand held inspection lamp stowed in the dummy tank, jack plug and flashing indicators. Phil warns anyone aiming to do a similar job that such parts are rare and expensive today. His Leader cost a whopping £4050 plus his time to restore.

Although the alternator can cope with extra loading, the Leader's crude electrical charging system is one of its weak points. Turning on the headlamp switches in an extra coil, when the continuous extra charge resulting from long fast cruises can boil the battery. An owner not concerned with utter originality is well advised to use a modern solid state regulator. Electronic ignition is also recommended, for although the twin contact breaker points should allow accurate timing, any error detracts from smooth running.

There is nothing like an emergency for discovering how well you are getting on with a test machine. In this case it was a car emerging from a farm entrance on a narrow lane, its driver blind to the Ariel Leader's bright finish and enormous frontal area. Lashing rain and mud on the road did not help.

Somehow we survived, the Ariel's capability as an all-weather transport probably having helped us escape disaster. The screen and legshields catch the worst of the weather, leaving the rider undistracted and comfortably in control. Safe handling inspires confidence, allowing you to concentrate fully on road conditions, and Ariel's flexible 250cc twin-cylinder two-stroke engine offers instant pick-up on demand. Braking is not so marvellous, but the lack of bite may have saved the day on that treacherous mud.

It's a good job nothing untoward happened, for this concours winning Leader can claim to be the smartest example in use anywhere. A 1963 model, it has been restored with no expense spared by Ariel two-stroke super-enthusiast Morris of Oswestry, Shropshire. Humming around the county's rural byways brought home what a pleasantly useful machine the Leader is.

Starting is easy except from dead cold, when several kicks are needed despite a butterfly choke device, and the engine feels smooth on a steady or rising throttle. With indicators and mirrors for safety, complemented by loads of room to carry things, it's such a user friendly mount you wonder why so few Leaders appear at classic events.

The reason has to be the Ariel's image problem. All-enveloping bodywork makes it look like a giant scooter. Turn up at a motorcyclists' pub on a Leader and people are more likely to smirk than look on in awe.

When conceived in the Fifties, the ultra-sensible Ariel made sense. No major factory could thrive by only selling to the converted. In post-war Britain a motorcycle was still a serious transport option rather than a pure leisure vehicle. Finding new customers was the key to a factory's commercial success and that meant demonstrating a two-wheeler's convenience as a mode of transport.

Introduced in 1958, Ariel's Leader wasn't the first attempt at an all weather tourer for the rider expecting clean hands and dry trousers. But its radical design was one of the boldest re-thinks of the two-wheeler ever made by a mainstream British factory.

The men at Selly Oak, Birmingham, led by general manager Ken Whistance and designer Val Page, had the courage to abandon the convention of a pedal cycle derived tubular frame. They opted to use a car-type welded fabrication of steel pressings to form the chassis.

It's a neat idea. The Ariel 'beam' incorporates the steering head at its front end and rear suspension unit top mounts at the rear. On the underside, integral brackets carry the com-

PHOTOGRAPHY MARTYN BARNWELL

At a glance

1963 Ariel Leader

Engine type two-stroke twin
Bore x stroke 54 x 54mm **Capacity** 247cc
Transmission four-speed foot change, wet clutch
Frame pressed steel fabrication **Suspension** trailing link
front fork, swinging arm rear suspension
Weight 340lb **Wheelbase** 51in **Seat height** 30in
Petrol tank 3gal **Top speed** 68mph
Petrol consumption 50mpg
Price new £210 **Guide price now** £650-£2000

Club contact Ariel Owners' Club, Membership Secretary
Andy Hemingway, 80 Pasture Lane, CLayton, Bradford
BD14 6LN (01274 882141)

Ariel's Leader is one of the boldest re-thinks of the two-wheeler ever made by a mainstream British factory.

bined engine and gearbox unit, and the swinging arm pivot. In the hollow interior is a fuel tank, keeping the weight usefully low down.

The Leader has trailing-link front suspension with short pivoted links acting against self contained spring and damper units in each fork leg. The mechanism proves itself on the road, but its pressed steel enclosures look ungainly compared with the clean lines of a typical telescopic fork.

Ariel's upper fork is radically different, too. Instead of a normal layout with two stanchions yoked above and below the steering stem, the Leader's fork is more like that of a pedal cycle. A bridging piece above the wheel has a single steering stem fixed to it, which passes through the headstock. The handlebar is fixed to its top by splines.

Copious mudguarding and weather protection is provided by metal pressings including legshields — a turn-off for any sporty rider, although Fifties commuters favoured them for protection from the elements. The acres

of panelling and the eye-height windscreen forced Ariel to create a bold overall style for the Leader. The success of the exercise can be judged by admiration shown for the Leader today by non-motorcyclists. If the Ariel was a car it would have a huge cult following.

Installing a two-stroke engine in the Leader was just as radical a departure for Ariel, a firm known for its sturdy ohv singles and the

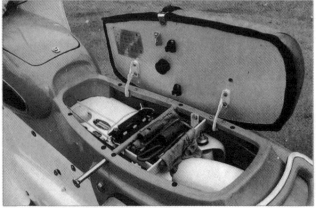

Under seat compartment contains fuel tank at the front, battery and toolkit. Telescopic grab handle helps putting the Leader on its stand.

1000cc Square Four luxury tourer. Although the 54 x 54mm 180-degree stroker twin was inspired by the German Adler design, it still exhibits plenty of original thinking.

The crankcase and gearbox are contained within a single casting although there is an air gap between the housings. The casing is designed so that its internals can be readily removed from the side.

Each cylinder has its own pressed-up crankshaft with full circle flywheels. Their inner mainshafts are mated together by a tapered joint supported in the centre main bearing ballrace. An Allen bolt inserted through the right hand crank's hollow mainshaft secures the joint, pegged by a Woodruff key to maintain 180-degree displacement. The cranks and their double-row roller big-end bearings can be withdrawn through detachable crankcase end covers. The Burman gearbox internals can be taken out from the right side after the outer and inner covers have been removed.

Leader's detractors forget that it was voted *Motor Cycle News* Machine of the Year - 1959.

Further reading

Here's what we have about the Ariel Leader in photocopy form from our archive. Prices include postage *

The MotorCycle road test 15 December 1960. £2.50.

MotorCycling road test 7 August 1963. £2.50.

Owners guide for Ariel Leader and Arrow. September 1962. 53 pages. £5

Spare parts list March 1961. 47 pages. £4.50

Write to: Richard Rosenthal, *The Classic MotorCycle*, 20-22 Station Road, Kettering, Northants NN15 7HH. Make cheques payable to *The Classic MotorCycle*, or call with your Access/Visa number of 01536 386790.

*SUBSCRIBERS GET 10% DISCOUNT

The cylinders tilt forward at 45 degrees, helping to make a squat unit that can tuck closely under the chassis beam. Air enters the bodywork between the legshields to cool discrete cast iron cylinder barrels and alloy heads. An upward-projecting part of the main engine casting acts both as chassis hanger and inlet manifold. It supports the ⅞in bore Amal Monobloc carburettor and contains the intake duct for mixture to the crankcases. Two single garter seals — or originally a double seal — to the right of the centre main bearing separate the two primary compression chambers.

A Burman clutch driven by a single row primary chain in an oil-tight casing is easily adjustable using a slipper tensioner. The left mainshaft carries a flywheel outboard of the engine sprocket and twin contact points for the coil ignition system are housed in the outer primary drive cover. A Lucas alternator is sited at the other end of the crankshaft.

Producing 17.5bhp with the squish combustion chambers introduced from 1961, the engine is potent enough to carry the weight of the bodywork and the numerous optional extras on this example. But only just. Because of the sound handling and responsive throttle, it is tempting to push the Ariel hard, when it tends to smoke excessively and fuel consumption sinks below 45mpg. Carrying a pillion passenger, whose footrests undulate with the swinging arm, just adds to the strain.

The Leader would be taken more seriously if it had a muted ohv engine: smoke and cacophony tend to spoil its aspirations to sophistication. Originally a 25:1 petroil mix was recommended, but with modern oils 35:1 should be safe for pouring in the 3 gallon fuel tank's filler under the hinged dualseat. Owner Phil Morris revels in the smoke and noise as being all part of the fun.

Ariel styled a dummy fuel tank into the space between seat and handlebars to offer a weatherproof luggage compartment. Its hinge-up lid has a crude lock and inside there is a steering lock lever and a pull wire release for unlocking the hinged seat. Another clever feature is the telescopic grab handle to assist in putting the Leader on its centre stand. Retracted below the seat on the left, it can be fiddly to operate with a damp gloved hand.

Owners of standard machines must learn to live with the weedy 6in drum brakes and unusually long travel at the gear lever, although the gearbox itself is a sturdy item. Our day was spoiled when the Leader's clutch began to lose its grip, but this is apparently a rare occurrence on the model.

The Leader's detractors forget that it had many friends, being voted *Motor Cycle News* Machine of the Year in 1959. And thousands of learners enjoyed themselves on the Arrow, the unenclosed version Ariel made from 1960 to maximise sales. By 1961, 25,000 of the two stroke twins had been turned out and production survived transfer to BSA's plant in 1963 — continuing until 1965. A fully equipped Leader as smart as this can be a showpiece and a working roadster all at once. ∎

Crankcase and gearbox are a single casting, designed so that their internals can be removed from the side.

250cc Arrow from Ariel's 1960 brochure. Frame pressings are electrically welded. Dummy tank shell support headlight.

icture this. A beam frame running from headstock to swinging arm pivot, integral fuel tank, trailing link forks, inclined 250cc two-stroke engine and 16 inch wheels. You could be forgiven for conjuring up a mental picture of some state of the art race replica from either Italy or the Orient. In fact this description fits a British machine which has just celebrated its 40th birthday – the Ariel Leader and subsequent Arrow.

By the 1960s the Ariel company was an integral part of the BSA empire but retained an independent identity throughout its range. Indeed Ariel's legacy is a reminder of what a radical and forward thinking concern it was. The Leader and before that the Square Four are just two examples of machines well ahead of their time. It is surprising that the marque has never taken on the legendary status of Norton, Triumph and BSA.

The Leader originated from the drawing board of Ariel's veteran designer, Val Page, in 1955, the brief being simply an ultra modern, all weather machine. Page's brilliant interpretation resulted in the boxed beam chassis formed from two edge welded pressings, from which the engine was underslung, suspended at just two points, the rear of which doubled as swinging arm pivot. There was extensive use of pressed steel, much of it produced by the BSA subsidiary, Carbodies of Coventry, including dummy tank, legshields, headlamp and tail cowling and the all encompassing side panels. The front fork stanchions were also enshrouded within a steel pressing. The dummy tank served as parcel space while the fuel tank proper nestled within the chassis beneath the hinged dual seat.

Even the engine looked radical, canted forward at 45 degrees, alloy heads on iron barrels with angled finning to run horizontal in the air flow, a one piece crankcase and gearbox into which the built up crankshaft assembly was

fitted as two halves before being fastened together with a draw bolt. Likewise the Burman made four speed gears were built up in situ.

Page said that the 54mm x 54mm square dimensions of the engine "owed little to sporting pretentions" and were more or less a mechanical compromise within the confines of crank throw, space available to bolt up the cranks and the wall thickness between the bores for transfer passages. Since then however, these dimensions have featured regularly in many two-stroke sports machines.

The fork design also followed Page's radical thinking, a bicycle styled arrangement, devoid of yokes at the top with hydraulically damped spring units concealed within the pressings, mating up to trailing links at the bottom, arranged to maintain constant wheelbase. The Leader was launched in the summer of 1958 at a retail price of £209 11s 7d including purchase tax.

It was a very bold move by Ariel MD Ken Whistance, to go ahead with the venture, for it was unchartered territory and the tooling costs involved must have been enormous.

With the Leader, Ariel's eggs were firmly in one basket and although it sold reasonably well figures did not reach the hopes of the management. So in December 1959, a second version, the Arrow, was launched. The brainchild of Page's assistant, Bernard Knight, the Arrow was little more than a Leader stripped to the bare necessities but its appearance did go some way to appealing to the younger riders of the day. Also, the removal of some of the pressings and the resultant loss of some 50lbs, enhanced the machine's performance considerably and at just £167 it was the cheapest 250 on the market.

The Leader was voted MCN Machine of the Year in 1959 and the Arrow followed suit in 1960. In 1961 Ariel went for the hat-trick with

the announcement of the Sports Arrow. They were successful, thus proving the basic excellence of the design. Almost immediately dubbed the Golden Arrow, because of its dummy tank colouring, this glamorous version sported, among other things, whitewall tyres and red hand grips and was quite lively too, with a 1 1/16in Amal Monobloc (as opposed to the 7/8in of its predecessors), suitably modified ports and compression lifted to 10:1 from 8.25:1. The Golden Arrow gave a genuine 20bhp and top speed of about 80mph, yet it could still achieve more than 50mpg even under hard working conditions. The Golden Arrow cost £190 15s 7d.

By 1963, motorcycle sales in general were falling and BSA brought Arrow and Leader production into their main Small Heath works and closed the Grange Road, Selly Oak, Ariel factory. Their sales were slowing too and overseas markets were reluctant to accept the pressed steel principle, though within months, similar ideas were being welcomed from the Orient. Some examples, such as the 'step-through' Honda, are with us to this day.

A final base model Arrow, identical except for a 199cc engine, was introduced in 1964, the sales pitch supposedly aiming at the cheaper 'under 200cc' insurance rate. In reality it was a stock clearance exercise and all production ceased in 1965.

My earliest recollections of the Arrow stem from my Nottinghamshire home village where, during the latter part of the 1960s, a handful of would-be 'Rockers' – influenced no doubt by the racing successes of Mike O'Rourke and Peter Inchley – ran brightly painted, café racer style Arrows, fitted with ear splitting expansion chambers that gave forth much smoke. Now upright citizens, they all speak highly of the machine's handling, if not of its performance.

EXHILARATING

ARIEL *Arrow*

A discarded Ariel Arrow field bike proved an irresistible challenge to Brian Cope but, with a little effort he soon turned it into his wife's favourite machine.

Nigel Clark takes a ride and looks back at 40 years of the beam frame two-stroke

Narrow engine, primary and generator are a legacy of its predecessor's (the Leader) enclosures. Cylinder finning was practical but radical style wise for the early 1960s.

Yokeless bicycle style trailing link front fork maintains constant wheelbase .

Removal of tool box from within dummy tank gives access to comprehensive parcel space. Fiddly perhaps but practical. Note 200 badges on dummy tank.

Fulfilling a youthful dream

1964 budget model 200cc Arrow was final machine of the range. Other than capacity, badges and colour scheme it was identical to the rest. Janet's Arrow began life in this form, compare it to the top of the range 250cc Golden Arrow shown below.

Fuel tank is an integral part of the beam frame construction and is found adjacent to the battery compartment beneath the hinged dual seat. Easy access to rear shock absorber, from above mudguard section permits simple removal.

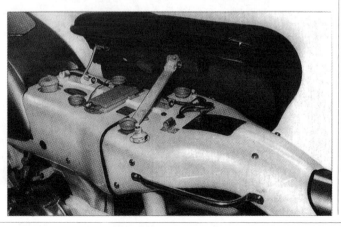

Until I met Brian Cope, I had never ridden an Ariel Arrow, so where better to make my inaugural ride than on a beautiful warm and sunny day on the Isle of Man, where Brian and his charming wife Janet now reside.

Although hailing originally from Lincolnshire, Brian was the Island's Chief Veterinary Officer, up to his retirement in July 1998. The Copes are well known for the active part they play in vintage circles and Brian's ability as a restorer is highly respected. Studying his many machines, I was immediately put at ease because they are all quite perfect. The Ariel, which is actually Janet's machine, fired after only half a dozen or so light kicks and as Brian warmed it up, I gleaned a little about its background.

It began life in 1964 as the budget 200cc model but almost ended its days as a field bike. Brian spotted it lying against a tree, seized and unwanted, at the back of a garage in Fulstow, Lincs. The main frame beam was sound but the rear mudguard, chainguard, toolbox lid, gearbox cover and dummy tank were missing. Among parts sourced, Brian found a pair of dummy tanks, each with one side rotten. These were cut in half and the good halves welded together and finished in traditional Cherokee red. I challenge anyone to 'see the join'. The engine has been bored out to 250cc and fitted with standard pistons and the carburettor at 1 1/8in is slightly larger than standard. Brian has also chosen to gear up with a bigger gearbox sprocket.

The first thing to strike me as I sat astride the Arrow was its diminutive size. I am only of 31in inside leg but I could easily stand flat footed without the machine touching my thighs. There's little wonder that Janet favours this particular machine.

I sat for a few seconds to familiarise myself with the basic controls before pulling in the featherlight clutch and silently engaging bot-

At a glance

1964 Ariel Arrow

Engine type	two-stroke vertical twin
Bore x stroke	54mm x 54mm
Capacity	247cc
Compression ratio	10:1
Transmission	4 speed
Brakes	6 inch sls front and rear
Power output	20bhp approx
Tyre size	3.25 x 16 front and rear
Weight	275lb approx
Market value	£300 (rough) - £1600 (concours)

Club contact Ariel OC, Andrew Hemmingway, 80 Pasture Lane, Clayton, Bradford, West Yorks BD14 6LN.

Original sales brochures Mono copies available at £3.50 per A4 sheet. Contact The Classic Motorcycle, PO Box 99, Horncastle, Lincs LN9 6LZ. Tel: 01507 525771.

Superb Cherokee red and Old English White finish belie the fact that this Ariel was once a field bike. A credit to Brian Cope's restoration skills.

tom gear on the long pedal. I made a mental note 'one-up, three-down like the Norton'. After a couple of years on a Bonneville's up for up system, it's very easy to forget. A little throttle was all that was necessary to burble smoothly away. There was an unexpectedly wide gap between first and second which came as a surprise. In fact ratios between all four gears are wide.

The lightness of the bike and especially the steering came as another surprise and the twitchy effect was a little unnerving at first. As I headed off out of Glen May and onto the coast road, the pace of the Arrow quickened as the engine reached a better working temperature. Allowing it rev out a little more made much more sense of the gearbox ratios. It was impossible to bear the ball of my right foot onto the footrest as my heel fouled the fixed kickstart but that was a minor hindrance

The Arrow's proud owner, Janet Cope on her GTP Velocette.

as use of the instep on the rest made for an easier gear change.

Dropping down a steep hill to an evil hairpin around the narrow gable wall of a building, those trailing links worked a treat under hard braking, keeping the plot in a straight and stable line with no discernible dive. Within 15 minutes I had come to terms with the Arrow's nimble feel and was beginning to enjoy myself.

The suspension coped easily with the odd rough patch on the road and I soon learned that to maintain momentum on the ups and downs of the twisty road, a little jig had to be danced on the gear pedal, in true two-stroke fashion. This is not to say however that the engine lacked torque, on the contrary, the excellent torque figures were obviously taken into account when the gear ratios were designed and Brian has taken this a step further by carrying even taller gearing than standard. It was simply that the road chosen was extreme in its contours and would have tested the pulling power of even the best four-stroke.

In deference to the machine's age, I did not cane it too hard through the gears but on one reasonably flat section, I opened it up and soon saw an indicated 70mph as the Arrow began to breathe deeper. I glanced over my shoulder and laughed out loud. There was the two-stroke oil induced fog that I recalled from my childhood. I reckon I would have to experiment with high quality, lean mix, chainsaw oil if the Arrow were mine. Nevertheless, it wasn't going to seize that was for sure!

Becoming accustomed to the front brake's only adequate retardation capa-

bilities, it was down a gear with a long and leisurely change and a big blip of the throttle mid way, drop into the corner as steady as a rock and power out while still heeled over. The little Arrow handled like a dream and cried out to be thrown around the Island's traffic free twists in complete abandon. I had the hang of it now and was having some serious fun.

Half an hour later I made my way back to the Cope residence with a grin on my face as wide as Douglas promenade. I switched off the engine, dismounted, placed a foot on the centre stand tang and with an effortless pull, the perfectly balanced machine rolled gently onto its stand. It seemed a fitting finale to the little bike's display.

The timing of the Arrow's arrival, its short life, lack of development and the reluctance of the buying public to adopt its virtues, seem all the more tragic when one thinks of the imminent onset of the evil handling two-strokes from Japan which, in contrast, were so eagerly accepted.

Stepping back to his youth, Clark enjoys his first ride on an Arrow. Better late than never!

Keeping It In The Family

The Arrow was Selly Oak's great white hope. The factory put all its eggs in the two stroke basket – and it nearly paid off. **Roy Poynting** *samples a well travelled – but totally authentic – example.*

Regular readers will be familiar with our occasional features on motorcycles which are 'Authentic and Unrestored.' The two attributes often go together; but there is always an exception to prove the rule. This Ariel Arrow is as authentic as any 40-year-old machine can be – while still being in first class running order – and yet it has been totally restored. In fact it has been restored twice!

How then, can we be sure it is authentic? Because owner Roy Houghton has known and maintained the Arrow from the day it was first put on the road in 1960, and it was he who undertook both restorations. The Arrow was originally owned by Roy's father, who bought it from Alec Bennett's dealership in Southampton. Coincidentally, Roy was then employed as a mechanic in the car branch of the same company. Earlier, he had served his apprenticeship there, before

Unconventional trailing link front suspension is concealed behind styling 'spats.'

spending his National Service working on tanks with the Royal Engineers.

The Ariel was used day in and day out, to transport Mr Houghton Senior to and from work. He was evidently a motoryclist of catholic tastes, as the Arrow was preceded by a substantial Red Hunter and a featherweight New Hudson autocycle. He took care of his machines, carefully wiping the Arrow down every night when he put it away. When it needed servicing, it was done by Roy. "Nobody else has ever laid hands on it," says Roy, "that is how I know it is totally correct. For example, some people say that the hooter should not have a black centre, but that is how it always was."

Nit pickers might also think that the fact that the ignition switch is black, while the lighting switch is grey, indicates a sloppy restoration. But that is part of the machine's history too. "The original switch failed in about 1961," Roy recalls, "and at that time Ariel could only supply black ones.

As a result of a holiday encounter with an American on an Italian camp site, Roy emigrated to the United States in 1968. In California he found a better paid job with a British Leyland dealership, and stayed there while the British car industry did its best to follow our motorcycle companies into oblivion. Luckily for Roy, his bosses chose to major on Jaguars – which remained popular during his stay.

Naturally, Roy and his wife visited the old country from time to time. And in 1973 his father announced that since he had not ridden the Ariel for a while, he was getting rid of it. "I'd like to take it over," said Roy, perhaps expecting to be given the machine, but his father was no sentimentalist. "I've been offered £30

Roy Poynting enjoys the Arrow experience. The concept of the Ariel strokers was bold and perhaps deserved more success.

Partial engine enclosure helped give the Arrow 'clean appeal' to non-motorcyclists.

by your old company, Alec Bennett's, and you can have it if you match their offer," he said.

Roy forked out the money, and took the Arrow back to the States. He found that the paintwork under the tank had been worn away by his father's nightly wiping down routine, which doesn't say much for the quality of the finish applied by Ariel. And during the time the Arrow had not been used, the right hand piston had seized in its bore. The bore was unworn, and fitting new standard-sized pistons took no time at all. "That is the only time the engine has needed repairs in its 26,500 miles," smiles Roy. He did a respray himself with an airless spray gun, and had some re-chroming done which still looks good a quarter of a century later.

Roy never put the machine on the road in America, because he found the classic scene quite different there. "We took it to lots of shows," he remembers, "but there were no road runs, we just rode it in arena demonstrations." Roy's wife, Doreen, was a motorcyclist too, and took the saddle in some of the parades. The Houghtons returned home when Roy retired in the early Nineties, and the Ariel came too. With the classic boom at its peak here, and plenty of road runs to use the Arrow on, it was time for its second rebuild.

This time, Roy took no short cuts. He completely dismantled the engine and found that everything – including the original bores and the replacement pistons – was in good order. He split the crankshaft assembly, though and replaced the seals just to be on the safe side. A few parts were re-chromed locally, and the paintwork was re-sprayed by a friend in the trade. He accurately matched the original Dark Seal Grey and the colour which I would describe as pale blue – if I didn't know that Ariel termed it Light Admiralty Grey.

drive it hard to get the best out of it. At small throttle openings, the silencing is so good that you are unaware of the inevitably erratic firing, and the power pulses are still frequent enough to merge into smooth propulsion.

The Arrow was about the hottest and most popular quarter litre British bike on the market in the early Sixties. Its combination of racy modern looks, adequate performance and good handling was sufficient to make a legion of young fans feel as if they were riding a proper motorcycle, even when their choice of machine was restricted by their L plates.

Roy, himself, has been booked while riding the Arrow, but not for speeding. An officious copper summonsed him for wearing his old Moby crash helmet with its 'flat hat' styling. "I knew I was in the right," says Roy, because it had a BSI label, but the Police did not agree." Roy's plight became a bit of a cause celebre, and it was publicised in the national magazines at the time. Finally, the VMCC supplied an authoritative interpretation of the law, and the Police had to reluctantly back down. Before that though, they went as far as to fix a date for a court case, and caused Roy a lot of unnecessary worry.

If you did want to speed, the stiff box section chassis certainly provided the basis for excellent handling. This is one of those machines on which you don't have to make a conscious effort to choose a good line round a bend – it just seems to happen. Despite the small wheels, ground clearance is ample for fairly ambitious cornering angles.

Ready for the off come rain or shine. An Ariel Arrow makes a very practical everyday machine.

Putting the Arrow back on the road, Roy was dismayed to find that the previously smooth motor was now a vibrator. "I hadn't realised how critical the crankshaft alignment was," he says ruefully. "The two halves are pulled onto a taper by a through bolt and, although I'd kept within the specified tolerances, it wasn't good enough." The whole motor had to come down again, and this time Roy aligned the crank to within half a thousandth of an inch at all points.

The gain was well worth the pain. When I ride the Arrow, I find its smoothness remarkable; even judging it by twin two-stroke standards. The engine revs so willingly and unobtrusively, that it has the effect of making the machine appear more powerful than it is. Because there is no vibration period to avoid, or flat spots to work through, it seems like no time at all before I am travelling at quite respectable speeds. Not that you have to

Amal Monobloc carburettor is well tucked away.

A new design from the ground up, the Arrow was a brave attempt to come up with a genuinely new type of machine.

Strangely, straight line steering is not equally precise. Roy says that it has only been like this since he changed to the block pattern front tyre and intends to switch back to a ribbed tread.

By universal agreement, the Arrow's brakes are barely adequate. Roy points out that the front brake is one of the ways of identifying an early Arrow like his. The torque arm's anchorage point was moved well up the fork stanchion in 1961. Another more obvious change that year was the repositioning of the spark plugs in the centre of the cylinder heads, indicating a change to a higher compression squish head design.

The other unarguable failing of Ariel's lightweights is the gear change. As they had for many years, Ariel remained faithful to Burman, and utilised slightly modified internals from the CP gearbox. Burman gearboxes never provide hair trigger action, and in this incarnation, require such an extreme movement that changes between the lowest two gears usually only get as far as neutral.

Still, what is so extraordinary about the Ariel Arrow (and its Leader

sibling) is not that they have these foibles – with the exception of the brakes, you would soon get used to them – but that they were so nearly right straight out of the box. In hindsight, the launching of the futuristic Leader in 1958, a decade after Velocette nearly signed its own death warrant with the similarly enclosed LE, was either breathtakingly brave, or extremely rash.

Equally surprising is that the Leader was generally accepted by the conservative British public. And launching the pseudo conventional Arrow just two years later – to cater for those who would not be seen dead on an, 'overgrown scooter' – was a masterstroke.

Traditionalists were undoubtedly sceptical about the capability of the new Ariels, for this was an era when small capacity was synonymous with feeble performance. They had to take notice when an Arrow tuned by Hermann Meier, and ridden by Mick O'Rourke, finished seventh in the 1960 Lightweight TT. It must have considerably enhanced both the

Air filter housing is tucked in out of harm's way.

Fact File

1960 Ariel Arrow

Engine type	two-stroke parallel twin
Capacity	249cc
Bore x stroke	54mm x 54mm
Output	16bhp at 6400rpm
Compression ratio	8.25:1
Carburettor	⅞ in Amal Monobloc
Ignition	battery/coil
Lubrication	petroil mix
Gearbox	Burman four speed
Tyres	325 x 16in
Brakes	6in sls drums
Seat height	29in
Wheelbase	51in
Weight	270lb
Top speed	70mph (est)
Price new	£168
Price guide now	£1000-1500

Club contact Ariel Owners Club, Secretary, Andy Hemingway, 80 Pasture Lane, Clayton, Bradford, West Yorks, BD14 6LN.
Vintage Motor Cycle Club, Allen House, Wetmore Road, Burton upon Trent, Staffs, DE14 1TR.

Further reading We can supply Road Test No. 99 Ariel Arrow, 249cc, 24.11.60. Owner Guide for Ariel Leader and Arrow, 53 pages, £15.00. Spare parts for Ariel Leader and Arrow, 1961, 50 pages, £15.00.

Roy Houghton enjoys the Ariel Arrow he has looked after from new.

reputation and sales prospects of the street version.

The styling successfully concealed just how unorthodox the machine was. Trailing link forks were an unknown quantity for the British public, but they hid behind spats and could soon be forgotten. The beam type pressed steel frame precluded the use of conventional forks, but the bicycle-type handlebar/headstock arrangement was invisible in the Leader, and accepted by the time the Arrow appeared. The beam-frame itself was disguised by bodywork, and blended unobtrusively into the rear mudguard on the Arrow.

The petrol tank is sensibly tucked away inside the frame pressings, where – although restorers find its removal difficult – it lowers the centre of gravity and is protected in the event of a collision. In everyday use it is easily accessed for refilling, as the dual seat with its unusual – and original – plywood base simply swings up out of the way. However, the Ariels would look weird, and feel scooterish, without something in the conventional tank position. A dummy tank is the answer.

It looks good, gives something to grip with your knees, and provides a convenient place for a toolbox. The tool tray itself is quickly removable for access to the electrics, which are mounted alongside the beam frame, well away from the elements.

By slimming the dummy tank at the front and mounting the headlight between tank extensions formed into brackets, the illusion of conventionality is maintained. The Arrow completely avoids the slightly hunch-shouldered look of the similarly conceived Douglas Dragonfly. The fact that the rather inadequate 6in headlight doesn't turn with the handlebars, didn't seem to worry owners too much. It is certainly not a problem for Roy Houghton who happily uses his bikes on local club runs in the daylight.

Any lightweight Ariel provides reliable handling and sprightly performance. Combine those features with a fine second restoration and you have an unusual machine. Add in a history of one-man maintenance and one-family ownership, and Roy Houghton's Arrow must surely be unique. ∎